Letters For Special Situations

Anne McKinney, Editor

PREP PUBLISHING
FAYETTEVILLE, NC

PREP Publishing
1110 ½ Hay Street
Fayetteville, NC 28305
(910) 483-6611

Copyright © 2012 by Anne McKinney

Cover design by David W. Turner

All rights reserved under International and Pan-American Copyright Conventions. No part of this book may be reproduced or copied in any form or by any means—graphic, electronic, or mechanical, including photocopying, taping, or information storage and retrieval systems—without written permission from the publisher, except by a reviewer, who may quote brief passages in a review. Published in the United States by PREP Publishing.

Library of Congress Cataloging-in-Publication Data
Letters for special situations / (edited by) Anne McKinney.
       p.   cm.
  ISBN 978-1475094350; 1475094353 (trade paperback)
  1. Commercial correspondence. 2. Business writing.
3. Correspondence. I. McKinney, Anne, 1948-
HF5721.L395   1999
808'.066651—dc21   99-11353
                                                                         CIP

Printed in the United States of America
First Edition

By PREP Publishing

Business and Career Series:

RESUMES AND COVER LETTERS THAT HAVE WORKED

RESUMES AND COVER LETTERS THAT HAVE WORKED FOR MILITARY PROFESSIONALS

RESUMES AND COVER LETTERS FOR MANAGERS

COVER LETTERS THAT BLOW DOORS OPEN

GOVERNMENT JOB APPLICATIONS AND FEDERAL RESUMES

LETTERS FOR SPECIAL SITUATIONS

Judeo-Christian Ethics Series:

SECOND TIME AROUND

BACK IN TIME

WHAT THE BIBLE SAYS ABOUT…Words that can lead to success and happiness

A GENTLE BREEZE FROM GOSSAMER WINGS

BIBLE STORIES FROM THE OLD TESTAMENT

TABLE OF CONTENTS

LETTERS FOR SPECIAL SITUATIONS

Introduction 1

1. Formatting Your Letters 3

2. Addressing Your Letters and Writing Your Salutation 6

3. Letters of Appeal (also see Letters of Complaint) 11
   A. Appeal of a court action 12
   B. Appeal of a dismissal from a job 13
   C. Appeal to a corporation from a franchisee challenging a fine and employment policies 14
   D. Appeal of a supervisor's rating 16
   E. Appeal of a company's failure to pay retirement funds 18
   F. Appeal to a teacher about a child's grade 19
   G. Appeal to the housing board 20
   H. Appeal of a transfer 21
   I. Appeal of a military medical board decision 22
   J. Appeal of a supervisor's rating 24
   K. Appeal of a suspension 26
   L. Appeal of a false accusation 28

4. Letters of Application, Personal Statements, & Essays 29
   A. Letter of application for admission to medical school 30
   B. Letter of application for admission to physician's assistant program 32
   C. Letter of application for dental school 34
   D. Essay "My Greatest Personal Failure" 36
   E. Essay "My Greatest Professional Risk" 37
   F. Letter of application for the Peace Corps 38
   G. Letter of application to medical school 40
   H. Letter of application to law school 42
   I. Letter of application for a superintendent of schools position 44

5. Business Marketing Letters and Press Releases 45
   A. Business estimate used by a cleaning company in marketing its services .. 46
   B. Business proposal by a resume-writing and outplacement service 47
   C. Letter of introduction used by a specialty steel company 48
   D. Letter expressing "thank you" to existing customers 49
   E. Letter of welcome to new customers 50
   F. Letter used in a chain letter mailing 51
   G. Press release for an art gallery 52
   H. Press release for a new book 53
   I. Letter marketing a courier service 54
   J. Letter following up on an initial verbal proposal 55
   K. Letter used to accompany a business resume 56
   L. Business resume 57
   M. Letter used to market a landscaping service 58

6. Career-Changing Letters 59
  A. From dental assisting to flight attendant (see also p. 83) 60
  B. The direct approach 61
  C1. Answering blind ads 62
  C2. Answering ads with names and addresses 63
  D. All-purpose cover letters, seeking management trainee position 64
  E. Responding to recruiters 65
  F1. All-purpose cover letters, background in criminal justice 66
  F2. All-purpose cover letters, entering pharmaceutical sales field 67
  F3. All-purpose cover letters, sales and accounting skills 68
  F4. All-purpose cover letters, communication and customer service skills 69
  F5. All-purpose cover letters, sales skills and versatility 70
  F6. All-purpose cover letters, military professional in transition 71
  G. Young professional emphasizing strong personal qualities 72
  H. College graduate seeks her first professional job 73
  I. From profit making to human services 74
  J. From commercial sales to health care 75
  K. From government to academia 76
  L. From aviation to sales 77
  M. From food industry to accounting and finance 78
  N. From private to public sector 79
  O. From retail to retail-related 80
  P. From managing people to managing money 81
  Q. From the grocery industry to a career in human resources 82
  R. From small business management to flight attendant (see also page 60) 83
  S. From social services to academic administration 84
  T. From store manager to fireman 85
  U1. Entrepreneur seeking a new industry 86
  U2. Entrepreneur seeking a new challenge in automotive industry 87
  U3. Entrepreneur returning to previous field 88
  V1. Seeking first job in chemistry field 89
  V2. Seeking first job in computer science 90
  V3. Seeking first job in publishing or advertising 91
  V4. Seeking first job utilizing history degree 92
  V5. Seeking first job in media journalism and English 93
  V6. Seeking first job in nursing field 94
  V7. Seeking first job in social services field 95
  W1. Seeking to advance in retail 96
  W2. Seeking a career change from retail 97
  X. Seeking to return to public health field or to university teaching 98

7. Collections Letters 99
  A. Collections letter #1 100
  B. Collections letter #2 101
  C. Collections letter #3 102
  D. Collections letter #4 103
  E. Collections letter #5 104
  F. Collections letter #6 105

8. **Letters of Complaint (also see Letters of Appeal)** 106
   A. Letter seeking ownership of insurance agency 107
   B. Letter complaining about unprofessional legal representation and refusing to pay in full 108
   C. Letter to Senator Jesse Helms about a father's medical benefits 112
   D. Letter to Department of Transportation with copy to Attorney General 114

9. **Letters in Confidence** 115
   A. Letter #1 expressing interest in employment 116
   B. Letter #2 expressing interest in employment 117
   C. When they ask for salary requirements 118
   D. When they ask for salary history 119
   E. Letter expressing interest in a competitor 120

10. **Letters as Bids** 121
    A. Bid from a building subcontractor 122
    B. Bid from a professional sign company 123

11. **Letters related to Consumer Credit and Finance** 124
    A. Letter to credit bureaus requesting fraud alert on your credit file after a robbery 125
    B. Letter to Trans Union Credit Bureau 126

12. **Follow-up Letters** 127
    A. Follow-up letter #1 from retailer 128
    B. Follow-up letter #2 from retailer 129
    C. Follow-up letter #3 from restaurateur seeking accounting job 130
    D. Follow-up letter #4 from MIS manager 131
    E. Follow-up letter #5 to pharmaceutical company 132
    F. Follow-up letter #6 from MIS manager 133
    G. Follow-up letter #7 from a retail executive seeking internal promotion 134
    H. Follow-up letter #8 from retailer 135
    I. Follow-up letter #9 to consumer products company 136

13. **Last Will and Testament** 137
    Letter expressing the final wishes of Chandler McDoogal, Jr. 138

14. **Legal Letters and Notices** 139
    A. Child custody proposal 140
    B. Letter of support and affidavit 141
    C. Legal financial agreement in a divorce settlement 142
    D. Letter of notice regarding an option agreement 143

15. **Letters of Apology** 144
    Letter of apology from one business to another 145

16. **Letters of Appreciation** 146
    Letter of praise for an employee and a company 147

17. Letters of Introduction **148**
A. Letter of introduction from a consultant 149
B. Letter of introduction from a business introducing its services 150

18. Letters of Invitation **152**
A. Invitation to a job fair 153
B. Invitation to an Eagle ceremony 154
C. Letter of invitation to a meeting 155

19. Letters of Negotiation **156**
A. Letter negotiating an insurance settlement 157
B. Letter negotiating final payments when subcontractor failed to complete a job 158

20. Letters of Nomination **160**
Letter nominating an individual for a leadership award 161

21. Letters of Notice **162**
A. Letter of notice to real estate commission 163
B. Notice from a treasurer regarding a bank account 164
C. Notice regarding lapsed alimony payment 165
D. Notice of a sealed bid land and timber sale 166
E. Notification & Certificate of Destruction 167

22. Letters of Opposition **168**
Letter of opposition to a rezoning proposal 169

Letters of Recommendation (see Reference Letters, page 200)

23. Letters of Regret and Condolence **170**
A. Letter of condolence to an employee whose husband died 171
B. Letter of regret to a job applicant 172

24. Letters of Reprimand **173**
A. Letter of reprimand to an employee 174
B. Reprimand and memo to the file 175

25. Letters of Solicitation **176**
A. Letter of solicitation on behalf of disadvantaged children 177
B. Resume used as a method of soliciting funds for business sponsorship 178

26. Letters of Support **179**
Letter of support on behalf of a party in a child custody dispute 180

Letters of Termination (see letter on page 158-159 as well as the letter on page 174)

27. Letters of Understanding and Intent **181**
A. Letter of intent and investment agreement 182
B. Letter of understanding and services agreement 183
C. Letter of understanding and agreement with independent subcontractor 184

28. Letters of Welcome 186
Letter of welcome from a church 187

29. Letters to Public Officials 188
A. Letter to a senator requesting a letter of congratulations for an Eagle Scout 189
B. Letter to a senator requesting an appointment to a military academy 190

30. Minutes and Agendas 191
A. Agenda for a fraternal organization meeting 192
B. Minutes of the meeting of a fraternal organization 193

31. Networking Letters 194
Networking letter sent to an industry colleague 195

32. Postponement Requests 196
Letter requesting postponement of an interview 197

33. Promissory Notes 198
Promissory note 199

34. Reference Letters and Letters of Recommendation 200
A. Letter of reference for a respected office manager 201
B. Letter of reference from a business professional 202
C. Letter of reference from a friend 203
D. Letter of reference from a supervisor 204
E. Letter of reference from a teacher 205

35. Relocation Cover Letters 206
A. Cover letter for a nurse relocating to a new town 207
B. Cover letter for a versatile young manager 208
C. Cover letter for a food service professional relocating to New Hampshire 209
D. Cover letter for an office professional relocating to Iowa 210
E. Cover letter for an office professional relocating to New York 211

36. Requests for a Raise 212
A. Letter from a comptroller requesting a raise 213
B. Letter from a production worker requesting a raise 214

37. Requests for a Transfer 216
Request for a transfer because of a supervisor 217

38. Requests for Financial Aid 218
Letter requesting financial aid for a mother with Alzheimer's 219

39. Requests for Promotion 221
A. Formal letter in military style seeking promotion to lieutenant 222
B. Letter requesting an internal promotion in an educational system 224
C. Letter requesting promotion within the United Way 225
D. Request for promotion within state government 226
E. Request for promotion and consideration for multiple job openings 227

40. Requests for Reconsideration 228
  A. Letter requesting reconsideration for a sales job 229
  B. Letter requesting reconsideration by the CIA for a job as a Special Agent 230

41. Resignation Letters 231
  A. Letter of resignation because of medical reasons 232
  B. Letter of resignation from a CPA firm 233
  C. Letter of resignation from a car dealership 234
  D. Letter resigning from a restaurant position 235

42. Writing to Publishers, Editors, and Literary Agents 236
  A. Letter from a pre-published author who wishes to write a children's series 237
  B. Query letter describing a manuscript 238
  C. Synopsis for a novel 239

Introduction To This Book

The theory behind this book is that **your best teacher is an excellent example**, and this book aims to provide you with dozens of clear and readable examples of the letters required in the special situations in life.

"A Picture Is Worth a Thousand Words."
Although we don't claim that this book contains an example of every letter you might need to write in life, you will find helpful examples of many letters which you will need to compose. When you next find yourself in need of writing a **letter of complaint,** you will have a handy reference in this book. When you have a friend to whom you would like to write a **letter of condolence,** you can use this book to help you figure out what to say. If you have someone who owes you money and you want to write a **collections letter,** you can find samples of collections letters varying in tone and levels of aggression.

Do you wonder how to address letters to prominent officials? You can find the proper salutation when writing to VIPs and titled people in this book.

Do you wonder how letters are written to obtain an appointment to a military academy?

Would you like to see how **letters of support** are written so that they can be used in legal proceedings as official statements and affidavits?

When you next need to write a **letter of reference** for an employee, would you like to reduce the time it takes by borrowing techniques from a few examples from this book?

Have you ever wanted to write a **letter of opposition** to a zoning request? Have you ever wanted to write a **letter of reprimand** to an employee? Do you need to prepare meeting minutes and agendas for the clubs and organizations to which you belong?

When you next go **job hunting,** wouldn't it be nice to model your cover letters based on real cover letters written by professional writers? If you are relocating to another town, would you like to see how to write cover letters directed at employers in another town and possibly in another state? If you need to resign, would you like to see some examples of great **letters of resignation?** Would you like to write a **letter requesting a raise?** If you want to **reschedule an interview,** or if you want to reopen a door which you closed previously, would you like to see how such a letter should be phrased? If you want to write a **letter to request consideration for internal promotion,** would you like to see the wording used successfully by other people?

Have you been treated unfairly in some way, by a business or individual, and would you like to appeal or protest their actions? Check out the letters in the **Appeals Section.**

The purpose of this book is to enrich your life and help you deal gracefully with many of the special situations in life which require you to write a letter. If you are looking for a type of letter which isn't in this book, call our editors at 910-483-6611 and we will try to give you some advice. In the meantime, good luck with all your letters in life! And we are hoping that this book will be of tremendous value to you in business and personal matters!

ANATOMY OF A LETTER

Date

Addressing the Cover Letter: It's best to get the exact name of the person to whom you are writing. This makes your approach personal.

Exact Name of Principal
Exact Title
School Name
School Address
City, State zip

Dear Exact Name (or Dear Principal if you don't know the Exact Name):

First Paragraph: The first paragraph explains why you are writing the letter.

With the enclosed resume, I would like to introduce myself and initiate the process of being considered for a position as a Mathematics Teacher in your high school.

Second Paragraph: Here you have a chance to give some details about yourself or your motivation for writing.

As you will see from my resume, I recently graduated from the University of Rhode Island with a B.S. degree in Mathematics which I earned **Magna Cum Laude**. I am especially proud of graduating with honors since I was combining a rigorous academic curriculum with a demanding work schedule which involved me in handling a variety of managerial, accounting, and customer service responsibilities.

Third Paragraph: In the third paragraph, you can continue "selling" your concept or reason for writing.

Although I graduated in May 1999 with my B.S. degree, I am 27 years old and offer considerable experience in working with children of all ages. I personally am a wife and mother and would bring to the classroom much understanding of the learning styles of children. I feel I would be skilled in classroom behavior management, and I offer a maturity which younger college graduates might not have. I am a responsible individual known for my well organized work habits and disciplined style.

Fourth Paragraph: Here you have another opportunity to reveal facts which will impress or persuade your reader.

I am deeply committed to a career in the teaching profession, and I intend in my spare time to earn my Master's degree in Mathematics and then a Ph.D. I am a highly motivated hard worker, and I feel my own strong values could be an inspiration to high school students. Although I have earned my degree in Mathematics with high honors, I am fully aware of how difficult mathematics is for many people, and I excel in translating abstract concepts into understandable language.

Final Paragraph: This is an important paragraph in your letter. You have to let the reader know what the next step is.

If you can use a vibrant young teaching professional who could enhance the fine reputation of your school, I hope you will contact me to suggest a time when I could make myself available for a personal interview. I can provide outstanding personal and professional references.

Sincerely,

Marcia Vivero

Alternate Final Paragraph: It's more aggressive (but not too aggressive) to let the employer know that you will be calling.

Alternate Final Paragraph (could be substituted for the final paragraph above):
I hope you will welcome my call next week when I try to arrange a time when we might speak briefly in person about your upcoming needs and my desire to become part of your teaching staff.

Formatting Your Letters

There is not just one style of formatting a letter. On the pages which follow, we give you two excellent examples of formats to use when you set up your letter. Which one you choose depends upon the tone you want to create and your own personal style.

The editor tends to use the semi-blocked style throughout this book, although there are situations when the blocked style seems appropriate. For example, we think the blocked style works well in military-style letters such as the letter of appeal of a military medical board's findings in the Letters of Appeals section.

Those who like the semi-blocked style say they feel a letter is more readable and has "room to breathe" on the page when the paragraphs are indented.

It doesn't matter which style you use, however. You should choose a format which you like the most and which seems to suit the type of letter you are writing.

Always type or word process your letters; handwritten letters usually do not look businesslike, and handwriting is often hard to read. E-mailed correspondence is more informal and is often not considered a substitute for a typed or word-processed letter.

It's important to date every letter you write. In this way, if your letter ends up on someone's desk, the reader will be able to see how recently you wrote it.

Here are some tips on a few recurring problems and errors in letters. **Where do you put commas when you have items in a sequence?** We like a comma placed after every item in a sequence; for example, place a comma after the names of cities such as Los Angeles, New York, Chicago, and Dallas. The second tip pertains to a common problem to watch out for. **Proofread your letters carefully to avoid repetition of words and phrases as well as misspelled words and grammatical errors.** In other words, after making sure that you have no spelling errors, read your letter to make sure you haven't used "very" (or any other word) five or six times. In addition to a dictionary, a thesaurus is a handy tool for writers because it shows synonyms you can use to avoid excessive repetition. **Avoid confusing its and it's.** This is a common mistake in letters, and you should learn the difference between these words. "It's" is an abbreviation for "it is" whereas "its" is possessive. For example, "The bassett hound took its dog bone into the center of the yard and dug a hole in the ground because it's a champion hunter and by instinct knows how to guard and hide its booty." When you show your reader that you know how to properly use simple words which are commonly confused with their "lookalikes," you are inspiring confidence in your reader and coming across as an educated person who pays attention to details.

Blocked Letter

Date

Inside address

Exact Name of Person
Title or Position
Name of Company
Address (number and street)
Address (city, state, and zip)

Salutation

Dear Exact Name of Person: (or Dear Sir or Madam if answering a blind ad.)

The blocked letter is not the style you will see in the majority of letters throughout this book. In the blocked letter, everything is blocked against the left margin.

I would appreciate an opportunity to talk with you soon about how I could contribute to your organization through my proven accounts management, customer service, and public relations skills.

You will see from my resume that I began working with Revco when I was 16 years old; I continued my employment with Revco while attending college and was promoted to Pharmacy Technician while earning my Bachelor of Business Administration degree. After college graduation, the university where I earned my degree recruited me for a job in its admissions office, and I excelled in handling a wide variety of administrative and public relations tasks.

Body

Most recently I have worked full-time as an Account Representative while going to school at nights and on the weekends to earn my MBA, which I received in May 1999. I was handling key accounts worth more than $2 million annually for my employer and was being groomed for rapid promotion into a higher management position.

I have, however, relocated permanently to the LaFayette area because I recently married and my husband owns and manages his own business in this area. I am seeking an employer who can use a highly motivated individual with very strong communication, sales, customer service, and public relations skills. Because I earned both my undergraduate and graduate degrees while excelling in demanding professional positions, I have acquired excellent organizational and time management skills which permit me to maximize my own productivity.

If you can use a self-starter who could rapidly become a valuable part of your organization, I hope you will contact me to suggest a time when we might meet to discuss your needs and how I might serve them. I can provide excellent personal and professional references.

Yours sincerely,

Signature

Louise Patton

cc: Thomas Crane

Date

Exact Name of Person
Title or Position
Name of Company
Address (number and street)
Address (city, state, and zip)

Dear Exact Name of Person: (or Dear Sir or Madam if answering a blind ad.)

    I would appreciate an opportunity to talk with you soon about how I could contribute to your organization through my proven accounts management, customer service, and public relations skills.

    You will see from my resume that I began working with Revco when I was 16 years old; I continued my employment with Revco while attending college and was promoted to Pharmacy Technician while earning my Bachelor of Business Administration degree. After college graduation, the university where I earned my degree recruited me for a job in its admissions office, and I excelled in handling a wide variety of administrative and public relations tasks.

    Most recently I have worked full-time as an Account Representative while going to school at nights and on the weekends to earn my M.B.A., which I received in May 1999. I was handling key accounts worth more than $2 million annually for my employer and was being groomed for rapid promotion into a higher management position.

    I have, however, relocated permanently to the LaFayette area because I recently married and my husband owns and manages his own business in this area. I am seeking an employer who can use a highly motivated individual with very strong communication, sales, customer service, and public relations skills. Because I earned both my undergraduate and graduate degrees while excelling in demanding professional positions, I have acquired excellent organizational and time management skills which permit me to maximize my own productivity.

    If you can use a self-starter who could rapidly become a valuable part of your organization, I hope you will contact me to suggest a time when we might meet to discuss your needs and how I might serve them. I can provide excellent personal and professional references.

    Yours sincerely,

    Louise Patton

cc: Thomas Crane

Semi-blocked Letter

Date

Three blank spaces

Address

Salutation

One blank space

Body

One blank space

Signature

cc: Indicates you are sending a copy of the letter to another person

Addressing Your Letters and Writing Your Salutation

When you write a letter for business, personal, or social reasons, the first problem you are likely to encounter is figuring out how to address the person to whom you are writing. In general, the form of a letter was shown on the preceding pages, and we will now show you how to address various officials in church and government so that your salutation can be correct. There are many excellent books you may consult if you are looking for more guidance in this area. We recommend the following book which you can consult in your library: *Protocol: The Complete Handbook of Diplomatic, Official and Social Usage* by authors Mary Jane McCaffree and Pauline Innis, published by Devon Publishing Co., Washington, DC. Please note that you may need to visit your reference librarian to obtain the correct zip code of the official to whom you are writing. Throughout this book, you will see numerous examples of the proper format for business and social letters. Just follow the style of the letters in this book and you will not go wrong.

A problem many of us encounter in business is how to handle proper names and greetings in a business letter. The most important rule here is to spell the person's name correctly!

Some common problems we encounter relate to women's names, and here are some brief rules about that and other common issues:
- If you don't know if the woman to whom you are writing is married or single:
  Dear Ms. Smith:
- If the person to whom you are writing is a medical or academic doctor:
  Dear Dr. Smith:
- If you don't know the name of the person to whom you are writing:
  Dear Sir or Madam:
- Never use the first name as the salutation in a letter:
  Dear Mary Smith:

ADDRESSING LETTERS TO U.S. GOVERNMENT OFFICIALS:

Writing to the President:
The President
The White House
Washington, DC 20510
Dear Mr. President:

Writing to the Vice President:
The Vice President
United States Senate
Washington, DC 20510
Dear Mr. Vice-President:

To the Chief Justice:
The Chief Justice of the United States
The Supreme Court
Washington, DC 20543
Dear Mr. Chief Justice:

To an Associate Justice:
Mr. Justice Smith
The Supreme Court
Washington, DC 20543
Dear Mr. Justice:

To a U.S. Senator:
The Honorable Anne Smith
United States Senate
Washington, DC 20510
Dear Senator Smith:

To a U.S. Representative:
The Honorable Anne Jackson
The United States House of Representatives
Washington, DC zip code
Dear Mrs. Jackson:

To the Speaker of the House of Representatives:
The Honorable James Jones
Speaker of the House of Representatives
Washington, DC zip code

To U.S. Government Officials:
Mr. James Jarvis
Title
Address zip code

To the Governor:
The Honorable James Ray Jarvis
Governor of (State)
Address
City, State zip code
Dear Governor Jarvis:

To the Lieutenant Governor:
The Honorable Meredith Jones
Lt. Governor of (State)
Address
City, State zip code
Dear Mrs. Jones:

To a State Senator:
The Honorable James Ray Jarvis
The State Senate
State Capitol
Address zip code
Dear Senator Jarvis:

To a State Assemblyman or Representative:
The Honorable Meredith Jones
House of Representatives (or The Assembly)
State Capitol
Address zip code
Dear Mrs. Jones:

To a Federal Judge:
The Honorable James Ray Jarvis
United States District Judge
Address zip code
Dear Judge Jarvis:

To a State or Local Judge:
The Honorable Meredith Jones
Judge of Superior Court
Address zip code
Dear Judge Jones:

To a U.S. Ambassador:
The Honorable Kyle Smith
American Ambassador
American Consul-General

Dear Mr. Ambassador:
or Dear Madam Ambassador:

To a U.S. Consul-General, Consul, Vice-Consul, or Charge d'Affaires:
Kyle Smith, Esq.
or American Consul
or American Vice-Consul
or American Charge d'Affaires
Dear Sir:
or Dear Madam:

To U.S. Delegate to the United Nations:
Mr. James Ray Jarvis
Chief of the United States Mission to the
United Nations
Dear Mr. Jarvis:

To the Ambassador to the U.S.
His Excellency James Ray Jarvis
Ambassador of (Country)
Note this exception: Address British officials as
British Ambassador, British Minister, etc.
Dear Mr. Ambassador:

To the Foreign Minister:
The Honorable James Ray Jarvis
Dear Mr. Minister:

To a Diplomatic Official with a Personal Title:
His Excellency, Count James Ray Jarvis
Ambassador of (Country)
Dear Mr. Ambassador:

**To the Secretary-General
of the United Nations:**
His Excellency James Ray Jarvis
Secretary-General of the United Nations
Dear Mr. Jarvis:

To the President of a Republic:
His Excellency Meredith James
President of the Republic of (Country)
Dear Mr. President:

To the Prime Minister of Great Britain:
The Right Honorable James Ray Jarvis
Prime Minister
My dear Mr. Prime Minister:

To the Prime Minister of Canada:
The Right Honorable Kyle Smith
Prime Minister of the Dominion of Canada
My dear Mr. Smith:

ADDRESSING MILITARY OFFICERS AND ENLISTED SOLDIERS:

Please note that only the first example shows the complete style of addressing a military professional, with full rank and full name followed by a comma, and then the abbreviation of the branch of service:

If he or she is **Army**:	General James Ray Jarvis, U.S.A.
If he or she is **Army Reserve**:	Major Andrew Smith, U.S.A.R.
If he or she is active-duty **Navy**:	Lieutenant Commander Nancy Smith, U.S.N.
If he or she is in the **Naval Reserve**:	Warrant Officer Jackson Smith, U.S.N.R.
If he or she is in the **Coast Guard**:	Lieutenant Amy Warren, U.S.C.G.
If he/she is in the **Coast Guard Reserve**:	Lieutenant Samuel Anthony, U.S.C.G.R.
If he or she is in the **Marine Corps**:	Captain John Smith, U.S.M.C.
If he/she is in the **Marine Corps Reserve**:	Captain Jennifer Wallace, U.S.M.C.R.

When the addressee is retired: put (Ret.) after the service initials:
General James Ray Jarvis, U.S.A. (Ret.)

General James Ray Jarvis, —
Dear General Jarvis:

Lieutenant General James Ray Jarvis, —
Dear General Jarvis:

Major General James Ray Jarvis, —
Dear General Jarvis:

Brigadier General James Ray Jarvis, —
Dear General Jarvis:

Colonel James Ray Jarvis, —
Dear Colonel Jarvis:

Lieutenant Colonel James Ray Jarvis, —
Dear Colonel Jarvis:

Major James Ray Jarvis, —
Dear Major Jarvis:

Captain James Ray Jarvis, —
Dear Captain Jarvis:

First Lieutenant James Ray Jarvis, —
Dear Lieutenant Jarvis:

Second Lieutenant James Ray Jarvis, —
Dear Lieutenant Jarvis:

Chaplain James Ray Jarvis, —
Dear Chaplain Jarvis:

Fleet Admiral Amy Smith, —
Dear Admiral Smith:

Vice Admiral James Ray Jarvis, —
Dear Vice Admiral Jarvis:

Rear Admiral Amy Smith, —
Dear Admiral Smith:

Commander James Ray Jarvis, —
Dear Commander Jarvis:

Lieutenant Commander Amy Smith, —
Dear Commander Smith:

Lieutenant James Ray Jarvis, —
Dear Lieutenant Jarvis:

Ensign Jane Smith, —
Dear Ms. Smith

Captain James Ray Jarvis, —
Dear Captain:

Airman John Jones, —
Dear Airman Jones:

Corporal John Jones, —
Dear Corporal Jones:

Master Sergeant Amy Smith, —
Dear Sergeant Smith:

Midshipman James Ray Jarvis, —
Dear Midshipman Jarvis:

Petty Officer Amy Smith, —
Dear Ms. Smith:

Private James Ray Jarvis, —
Dear Private Jarvis:

Seaman Amy Smith, —
Dear Seaman Smith:

Specialist James Ray Jarvis, —
Dear Specialist Jarvis:

Warrant Officer Amy Smith, —
Dear Ms. Smith:

ADDRESSING MEMBERS OF THE CLERGY:

To the Anglican Archbishop:
To His Grace
The Lord Archbishop of (Area)
Dear Archbishop:

To a Bishop:
The Right Reverend James Ray Jarvis
Dear Bishop:

To the Protestant Archdeacon:
The Venerable James Ray Jarvis
The Archdeacon of (Area)
Diocese of (Area)
Dear Archdeacon:

To an Academic or Seminary Dean:
The Very Reverend James Ray Jarvis
Dean of (Seminary)
Dear Dean Jarvis:

To a Protestant Minister or Priest:
The Reverend James Ray Jarvis
Dear Dr. Jarvis (if a Ph.D.)
or *Dear Mr. Jarvis:*

To a Rabbi:
Rabbi James Ray Jarvis
Dear Rabbi Jarvis
or *Dear Dr. Jarvis (if a Ph.D.)*

To The Pope:
His Holiness The Pope
Vatican City
Italy
Your Holiness:

To a Cardinal:
His Eminence James Ray Jarvis
Archbishop of (Area)
Dear Cardinal Jarvis:

To the Archbishop:
The Most Reverend James Ray Jarvis
Dear Archbishop:

To a Bishop:
The Most Reverend James Ray Jarvis
Dear Bishop:

To an Abbot:
The Right Reverend James Ray Jarvis
Dear Father Jarvis:

To a Canon:
The Very Reverend Canon James Ray Jarvis
Dear Canon Jarvis:

To the Monsignor:
The Right (or Very) Reverend Msgr. James Jarvis
Dear Monsignor Jarvis:

To the Superior of a Brotherhood:
The Very Reverend James Ray Jarvis
Title
Dear Father Superior:

To a Sister Superior:
The Reverend Sister Superior
Dear Sister Superior:

To the Mother Superior of Sisterhood:
The Reverend Mother Superior
Name of Convent
Dear Reverent Mother:

To a Brother:
Brother James Ray Jarvis
Dear Brother Jarvis:

To a Priest:
The Reverend James Ray Jarvis
Dear Father Jarvis:

To a Sister:
Sister (Full Religious Name)
Dear Sister:

To a member of the Convent Community:
Mother (Full Name)
Name of Convent
Dear Mother (Last Name):

Letters of Appeal
(also see Letters of Complaint)

Sometimes it's necessary to write a letter of appeal if you feel you encountered a situation in which you were shortchanged. The matters which are being appealed in this section range from medical issues to career-threatening problems.

Giving the details is important.

A main thing to keep in mind when writing an appeals letter is that you need to give as many details, dates, specific names, and so forth as possible so that the individual reading your letter of complaint will clearly follow your train of thought and be persuaded by your point of view. If the facts are on your side, make sure you give the facts in very detailed and explicit ways. It's OK to show your emotion in such a letter but make sure you don't substitute emotion for factual information.

Remember that you are writing to persuade, not just complain.

A letter of complaint is similar to an appeals letter, but they are different in one major respect: often a complaint letter is written to ventilate your negative feelings about an incident, or to express your objections to a proposed change, whereas an appeals letter is often written in an attempt to get a decision overturned or changed in your favor. You must persuade your reader in an appeals letter.

State your request, expectation, or recommendation clearly.

In the letters that follow, you will notice that the writers clearly state, often more than once, the outcome they are seeking. For example:

- "We request an additional 120 days for completion of this project."
- "In conclusion, we feel that after you review the facts and the company's policies, you will determine that there has been no violation of company policy and will make the decision to return the territory in question to our division."
- I wish to continue in my employment with General Life of California, and I hope you will review my circumstances and permit me to become reinstated with the company."

Before you write a letter of appeal, write down the result you hope will be achieved by the letter you are writing, and state very clearly for your busy reader the action you hope he or she will take.

Be as clear and concise as you can be.

If your reader is confused after reading your letter of appeal, he or she may do nothing. A good way to test whether or not your letter "makes sense" is to read it out loud to someone else and see if that person understands your point of view and would be persuaded to take the action you desire. Remember that writing and rewriting are the keys to a great letter!

ATTENTION: Clerk of Superior Court

SUBJECT: Notice of Appeal

DATE: Date

Dear Sir or Madam:

Formal request for an appeal

I am requesting an appeal on the case of Dorothy Smith vs. Billy Newton which was scheduled for Monday, December 30, 1999, at 10:50 A.M. in the Dragon County Courthouse, Room 64.

Summons was not served on me personally

My reason for this appeal is that I had not been properly served the summons and there was never an attempt made to collect the past due amount of money. I had been in San Diego, CA, working at General Electric. A neighbor of mine informed my family of the summons to appear in court.

My desire to settle the matter

Prior to that, I had been in contact with Ms. Angela Davis (483-6611) of Best Mortgage Brokers to make an attempt to purchase a home. Mrs. Smith was well aware of this. Because I was not served the summons, I was, therefore, deprived of my due process and right to appear in court to present my case. The judgement rendered against me has placed me and my family in a financial "straight jacket." I would like to settle this matter as soon as possible with both Dorothy Smith and Dragon County. I would like to appear in court on this matter.

Thank you for your time and consideration of my formal request for an appeal of the case.

Yours sincerely,

Billy Newton

APPEAL OF A COURT ACTION

Appealing a court summons

It's often simply a matter of writing a letter such as this one if you feel a court action has been taken "behind your back." In this case, he alleges that the summons was not properly served, so he appeals for an opportunity to have his "day in court" and to present his case.

TO: Mr. Mark Coaglet
    President, Best Life of Georgia

FROM: Ayanna Stevenski

DATE: December 19, 1999

Dear Mr. Coaglet:

I am writing this letter to make you aware of circumstances out of my control which caused problems in my employment, and I am respectfully requesting that you review my previous circumstances and my radically transformed current situation and permit me to continue employment as an agent with Best Life of Georgia. Please accept this letter as a formal appeal of my recent dismissal from the company on grounds of instability and poor production.

I experienced problems due to medical prescriptions. Due to a failed marriage and a life-threatening ectopic pregnancy which required emergency surgery, I was put on Prozac for depression in December 1997. However, Prozac produced adverse effects, and rather than taking me off the Prozac, my physician prescribed 17 different mood-altering drugs to counteract the side effects of the Prozac. Subsequently I learned that this physician had been barred from three different hospitals. Prior to this I had never been in any kind of trouble. I have since been informed by several physicians that my aberrant behavior was due to a toxic reaction caused by the buildup of mood-altering chemicals which were administered and monitored incorrectly.

Subsequent employment with Best Life of Georgia. I was hired as an agent with Best Life of Georgia in May 1998. During my first three months of production, my mother died tragically, and this is the reason I did not make my quota with Jefferson Pilot. As the only child of parents who sacrificed greatly to raise me, I felt obligated to take three months off to help my father settle my mother's estate. When I returned to my employment as an agent with Best Life of Georgia, I was counseled on two separate occasions and given written warnings about the mood swings which I exhibited while I was on the job and which resulted in customer problems on two occasions. I truly believe that what was perceived of as mood swings by my supervisor were due to adverse effects of medications experimentally prescribed by my physician. After the second incident and my second warning, I immediately consulted another physician, and he insisted that I immediately discontinue all medications prescribed by the original doctor. Since I have been under the care of Dr. Phyllis Johnston of Grand Memorial Hospital, there have been no incidents.

My life is now stable and I am free of prescription drugs. I am now a happy and stable person, and I have discontinued use of the prescription drugs which caused my aberrant behavior. I am certain that I am capable of being a very successful agent for Best Life of Georgia. Please allow me to continue to serve a company that I have come to regard as "family" and that I wish to continue to serve with distinction. I humbly appeal my dismissal for cause and beseech you to feel compassion for unfortunate circumstances in my life which no longer exist. Thank you for your consideration.

APPEAL OF A DISMISSAL FROM A JOB

Appealing a job dismissal
A decision can often be reversed because of "mitigating factors" or because of circumstances outside your control. This letter intends to clarify the circumstances which produced the behavior that led to her dismissal, and she respectfully requests a second chance at employment with the company. Notice that she doesn't dispute that she behaved erratically; she simply wants to stress that the problem is behind her.

Date

Mr. Sam Smith
General Manager
Gracious Manner Nutrition Products
Address
City, state zip

Dear Mr. Smith:

This letter is written to respectfully request that you review the facts contained herein and reverse the recent company decision pertaining to the employment of James Ray Jarvis as well as the punitive fine levied on my franchise. I have been a loyal and profitable franchisee for more than 16 years, and I believe you are acquainted with my reputation as an honest and hard-working businessman.

We have not violated company policy.

On (exact date), I received a letter from Human Resources Vice President Jim Harding stating that flagrant violations of policy had been committed by our franchise in employing James Ray Jarvis; he informed me that he was recommending to the Board of Directors that our franchise be fined $10,000 while simultaneously being given an ultimatum to terminate the employment of James Ray Jarvis. I ask for your patient reading of this letter after which I feel certain you will reach a fair decision. This letter is an attempt to inform and explain to you that not only were there no violations of Gracious Manner policy on our part, but as a matter of fact, everything we did was in accordance with policy and based on information and advice given to us by our corporate office. Specifically, I received information and direction verbally and in writing from LaTonya Smith in Franchise Services, and we consulted extensively with her prior to employing James Ray Jarvis as an independent subcontractor. Please understand that I am not trying to get Ms. LaTonya Smith in trouble; I believe any errors on her part were innocent.

The facts suggest errors on the part of the corporate office.

The following is a list of the facts, as best as I can recall, which led to our employment of James Ray Jarvis on (exact date).

1. Mr. Jarvis responded to an advertisement we placed in our local newspaper on (exact date).
2. Mr. Jarvis's resume was reviewed, and he was invited to come in for an interview. The resume was in a functional format rather than a chronological format, and the dates and locations of Mr. Jarvis's previous employment were not apparent.
3. What was apparent from his resume was that he had the credentials we were seeking in a licensed electrician.
4. As is our normal company policy, on (exact date) we completed the paperwork required by our corporate office when we wish to hire an independent subcontractor in our franchise. The next step was for the corporate office to perform the necessary background investigation.
5. On (exact date) we received a fax from LaTonya Smith in the corporate office that the background check had been completed and that James Ray Jarvis was cleared for employment.

APPEAL TO A CORPORATION FROM A FRANCHISEE CHALLENGING A FINE AND EMPLOYMENT PRACTICES

Challenging the direct orders of the parent company is what this letter is all about. When you write such a letter, try to make a concise statement in the first paragraph about why you are writing, and then the succeeding paragraphs should "tell the tale" and recite the facts, especially the facts which will help to persuade the reader to take the action you are requesting.

6. We offered Mr. Jarvis employment on (exact date) at a rate of $10.75 an hour.
7. Mr. Jarvis commenced his employment with us on (exact date) and he has always performed as a model employee with a perfect record of attendance while performing work of the highest quality.
8. On (exact date), nearly six months after we hired Mr. Jarvis, we received an agitated call from Mr. Harding's secretary informing us that we had hired an individual with a record as a felon, and that we were in violation of company policy.
9. We responded that we had followed company procedures at every step of the way, and that the problem appeared to reside in the manner in which the background check had been conducted by the Human Resources Department. Mr. Harding's secretary replied that, although the application filled out by Mr. Jarvis stated that he was at the Central City Department of Corrections from 1996-99, Human Resources assumed that he had been an Electrician there. Although she had called the Department of Corrections to verify the time he was at the Central City facility, they would not provide any information and she failed to figure out that Mr. Jarvis had been incarcerated during that time and that he was in a prison apprenticeship program which had led to a diploma in Electrical Wiring and Installation.

The situation we are in is ludicrous.

With all due respect to you and to our fine organization of which I am proud to be a part, I believe that the corporate Human Resources Department is attempting to find a "scapegoat" so that it can be absolved of any responsibility for not being in compliance with our traditional corporate policy that felons are not offered employment as subcontractors. I believe the conventional wisdom has been that, because felons cannot be bonded, they must not be allowed to work unsupervised within any of our corporate facilities, as our electrical subcontractors must do. The fine print in our company manual states that any franchise which hires a felon will be fined $10,000! In the spirit of all that is fair and decent, I absolutely resist being levied with such a fine. The colonists overthrew the British for excesses such as this, sir. Please do not allow an overbearing and perhaps antiquated company policy to diminish the zest of, and perhaps cause the alienation of, your franchisees who are your bread and butter. Let's be fair, above all. For some reason of which fate may be a part, the background investigation failed to reveal the felony background of Mr. Jarvis. I am not interested in pointing a finger or finding a scapegoat; I want to find a solution to this problem.

What we recommend is as follows:

I believe the most fair and compassionate course of action is **not** to terminate Mr. Jarvis's employment, which I have been ordered to do by the corporate office. Mr. Jarvis is a rehabilitated individual and is remarried with a family of three to support. He has done an excellent job. I believe our entire policy toward hiring felons must be reexamined, and I believe we must support the right of felons to seek employment in our society. I humbly appeal the corporate office's decision to fine me $10,000 and to require me to fire Mr. Jarvis. Please evaluate these facts and render a decision consistent with your reputation as a fair individual and a strategic thinker.

With best regards,

Mason Woodward
Franchisee, District #10

APPEAL TO A CORPORATION FROM A FRANCHISEE CHALLENGING A FINE AND EMPLOYMENT PRACTICES

In the second page of this letter, you will see that the writer tries to make a multifaceted appeal. If one argument doesn't work on the reader, maybe another argument or fact will do the job. Notice that the final paragraph is a summary paragraph, which tells the reader what action you want him or her to take. Watch your tone throughout a letter of appeal; you don't want to alienate your reader by an arrogant tone.

RE: Formal Rebuttal of Supervisor's Evaluation

FROM: Madeline Knox, SSN 122-22-1111
       Assistant Manager, Unit 32, District #2

DATE:

APPEAL OF A SUPERVISOR'S RATING

Sometimes it is necessary to challenge a supervisor's performance appraisal of you, especially when you think it is lacking in merit. Often such performance evaluations affect your chances of future promotion, and the "numbers" assigned to you by an unfair supervisor can follow you around for a long time. There is a technique to challenging a supervisor's professional evaluation, and this letter is a model.

To Whom It May Concern:

As a hard-working and loyal employee of the ABC Company for the past seven years, I, Madeline Knox, wish to offer a rebuttal to the Satisfactory rating I received on my most recent quarterly performance evaluation, and I wish to appeal the rating. It is my desire that the Satisfactory rating be changed to an Excellent rating since Excellent is what I strongly feel I deserve. When I worked in District #3 for the company prior to my reassignment to District #2 six months ago, my managerial and customer service skills were always rated Excellent. They have not changed.

My customer service skills are excellent.

My customer service skills are Excellent instead of Satisfactory, as I was rated. Throughout each day and all year long, I greet all customers with a smile and pride myself on doing my part to assure that each customer has a cheerful day. At no time on my shift have I ever had a customer complaint. I disagree with the supervisor's rating that my customer service skills are Satisfactory and "in need of improvement." I take very seriously my job to provide the finest personal experience and professional service for our customers.

My managerial skills are excellent.

My managerial skills have never been formally tested to determine if they need improvement, and I feel that the "in need of improvement" rating I was given is incorrect and will impede my ability to rise into higher management ranks in the company. As an assistant manager I have certainly tried to make suggestions and recommendations that would improve profitability. However, it has been my experience that the assistant manager's opinion is frequently ignored. On my own initiative throughout 1999, I made numerous suggestions which I believe would have improved our profitability while eliminating slow-moving stock. For example, one of my first suggestions after I was reassigned to District #2 was that we evaluate all vendors' products with the intention of identifying the slow-moving items. My store manager agreed.

- The first vendor I approached about dead stock was Woodstock. I suggested that his company take out three types of beverage which were not selling. The vendor agreed and told me he would. Later, I was informed by my store manager that "we did not want to be short." I believe the vendor had gone over my head at the store level to reverse my suggestion. My attempts to change the product mix in District #2 have not been successful because my frontline management opinions about "what's moving and what's not moving" have not been listened to.

- On another occasion I was blamed for a problem which I believe was a clerical error in the shipping and receiving department. I ordered merchandise and completed the correct paperwork indicating that fact. In December 1999, my store received a double shipment, and I was blamed for this error.

I offer proven management potential.
In terms of advancement potential, I feel that I would make an excellent store manager if given the opportunity. In terms of "Potential to develop" and "Initiative"—two key rated areas—I feel I should have received the highest ratings. I am well known for my willingness to work irregular hours and fill in for other employees experiencing schedule problems so that our organization can capably serve customers and maximize profitability.

I request a formal hearing.
I can only surmise that a lack of the proper amount of time needed to observe my skills and abilities was probably the main factor in my receiving a lower evaluation than I deserve from my current supervisor and store manager. I certainly am not criticizing my store manager or anyone else personally in writing this rebuttal. I simply want to "set the record straight" so that my loyal and faithful service to the company can continue. It is my desire to serve the company in higher and higher levels of managerial responsibility. I respectfully request a formal hearing about this matter so that I can be questioned about my abilities and potential and a fair evaluation made of my performance.

Sincerely,

Madeline Knox

APPEAL OF A SUPERVISOR'S RATING

The final paragraph of an appeals letter can be very important. You want to adopt as conciliatory a tone as possible because your overall aim is reconciliation and compromise. Be aware that there are many things you should NOT do in a letter of appeal: (1) You don't need to say everything you think. (2) You don't need to insult or slander anyone. (3) You don't need to come across as persistently grumpy and irascible. Remember that you are not trying to make anyone angry in an appeals letter. It is a letter of appeal, not a letter of insult.

Date

Mr. James Jarvis, Chairman of the Board
XYZ Beverage Company
3528 Yorkshire Road, Suite 92
Grand Rapids, MI 80920

Dear Mr. Jarvis:

APPEAL OF A COMPANY'S FAILURE TO PAY RETIREMENT FUNDS

Often it's worth writing a great letter to try to resolve a problem before going to the trouble and expense of involving a lawyer. Notice the allusion to the possible involvement of a "third party" in the final paragraph of the letter. This letter is a request for fair treatment, and the writer presents a precedent for the company's taking the action which he is seeking. Notice that this individual has failed to get middle management to take appropriate action, so he is writing to the chairman of the board to make him personally aware of the matter.

I am writing this letter on behalf of myself and Denise Smith, whose signature also appears at the end of this letter. In January of 1999, both Denise Smith and I left the employ of XYZ Beverage Company of Grand Rapids. Both of us were 100% vested in the company's retirement plan. Two friends of ours, also employees of XYZ Beverage Company, told us that after they had been gone for one year, the company had paid them the funds in their retirement accounts. Ms. Smith and I each contacted the company and spoke with Kim Goforth. She told us that, after we had been separated from XYZ Beverage for a period of one year, she would send us the paperwork to fill out and we would then receive the funds in our retirement accounts. I asked her if there was a law that stated we had to wait one year, and she replied that the waiting period was in case we were to return to work with the company before that year was up.

One year and one month after we left the company, neither Ms. Smith nor I had received communication from the company or from Kim Goforth. We both called and were told by Kim Goforth that we would have to wait until a quarterly audit at the end of March. She said she would know how much we had in our retirements accounts at that time, and then she would send us the paperwork. Nothing happened, so we each called again. At that time, she told us that she guessed she must have "let it fall through the cracks." She then informed me that there was over $5,000 in the account, and that she would write a check that day if the amount was under the $5,000 limit. I asked her why didn't she just go ahead and write me the check anyway, and she said that the company would go broke if she just wrote checks to everyone.

The next time we spoke, Kim Goforth informed me that we would have to wait until the age of 65 before we could collect the funds in our retirement accounts. This contradicted what she had told us originally, regarding the one-year waiting period. When I asked Kim Goforth what would happen to the funds in my retirement account if I did not reach the age of 65, she could offer no answer at all. Since some of our coworkers unfortunately passed away before reaching that age, it seems she should have known how that situation had been handled in the past.

I finally told Ms. Goforth that in light of what had happened, Ms. Smith and I would have to get an attorney and pursue the matter through legal channels. She replied, "That would be 'cool'." Well, we don't think that would be "cool." Since we could not get this matter resolved by lower-level officials at XYZ Beverage Company, we are asking for your assistance in resolving this matter. We are hopeful that we will not need the services of a third party to resolve this matter.

Yours sincerely,

Denise Smith   Dennis Johnson

Date

Dear Mr. Forest:

It has come to my attention that David Douglas is struggling with some problems in your classroom, and I am hopeful these problems can be resolved through cooperation.

David brought home his progress report today and he has an average of 84 C largely due to the fact that you had recorded four zeros for work which he had turned in and which you had graded.

One of the zeros

When Douglas saw his progress report today, he knew immediately that the zeros were wrong. He retrieved from his bookbag and showed you one of the papers for which he had received a zero, and you took that paper on Metallurgical Processes on which you had written "A." Apparently this grade was not recorded in your gradebook.

Missing work sheet: Cyclops Law Problems Worksheet

This appears to be a missing grade which was not recorded in your grade book. David went home with Brian Murphy on 03/18/99 and completed the Cyclops Law Problems worksheet, which was turned in the next day. In your class students exchange papers and grade each other's, and David made a 100. David believes that fellow student Andrea Burgess graded this paper but he is not certain. This grade was not recorded in your gradebook, but David did the work and turned in the worksheet and Brian Murphy and his mother can verify the above. Brian remembers getting a 90 and remembers David getting a 100. Unfortunately, David cannot locate this paper because you did not give this paper back. It can be verified that David was in attendance on that day, that he completed the worksheet and handed it in, and the worksheet must still be in your possession. David did not earn a zero on this worksheet.

Two of the zeros

David made up two of the quizzes for which he had received a zero. He took two of the quizzes on March 25. He had taken the two quizzes previously but was told at the end of the two quizzes that he had used the wrong notes but would be allowed to make up the quizzes in time to affect this grading period. The two quizzes which David was required to make up he had made 100 on, and he believes he also made 100 on the makeups.

I have signatures from Brian Murphy and from Brian's mother verifying the fact that the worksheet was done and turned in. We are hopeful that you can find the worksheet. David feels that he has worked hard to earn an A in your class, and we are hopeful that these clerical errors can be corrected.

Sincerely,

Mary Sikes (David's mother)   David Douglas

Brian Murphy   Mary Murphy

APPEAL TO A TEACHER ABOUT A CHILD'S GRADES

There's something about putting your concerns in writing that makes people pay more attention to your problem. In this letter, a parent is writing to a busy teacher politely challenging a child's grades and providing facts which demonstrate that the teacher is in error.

XYZ BUILDING CONTRACTORS
1110 Hay Street, Haymount, Georgia 85723
Phone: 910-483-6611 E-mail: preppub@aol.com Fax: 910-483-2439

Date

Housing Board of Appeals
Street Address
City, State zip
Reference Project 654, Bid #05340

Dear Ladies and Gentlemen:

This letter is a formal request for an extension of 120 days for completion of a project which we have undertaken for the Department of Housing. It is our hope that we will make clear in this letter that we are seeking an extension because of reasons outside of our control, and we respectfully request the understanding of the Housing Board of Appeals and the granting of an extension of 120 days.

Equipment problems which led to the delay have been resolved:
The delays in completing the renovations are due to equipment availability problems caused by manufacturer stockout as well as unexpected manpower shortages of our electrical and plumbing subcontractors. Through resourceful problem-solving, we resolved equipment problems by ordering sinks and fixtures from a vendor in California rather than our usual source, which is experiencing shipping problems due to a labor strike. The equipment is expected to arrive within 10 days from the writing of this letter.

Resolution of labor problems:
The manpower problems have also been resolved. Both the electrical and the plumbing subcontractor we chose for this project are known for quality work and reliability. However, the electrical subcontractor was recently saddened by the loss of a key employee on November 30 of this year due to a fatal motorcyle accident, and the plumbing subcontractor experienced temporary problems due to a fire on December 5 of this year which caused our plumber to lose his facility. The plumber (Larry Jones & Company of Hope Springs) has recovered and, because of his excellent industry connections and problem-solving skills, has been offered assistance by his industry competitors in his difficult circumstances. Since all his tools and equipment burned to the ground, he has been loaned all necessary equipment to complete the project.

Request for an additional 120 days to complete the project:
We ask the Housing Appeals Board to take into consideration our company's reputation for quality work and our commitment to seeing this job through to completion. We remain committed to finishing the project in a high-quality fashion. Although we realize the normal action of the Department of Housing is to cancel a project which is more than 30 days in delay, we respectfully request an additional 120 days for the final completion of this project.

Sincerely,

Nancy and Buddy Smith

APPEAL TO THE HOUSING BOARD

There are rules and regulations which determine how you can "play the game" in business and government contracting situations. As you will see when you read this letter, this company fell victim to a county regulation that a contract can be cancelled when the contractor experiences delays of more than 30 days. A letter such as this one can initiate a formal review and present the circumstances which caused the delay.

Date

Mr. Bill McGowan
General Manager
Belk Department Stores
583 Cross Creek Road
Haymount, LA 87523

Dear Mr. McGowan:

This is a formal request for you to reconsider your decision to transfer me from the Belk Store in Livermore Mall to the store in Beaver Run Mall. My reasons are twofold:

1. The transfer poses a hardship to me. On my current schedule, I work from 3:15 until 11:15. This schedule permits me to keep my three-year-old grandchild. The transfer would require me to work in the mornings. Although you told me verbally that the Beaver Run store would work with my scheduling needs, the schedule which they have posted requires me to go to work at 6:30 a.m.

2. I am an outstanding employee and am doing an excellent job in my current position. I get along very well with all of my coworkers, employees, and the branch manager. I am very loyal to Belks and to my supervisor. I always work hard to ensure that the operation of the store runs smoothly. I have done, and continue to do, an excellent job at Livermore. To my knowledge, all employees enjoy working with me. I treat everyone fairly and show compassion toward all employees. I demonstrate a great deal of respect for my manager and she knows that she can always depend on me, no matter what the task.

I want to thank you for allowing me to communicate my feeling regarding this matter to you, and I hope that you will understand my position. I know that you are by reputation a caring and understanding general manager, and I am formally requesting that you allow me to remain at the Belk Store in Livermore Mall. This is where I believe that I can be of best service to Belk. During my fifteen years of service to Belk this is the first written request that I have ever made for a schedule consideration.

Yours sincerely,

Roseanne Wicker

APPEAL OF A TRANSFER

Sometimes a transfer in business can cause personal hardships. This letter is an attempt to appeal the decision of a supervisor to transfer a loyal employee to a mall which required her to work a less convenient schedule. This letter resulted in the employee being returned to her previous place of employment, because the supervisor understood her circumstances based on the facts she presented in the letter. Notice that she is very specific in the last paragraph about what she is requesting. When you write a letter of appeal, don't be vague about what you are asking your reader to do!

Date

SUBJECT: Rebuttal of MOS/Medical Retention Board Findings of Clark D. Emerson
THRU: President, MOS/Medical Retention board
TO: Commander
        99th Infantry Division
        Fort Defense, VA 12345

APPEAL OF A MEDICAL BOARD DECISION

There are rules and regulations which determine how you can "play the game" in the military, too. This young military professional is distressed because the medical board has decided that he cannot remain in military service because of a medical condition. He writes this memorandum of explanation providing information which he believes could result in the medical board's reversing its decision.

---

1. On May 5, 1999, there was a mandatory review of my medical profile by the MOS/Medical Retention Board. The recommendation of the board was that my case be referred to the Army's Physical Disability System because of some medical problems I have experienced. As you are aware, this in effect means that I must abandon my hopes and dreams for a military career. This is a memorandum of explanation which contains my formal request for an appeal of the board's decision.

2. The purpose of this memorandum is to provide additional information not already presented by me which I believe would give the board reason to reevaluate their decision so that I would have one of two options:
   a. Recommend to PERSCOM that I be reclassified from my current combat role to a personnel administration MOS. I provide in-depth details in this memo about the benefits to the U.S. Army of reclassifying me into the 23 Series Personnel Administration.
   Or
   b. Place me in a six-month Probationary Period. I provide a detailed explanation in this memorandum of how the medical condition in question in diminishing.

3. **I have received excellent evaluations throughout my military career; the medical condition reviewed by the board has never been mentioned on any of my performance evaluations and has never caused a problem for me on the job.** I respectfully suggest that, if my medical condition were so severe or restrictive that I should be considered for discharge or medical retirement, I would have experienced numerous on-the-job problems which would have been documented on my performance appraisals. Instead, my performance appraisals have described me as a hard worker and exemplary soldier. I began serving my country in the U.S. Army in 1995 and utilized my spare time in the evenings and on weekends to pursue my B.S. in Public Administration. I excelled in an administrative position in Ft. Sill, OK, from 1995-96; as an Artilleryman in Korea from 1996-97; as an Artilleryman (airborne qualified) at Ft. Campbell, KY, in 1997; and as an Administrative NCO at Ft. Campbell from 1997-present.

4. **My medical condition is improving and may be totally cured.** In the past six months, I have been under the care of Major Jenkins, who has prescribed very small doses of a medication called Zorinol, which helps to maintain body equilibrium. During my treatment with Zorinol, the medical problem which I have experienced called Dystasia has lessened. The condition which concerned the Medical Board was I had experienced two or three episodes monthly lasting from a few seconds to two minutes in which I experienced what appeared to be a mild form of epilepsy. I am very delighted that Dr. Jenkins has prescribed Zorinol from which I have suffered no side effects; there has been a dramatic reduction in this medical condition

because of this pharmaceutical product. In the last five months, I have observed a steadily decreasing incidence of the episodes: In the last five months I have experienced at most one episode a month, and I have experienced no episodes for the past month. **My condition seems to be either cured or in decline**—and I am hoping it is in remission totally—and I feel, at the very least, I should be allowed to remain in military service in a Probationary Period so that medical authorities can determine if my progress under this drug will lead to a permanent and full improvement.

5. **My chain of command has recommended that I be retained in a new MOS, and I have much to offer the U.S. Army in a Personnel Administration MOS.** With only one semester short of earning my college degree in Public Administration, I have much to offer the military if I were allowed to retrain into this MOS. While I have excelled as an artilleryman and paratrooper, I fully realize that the U.S. Army may not wish me to be assigned to a combat MOS because of my current and hopefully temporary condition. I am a team player and it is my heartfelt desire to serve the U.S. Army and my country in whatever capacity the medical board finds appropriate, and I would welcome the challenge of serving in a Personnel Administration MOS since I offer extensive education and professional skills in this area. My Battery Commander Captain Fred Paginol has fully recommended that I be retrained in this or another MOS and has urged that I be retained in military service.

6. **It is my desire to continue serving my country in the military as my grandparents, parents, and brother have done.** Both my grandparents and parents served with distinction in the U.S. Marine Corps and my sister also served in the U.S. Coast Guard. It has always been my deepest desire to be a contributing member of the U.S. Army, and I would like to ask the board to consider the new information which I present in this memorandum and grant me an opportunity to retrain in a new MOS or remain under observation before making a final decision on my case.

7. **I was feeling very nervous and anxious when I went before the medical board on October 5, and I did not express verbally the facts and findings which are presented in this memorandum of explanation.** I respectfully beseech that you consider this additional information which I did not present to the board and grant me the option of (1) either retraining in an MOS related to the personnel administration field or (2) remaining on a six-month probationary period so Dr. Jenkins and others can continue to observe the nearly miraculous effects of the drug Zorinol under which I believe I am making a full recovery. I do humbly thank the board for allowing me to present this additional information, and I hope you will alter the findings of the board made on May 5 in light of this new data.

Yours respectfully,

Clark David Emerson
886-78-2345

APPEAL OF A MILITARY MEDICAL BOARD DECISION

You cannot use a letter of appeal simply to whine and complain about the decision you didn't like. You must adopt a conciliatory tone and attempt to persuade the people in charge to change their minds and reach a new decision based on additional information or a different interpretation which you provide. *Here's a tip:* Don't wait, as this person did, to write a persuasive letter until *after* a board makes a decision which negatively impacts your career. It's much harder to get a medical board to change its mind, so create the persuasive "memorandum of explanation" as early in the process as you can.

Date

TO WHOM IT MAY CONCERN:

FROM: Fortuna Shilligren

This is a formal request for a full review of my recent performance evaluation, dated Tuesday, 6 April, and discussed with me on 7 April. During that discussion with my temporary supervisor, I made him aware of my concerns and disagreement with the ratings he had given me. The evaluation was prepared by Melvin Sony, a supervisor assigned to my department for only a six-month period. I have information to provide which I believe will lead to a correct adjustment in the numerical ratings Mr. Sony has given me ("2" is "exceeds expectations; "1' is "meets expectations.")

There are many of his <u>numerical ratings with which I agree</u>:
"CORE VALUES:"
2 **Integrity**
2 **Trust**
2 **Teamwork**

"MANAGEMENT ATTRIBUTES:"
1 **External Awareness**: I agree with this score, but I am working hard in my spare time to try to improve my understanding of technology and politics. I would like to take some computer classes to try to improve my computer skills and make myself a more valuable employee to Penney's in this regard.
2 **Customer Focus**
2 **Self Direction**

On the other hand, here are the "core values" and "management attributes" with which I disagree strongly and for which I request a reevaluation in order to establish the fact that I exceed expectations and deserve a "2."

CORE VALUES:
1 **Accountability:** I always take full accountability for my actions, and I am a model employee in this regard. My 17 years of loyal service to Penney's demonstrate my consistency in this regard, and I strongly feel I deserve a 2 in this area. On my own initiative I always assure that my area is properly stocked while maintaining the most effective merchandise presentation in order to optimize sales and turnover.

1 **Empowerment:** I continuously demonstrate my ability to work within broadly defined responsibilities, and I empower myself by taking action within reasonable boundaries. As an experienced retailer and loyal Penney's employee for 17 years, I am highly comfortable in independently taking action in order to improve customer service, profitability, merchandising effectiveness, and overall store image. On my own initiative, I take it upon myself to observe shoppette customers to deter shoplifting, and I am known for my vigilance in helping to deter theft and to help control expenses.

1 **Compassion:** As an Asian transplant to this country who is still working hard to refine my skills in the English language, I am well known for my sensitivity toward

---

APPEAL OF A SUPERVISOR'S RATING

You can compare this appeal letter with the appeal letter on page 16. In the case of this individual, she felt unfairly evaluated by a temporary supervisor who gave her lower performance ratings than she had ever received in her 17 years of working for the company. Without declaring war on the person who gave her the ratings, she tackled each measured area and provided information which she wanted the supervisor to use in revising his original numerical ratings.

others, especially toward those most in need of kindness and understanding and a helping hand. I have earned respect for my sunny disposition toward both employees and customers. In all my actions, I strongly exhibit the philosophy that all people should be treated with fairness, dignity, and respect.

1 **Risk Taking:** After 17 years of retailing with Penney's, I have become accustomed to working in an environment in which everything does not go as expected, since retailing is full of surprises and unexpected events. In situations when merchandise has not moved as quickly as buyers had expected, I am prompt in my willingness to help with appropriate markdowns and have volunteered my opinions in this area to my supervisors and to fellow employees.

1 **Creativity:** After 17 years of experience with Penney's, I have developed highly creative instincts regarding developing a new approach and suggesting better solutions when retail activities do not go as expected. I have volunteered my creative ideas in the area of employee scheduling as well as merchandising.

"MANAGEMENT ATTRIBUTES:"
1 **Leadership/Coaching:** I strongly feel I deserve a "2" in this area, as I pride myself on my ability to motivate, counsel, and coach other employees. I make a constant effort to improve employee awareness of the need for increased customer satisfaction, and I try to assure that new employees are happy and well trained in order to decrease turnover. I always show genuine respect for other employees, as I understand very well how it feels to come into a foreign country and learn a new language from scratch. I believe my experience as a foreigner has given me many skills that help me provide leadership and coaching to employees within Penney's.

1 **Problem Solving:** As an experienced retailer and loyal Penney's employee for 17 years, I am highly comfortable in independently taking action in order to solve problems related to improving customer service, profitability, merchandising effectiveness, and overall store image. On my own initiative, I have played a key role in solving problems and in developing suggestions that will increase opportunities for my employer. For example, on numerous occasions I have provided formal Employee Suggestions related to merchandise desired by customers which was not available in our store. I have been told by buyers that many of my suggestions influenced their buying decisions and promoted increased customer satisfaction and repeat business.

1 **Communication**: I continuously demonstrate my ability to communicate effectively with customers, and I hope this score was not assigned to me because my first language is not English. I am highly comfortable in independently taking action in order to improve customer service, profitability, merchandising effectiveness, and overall store image. On my own initiative, I take it upon myself to use my extensive product knowledge gained through 17 years with Penney's to cross-sell products.

I am making a formal request that my numerical ratings be reevaluated.

Sincerely,

Fortuna Shilligren

APPEAL OF A SUPERVISOR'S RATING

Even in a dispute, seldom is the other party wrong about everything. This individual creates a conciliatory tone and appears receptive to fair criticism when she says on page one that she believes her numerical score of (1) on External Awareness is correct, and that she intends to work hard to move her score in this area from a "meets expectations" to "exceeds expectations." By making this point, she makes it clear that she is not complaining about everything, across the board, which the supervisor thought.

Date

Subject: Rebuttal

To: Raphael Jorge D'Avila
     Plant Manager
     Callahan Mexican Originals

APPEAL OF A SUSPENSION

This appeal letter is intended to challenge a supervisor's decision to suspend a worker without pay for three days because of a coworker's accusation.

Dear Mr. D'Avila:

I, Samantha Greeson, am making the following statement on my own behalf in order to protest and refute the action taken by Melven Breeden, Superintendent, and Tom O'Brien, Supervisor for Callahan Foods, Inc. Melven Breeden and Tom O'Brien suspended me without pay for three days solely on the basis of the statement of accusation of a coworker and without any hard evidence at all.

The situation is as follows: on or about August 20th, 1999, after attending a meeting regarding safety in the workplace at 4 P.M., I observed one of my coworkers in clear violation of regulations regarding safety on production line nine, flour department. Coworker Delores was wearing an ankle bracelet on her leg which was not covered, and thus could cause possible danger to her. As Safety Representative and Relief Person, it was my responsibility to notify her of this violation, as wearing jewelry of any kind (other than religious symbols worn as a pendant) is a clear violation of company policy. I explained to coworker Delores that the bracelet was in violation of company policy, and she had to remove it from her leg. I relieved Delores so that she could go on break and remove the bracelet. After Delores returned from break, I noted that she returned to production line nine with the bracelet still on her leg.

After observing coworker Delores return to line nine with the bracelet still on her leg in spite of my informing her that it was a violation of company safety regulations, I reported the incident to Supervisor Donna Miller. Supervisor Miller stated that she would report the incident to Tom O'Brien for a written report of violation. After I talked with Supervisor Miller, another coworker, Jorge, approached me and asked me, "Why did you report that?" I explained to him that it was my job to report any violations of company safety regulations, to which coworker Jorge replied, "Why do you only tell on the Spanish workers?" I told him the safety regulations applied to all employees, regardless of race.

Coworker Jorge then stated that if I kept on "telling on them" (the Spanish people) I was going to lose my job. I told him that, as a Safety Representative, as long as I enforced the safety policies, I would not worry about losing my job. As we were having this discussion, another coworker, Eva, approached me and asked me if we were going to be working Friday. I stated to her that we were going to be working on that Friday. She expressed to me that Callahan had been sending people home because we didn't have enough work, and I replied that when I came to work for Callahan five years ago we had plenty of work, and everyone worked together as a team.

At this point, Jorge interrupted and said, "What? Are you talking about the Mexican people? I am not Mexican, I am from El Salvador." I told him it did not matter where you were from, we should all work together as a team regardless of race. This conversation took place while line nine was not operating. About 7:00 PM, line nine became operational again, and my lead, Carol Jensen, asked Jorge to tell Delores in Spanish to go to the office because Supervisor O'Brien wanted to see her. Jorge stopped next to Delores and spoke to her in Spanish. As I speak Spanish, I was able to understand him when he told her, "You have to go to the office because Samantha reported you for not removing the ankle bracelet. If you get written up, tell them about how she hates Mexicans."

About an hour passed, and then Jorge was called to the office. Shortly thereafter, my Supervisor, Tom O'Brien, asked me to take coworker Eva's place so she could go to the office. They questioned her about the conversation we had while line nine was not operating, which was a conversation among coworkers. One hour later (at approximately 9:15 PM), I was informed by the Superintendent, Melven Breeden, that I was in violation of company racism policies. This statement was made in the presence of my Supervisor, Tom O'Brien, with no warning and without giving me the chance to explain. Superintendent Breeden was only interested in the words of the coworker who was called to the office; I was given absolutely no opportunity to defend myself against these accusations.

I found Superintendent Breeden's open display of anger in the office to be highly unprofessional. I feel that the extremely biased and unprofessional manner in which he comported himself was completely out of line for someone who is supposed to be in a position of leadership. I have never been treated so badly by any supervisor, who would normally be expected to set the standards for professional behavior. Superintendent Breeden's loud, abusive tone of voice and the manner in which he lost his temper was totally uncalled for. Without being allowed to defend myself, the allegations made by my coworker were read to me and then I was asked to give up my ID card and was suspended for three days without pay. I feel that this was an unjust and unfair decision. I was never given a written copy of the warning, nor was I ever given the opportunity to rebut the accusations or to face my accusers.

This entire incident shocked and upset me. I could not believe that this action was being taken against me for the "crime" of doing my job and reporting a clear-cut, indisputable violation of company safety policies. I complied with Superintendent Breeden's orders and left the office to catch my ride home, as my work hours were over and I car-pool with someone; I had to go or I would have no way home. I have suffered mentally, emotionally, physically, and financially while trying to deal with this situation. I feel that this action was clearly wrong and that an injustice was done to me. I request that this matter be brought before the Plant Manager or a representative from Corporate Headquarters in order to reach a fair and equitable resolution. I lost three days of work for no reason. I am a single mother with five children and cannot afford to be out of work. This action taken by Superintendent Melven Breeden and Supervisor Tom O'Brien was not in compliance with company policy; it was unprofessional and unethical, and I request an apology and reinstatement with restitution of lost pay.

Respectfully yours,

Samantha Greeson

APPEAL OF A SUSPENSION

This is an unusual letter of appeal, since the writer is appealing the actions of her subordinates which led to an accusation of racial bias and a subsequent suspension.

Date

Subject: Docket #56098 NS

Clerk of Court
State of Louisiana
525 Country Club Drive
New Orleans, LA 80948

APPEAL OF A FALSE ACCUSATION

It's not fun to be falsely accused of anything, much less of being the father of a child who is not yours! This married man expresses his outrage over the allegation and he offers to go through the process of DNA testing to set the record straight.

Dear Clerk of Court:

I would like to make a formal rebuttal to the allegations of Felicia Jones, also known as Felicia Craven. I wish to provide facts and background information related to the false statement made by Felicia Jones that I am the father of her child.

I have never had a sexual relationship with Felicia Jones or Felicia Craven, and I am not, therefore, the father of Lenette Jones, born on September 23, 1998. Felicia Jones (Felicia Craven) is my half sister and, as a married man, I am deeply hurt—and angered—by her allegation. I can only assume that she has made this false statement because she is attempting to retain her status as a welfare recipient.

On August 3, 1999, I spoke to Mrs. Nancy Dunn by telephone about this matter because Mrs. Vicky Davidson was in court on that day and was unavailable to talk with me. As I made clear to Mrs. Dunn, I am willing to take a DNA test which could be performed here in Baton Rouge and then sent to the Independent Laboratory in New Orleans, Louisiana. I wish the court to know that I want to cooperate fully so that the record can be made clear that **I am definitely not the father of Lenette Jones.** I have provided my social security number to Mrs. Davidson already.

Once DNA testing has established that I am not the father of Lanette Jones, I would like to request that my name and all private and personal information, including my social security number, be expunged so that my good name can be cleared and so that no one, by chance, accident, or willful misuse, can use any information obtained from DSS or Social Service Support Enforcement or 22nd Judicial District Court of Lexington Parish for their own purpose or to tarnish my good reputation. Upon the conclusion of this matter and after the determination is made that I am not the father of Lanette Jones, I request that a Certified Letter be sent to me stating that all personal information, including my name and social security number, has indeed been expunged. I further request that the Court issue a strong reprimand to Mrs. Felicia Jones (Felicia Craven) for falsely accusing a married man whom she knows very well is not the biological father of her child.

Yours sincerely,

David Jackson
2nd Street South
Baton Rouge, LA 83456

Letters of Application, Personal Statements, & Essays

Sometimes it's necessary to write a letter of application. In the following pages you will see examples of letters and essays written as applications.

- You will see an application for medical school, which is actually more like an essay than a letter.
- You will see an application for the Peace Corps, which also is more like an essay than a traditional letter.
- You will see an application letter written by an individual who was applying for a Superintendent of School System position.
- You will see essays written for law school, and you will see an essay written for dental school.

In letters which are viewed as part of an application process, you are often asked to reveal your philosophy, values, ideas, and goals more than you do in a typical letter. Although these samples are provided to give you some ideas and insights, it's very important to come across as a unique individual. Be yourself!

Sometimes it's necessary to write a letter containing autobiographical information. In this section, you will see a letter used as part of the application process for law school which presents autobiographical information about the candidate for admission in an effort to explain slow academic progress. This letter is called a Personal Statement and is a formal part of the application process for many graduate schools. Personal Statements often provide an opportunity to explain erratic periods in your past.

In application letters and personal statements, you are trying to create a memorable image of yourself, and you are attempting to create, in words, a "picture" of yourself. Avoid cliched expressions which will make you appear the same as everybody else. Use words and phrases that will make you "come alive" and appear unique.

TO: Selection Committee, Medical School of Stanford University
FROM: Devlin Murphy
DATE: _____

RE: Application for Admission to the Stanford Medical School

My goal to become a medical doctor is a logical extension of my lifelong interest in saving lives, helping people, rescuing others, and excelling personally and professionally in all I do. My interest in medicine began when I was a child as I watched my Austrian grandfather devote himself as a physician to his patients in a rural setting. My interest in medicine intensified as I watched my sister, born with numerous birth defects, visit doctor after doctor and clinic after clinic in country after country throughout Europe. Throughout my childhood, I grew up overhearing medical theories and medical explanations and yearning for medical solutions which, in my sister's case, never came true. I look back upon my childhood and feel that I grew up in a medical laboratory of sorts.

A Passion for Helping Others is Evident in Everything I Have Done.

If my helping instincts were genetically determined and then environmentally encouraged, on my own initiative I have made life choices as an adult which reveal my genuine passion for rescuing, helping, and saving others. I have worked as a Veterinary Assistant for Krepp Veterinary Clinic, a job which places me in situations daily where I am trying to save the lives of our animal friends. In this job I have earned widespread praise for my excellent decision-making skills in emergency situations, and I have discovered that I have the ability to keep a cool head and think strategically in a crisis. In another job as a volunteer in a homeless shelter I have gained great satisfaction from helping people find safety and solace in an emergency shelter, and I have discovered that the health problems of family members was often what led to the financial ruin and subsequent homelessness of many of those individuals.

My Volunteer Activities Demonstrate My Dedication to Saving Lives, Molding Character, and Contributing to Social Justice.

Even as a youth, I volunteered my time in medical environments, as I worked as a Volunteer at the University Hospital in Los Angeles and as a volunteer at a nursing home. More recently, as a volunteer Police Officer with the San Diego Police Department, I organized the first police officer exchange between Austrian and American officers while helping citizens to arrange neighborhood watches, teaching children about safety issues using puppet plays and a police robot, and patrolling neighborhoods. As a volunteer EMT/Firefighter with the San Diego City Fire Department, I was constantly involved in saving people's lives while fighting fires and searching houses for victims. In 1999 I received the city's Outstanding EMT Award. My communication, listening, and counseling skills were refined in that firefighting job as I gave fire demonstrations at schools and child care centers. As a volunteer with Habitat For Humanity, I have derived much satisfaction from helping others, and that involvement has cemented my passionate belief that everyone has a right to (1) receive an education, (2) have adequate shelter, and (3) obtain medical care. As a Volunteer Rescue Scuba Diver with the San Diego Fire Department, I have searched for drowning victims and rescued survivors. I passionately believe that society's leaders must be involved in

---

APPLICATION FOR ADMISSION TO MEDICAL SCHOOL

Admission to medical school is a highly competitive pursuit. In such an application, before you write, it's a good idea to identify three different concepts which would be suitable themes for the application. You can't tell the admissions committee everything, so you'll have to decide which concepts, life situations, or unusual circumstances would allow you to reveal yourself in the most favorable light.

socially responsible ways in the community. I have worked tirelessly as a Cub Scout den leader with Boy Scouts of America helping boys aged seven and eight grow in self confidence and self discipline.

My Academic Achievements Reveal My Highly Motivated Personality as well as My Ability to Excel in Rigorous Academic Studies.

I have excelled in every training program in which I have participated, including EMT training, Police Academy Training, and Firefighting Training. In college, too, I have excelled and have a 4.06 average at the current time at San Diego State College where I am triple majoring in biology, chemistry, and sociology while earning my B.S. degree. I received the Chi Psi Award given to the top 3% of seniors and juniors, and I was named to *Who's Who in American Colleges*. I also received the Chemistry Award of the Year. My scholastic achievements have resulted in my induction into Alpha Chi Honorary as well as the honorary Psychology club, the honorary Biology club, and the honorary Sociology club. I always approach my studies in such a way that I try to maximize my learning experience, because I believe that our best educated scholar-doctors may one day be able to unlock the doors to some of our deepest medical mysteries. I am a highly motivated individual who always aspires to be at the top of my class and to be a leader in all I do.

I Offer a Character That Would Be a Credit to the Medical Profession.

I believe my character is well expressed in the types of activities and involvements I have chosen as an adult, which I have described briefly above. Principles of honor, integrity, and human kindness guide me in all my life decisions and human interactions, and I am very confident that I could one day be a medical doctor who would be a credit to the profession, a blessing to the communities I serve, an inspiration to medical staff and hospital employees with whom I would be working, and a source of pride to the institution from which I graduate.

Yours sincerely,

Devlin Murphy

APPLICATION FOR ADMISSION TO MEDICAL SCHOOL

Imagine how many applications have to be read and evaluated in order to find "the cream of the crop." Many people try to impress an admissions committee with "big words" and erudite expressions, but what an admissions committee is trying to do is to "meet you" through your application. You need to concentrate on finding a topic you can write about that will allow you to reveal your strengths, talents, and uniqueness. Watch your length! If an essay is supposed to be 500 words, make sure you are not overlength.

Felicia D'Allesandro
SSN: 000-00-0000

Letter of Application for Physician's Assistant Program

Valuable role models and influences

My desire to become a contributing part of the medical profession was aroused in me as a child, as I watched my mother, a Registered Nurse, serve her patients with selfless dedication. The many cards, letters, and gifts my mother continues to receive from her patients have indicated that her compassion and professional skills are appreciated. I have also watched as my mother and her colleagues spent many unnoticed hours after work discussing patient care and sharing their thoughts for improvements in the quality of nursing services. Another important role model for me was our family friend and our family doctor, Dr. Matthews. He donated his time unselfishly by traveling overseas to provide medical services to the poor, and I observed as a youth that Dr. Matthews seemed motivated by concern for humanity and treated medicine as his calling in life.

My decision to become a Surgical Technologist

I tested my desire to become involved in the medical profession when I volunteered at age 14 as a member of my church youth group at the Veterans Administration Hospital. Even as a youth, I was commended for my ability to work with patients in a professional manner that was unusual for a teenager. By the time I went to college, I knew that I wanted to become a medical professional.

Excellent academic performance in earning my A.S. degree/Surgical Technologist Diploma

I graduated at the top of my class with a 4.0 GPA in all my surgical technologist classes while earning my A.S. degree from Wormley Technical College in Decatur, GA. With excellent academic credentials and a reputation for excellent communication and human relations skills, I was one of only two students selected to work as a Surgical Technologist at Richland Memorial Hospital in Decatur, GA, prior to actually graduating from the program. This early work experience gave me valuable opportunities to assist surgeons, and it was at that point that I began to formulate my professional plan to one day become a Physician's Assistant. Working as a surgical Physician's Assistant is one of my goals within the PA field, but I am versatile and would enjoy rotating to other specialties including family practice.

Excellent reputation within my field

After graduating from Wormley Technical College, my husband and I moved to Kentucky, and I have been working from April 1995-present as a Certified Surgical Technologist at McDonnell Regional Hospital in Dixon, KY. I am highly regarded by all surgeons with whom I work because of my excellent technical knowledge, my absolute reliability, as well as my cheerful nature. I am currently specializing in cardiovascular surgery. I am specifically requested by many of the surgeons at the hospital.

APPLICATION FOR ADMISSION TO PHYSICIAN'S ASSISTANT PROGRAM

Sometimes your personal essay for admissions is weighted up to 60% of the admissions decision. What you write about and how you write weigh heavily in the admission committee's decision.

Why I want to be a Physician's Assistant

Although I am excelling as a Surgical Technologist, I desire more contact with patients than I currently have, and becoming a Physician's Assistant would give me an opportunity to work with patients. On my own time, I am learning Spanish and I plan to be bilingual in Spanish by the end of the Physician's Assistant program. Being able to speak Spanish will be of great value as I attempt to communicate with and help patients as a Physician's Assistant. I am constantly seeking to upgrade my knowledge and skills, and that is why I have availed myself of twice the required number of continuing education hours at McDonnell Regional Hospital. I am a current member of the Beta Beta Beta Biological Honor Society, and I am a member of the Association of Surgical Technologists. Although enrolling in a Physician's Assistant program requires a financial sacrifice for me since I will have to resign my full-time job as a Surgical Technologist, I am ready to make that sacrifice. I am confident that I can become a credit to the medical profession as a Physician's Assistant as I have been as a Surgical Technologist.

Yours sincerely,

Felicia D'Allesandro

APPLICATION FOR ADMISSION TO PHYSICIAN'S ASSISTANT PROGRAM

Beware of appearing greedy and self-serving in expressing your desire to attend a professional program. Admissions committees are seeking to admit individuals who will become distinguished alumni, so they are looking for candidates who have specific and ambitious goals for professional achievement. Don't tell admissions committees that you are seeking admissions because you are hoping to get a great job and a great salary!

LETTER OF APPLICATION FOR DENTAL SCHOOL

by David Martin

    To explain concisely why I am interested in the dental profession, I must begin with my childhood. From the time I was about ten years old, I spent most of my summers visiting with grandparents in Kansas where my grandfather is a small-town family dentist. This gave me a great opportunity to see first hand what a rural practice can be like by observing procedures as well as the business aspects of running a small practice. I was given a rare opportunity to observe and participate in lab work and sculpting and discovered that I possess a raw artistic talent as it relates to dentistry. This also gave me a chance to become moderately well versed in oral anatomy and oral procedures at a young age and to absorb and appreciate my grandfather's talent for making his patients feel comfortable. I became aware at a young age that I wanted to be a dentist and that, in my grandfather, I had a wonderful role model. I also know that I have the drive, intelligence, and natural qualities that would be needed.

    Presently I am volunteering in the office of Dr. Dixon Delbert's family dentistry practice in Wichita. Dr. Delbert has arranged for me to freely observe throughout his sophisticated practice which offers services related to endodontics, oral surgery, and periodontics. This has given me a chance to talk with professionals in varying dental specialties and to observe the contrast between a small practice like the one my grandfather runs and a large, modern facility.

    I believe my academic pursuits have prepared me well to enter the dental profession. I earned a B.S. degree in Marketing with a 3.34 GPA in my major at Georgia State University, and my undergraduate marketing degree equipped me with valuable insights into interpersonal relations. I feel my well-rounded personality would also be of value in the customer-and-employee relations aspect of dentistry, and I credit my involvements in high school as contributing measurably to my ability to interact socially with others in a gracious manner. In high school, in addition to being named to the National Honor Society and winning the Freshman English Student of the Year award, I was elected Sports Editor of the yearbook staff, was co-captain of the football and soccer teams, was captain of the golf and tennis teams, was selected for inclusion in *Who's Who Among American High School Students*, and was active in community service activities.

    As soon as I arrived at college, I became perceived as a campus leader and organizer; I was active in a philanthropic event that benefitted orphans and I held nine separate elected positions within my fraternity. In those elected positions I expressed not only my leadership ability but also my natural creativity; for example, I created several T-shirt designs which captured the spirit of certain events.

    My interpersonal skills have also been refined through jobs as a sales representative in a men's clothing store, phone representative for a marketing research firm, door-to-door salesman of educational books, and salesperson in a golf pro shop. I look back on my job with Southwestern Company as a major tool in refining my management skills; after a one-week training session, I was sent to a small town in Ohio and

---

LETTER OF APPLICATION FOR DENTAL SCHOOL

A spot at a professional school is a sought-after prize, and admissions committees read the applications to see the origin and history of your interest in the profession. They need to be assured that your interest in the field is genuine, and they need to be persuaded that you stand a chance of one day becoming an esteemed member of the profession.

had to find a place to live while functioning as an entrepreneur selling educational books door-to-door. It was like getting thrown into deep water and being told to "sink or swim," and I believe I changed from a boy into a man that summer.

Just three weeks after graduating from Georgia State University, I enrolled at Kansas City College in the program pursuant to a B.S. in Biological Sciences and have excelled in completing nine hours a semester while working 20 hours a week. At Kansas City College I have earned a 3.925 GPA and have been inducted into Beta Beta Beta, a national collegiate biology honor society in which invitations to become a member are based on grades, interest in the field, and faculty sponsorship. I have also joined the American Student Dental Association so that I can receive their publications and keep up with changes and new procedures in the dental profession. This semester I also completed Organic Chemistry I and Human Anatomy & Physiology courses at the University of Kansas with a 3.5 GPA.

One reason I feel I would be a credit to the profession of dentistry is that I believe I offer a rock-solid character. As a matter of personal philosophy, I try to live according to Christian values. I am known for my high ethical and moral principles, and I perceive of dentistry as a profession in which one can be of service to mankind and to the community.

In conclusion, I must emphasize that I was exposed to the dental profession at an early age and became fascinated with the possibilities of what I could accomplish with my artistic aptitude, intellectual abilities, and desire to enhance the quality of people's lives by providing quality dental care.

Yours sincerely,

David Martin

LETTER OF APPLICATION FOR DENTAL SCHOOL

Here's a tip: If there's anything you need to explain, such as a lackluster first semester freshman year, the letter of application is the place to do it.

ESSAY "MY GREATEST PERSONAL FAILURE"
WHARTON SCHOOL OF BUSINESS

ANGELA SMITH

LETTER OF APPLICATION FOR BUSINESS SCHOOL

A question like this makes you see clearly that the motivation of the admissions committee is to get to know you, and to see "the real you." This candidate was asked to write a series of seven essays about particular subjects to see the origin and history of her interest in the profession. Admissions committees need to be assured that your interest in the field is genuine, and they need to be persuaded that you stand a chance of one day becoming an esteemed member of the profession.

My greatest personal failure was not obtaining my college degree earlier in life. I regret not applying to a four-year, nationally ranked college directly out of high school. However, that did not appear to be an option for me when I was 18 years old because my parents strongly felt that all three of their daughters should fully fund their own education; in order to do so, I embarked on a path in life where I attempted to obtain my undergraduate degree while working full-time.

As a practical matter, I do realize, too, that I might have earned my degree in the "wrong" field (I was headed for architecture rather than business administration) had I not been seasoned and challenged by work experience. I have, however, been dogged in my pursuit of my degree because of my strenuous professional responsibilities and there have been many times during my undergraduate career when quitting seemed easier than persisting. Nevertheless, I have trained myself to acquire excellent time management skills and I am excelling academically with a 3.5 GPA, even though my time is encroached upon by the demands of being a military squad leader and shouldering an additional part-time job.

By experiencing the process of being a nontraditional student and realizing that it is possible to derive the same knowledge and enjoyment from night school as traditional students get from day school, I have empathy and support for anyone embarking on the same goal. A passionate believer in the value of education, I have already motivated two people in my squad to start college and have helped countless others navigate the bureaucracy required to enroll in college using the tuition assistance provided by the military. The forms and multistep process can be so intimidating that many soldiers quit and do not even give classes a chance. No matter what leadership capacity I am in, I will always encourage my coworkers and subordinates to better themselves by attending college and furthering their formal education.

My failure to attend college as an eighteen-year-old graduating high school senior has made me a more devoted and hungry student. I fully enjoy my classes and only miss due to unavoidable military commitments. I see some of the younger day students being expelled for violating my college's strict attendance policy and wonder if I would have been the same without the discipline enhanced in me by my four years of dedicated service in the military.

I attend college now for the pleasure of learning and expanding my horizons—not just as a means to an end. Although the actual degree means a great deal to me, gaining the knowledge and creatively applying that knowledge to solve practical business and social problems is the ultimate lure of the MBA.

ESSAY "MY GREATEST PROFESSIONAL RISK"
THE WHARTON SCHOOL OF BUSINESS

ANGELA SMITH

The greatest professional risk I have ever taken was to leave my stable, productive job to join the Army. Although sometimes I feel as though I took a step backwards, I realize that I would not have had the educational opportunities I have now because of the Army. Furthermore, the Army has given me a chance to utilize my leadership traits and refine my management skills in numerous supervisory situations which I would not have had the opportunity to do in the companies in which I worked prior to enlisting.

Because the Army is a "melting pot," the Army has also enabled me to work under often-austere conditions, under extremely tight deadlines, and with many types of personalities. Because I have chosen to combine full-time work with a demanding college schedule, I have become very efficient at managing my time within a schedule which looks like this:

Monday: 5:45 AM - 6 PM work; 8:00 PM - 10:45 PM classes at Waycross

Tuesday: 5:45 AM - 5 PM work; 5:30 PM - 10:45 PM classes at Waycross

Wednesday: 5:45 AM - 6 PM work; 8:00 PM - 10:45 PM classes at Waycross

Thursday: 5:45 AM - 5 PM work; 5:30 PM - 10:45 PM classes at Waycross

Friday: 5:45 AM - 6 PM work; lead military ceremonies on Friday PM

Saturday: Classes and studies until 6 PM; 6 PM - 3 AM waitress job

Sunday: Attend church at Jones Memorial Baptist Church; study

Furthermore, I take great pride in what I have achieved while serving my country and will continue to seek leadership positions even after I leave the military in February 1999. I plan on joining the Reserves upon leaving Active Duty and pursuing a commission to become an officer. I feel that this particular route will enable me to mesh together my enlisted experience as a soldier with my knowledge from my civilian education into a great leadership opportunity in the Army Reserves. It is my goal to continue providing leadership and to be of service as a leader in both the public and private sectors.

Although it was a risk to leave my job, home state, family, and friends, it is a move that revolutionized my life. I have matured extensively in the past four years and will enthusiastically seek to build upon these experiences in the corporate world once I receive my MBA from the Wharton Business School.

LETTER OF APPLICATION FOR ADMISSION TO BUSINESS SCHOOL

Similar to the question on the facing page, this question is designed to elicit a unique reaction and allow the admissions committee to "meet the real you." In the case of this individual, the admissions committee is bound to form a positive opinion of a hard-working young professional who has to efficiently manage every minute of the day to combine work with college.

LETTER OF APPLICATION FOR THE PEACE CORPS
Naomi Parkinson
SSN: 536-92-2198
Country Choice: Costa Rica

My reasons for wanting to become a Peace Corps volunteer

My reasons for wanting to serve as a Peace Corps volunteer are many. Although I have enjoyed life and have enjoyed various luxuries, I have always worked hard and feel that I have many talents and occupational skills which could be helpful to people in other cultures, and especially to those in developing cultures.

Of German descent, I speak German fluently and understand Polish, and I am very comfortable in multi-racial and multi-cultural situations. I feel I could contribute as a Peace Corps volunteer in three areas primarily:

1. **I can teach skills in business management,** especially small business management. Based on my 10 years of owning and managing a pet shop, I am well qualified to teach others how to board and groom pets professionally as well as how to ship pets domestically and internationally.
2. **In developing countries, many vendors could benefit from my knowledge and experience related to the organization and management of cooperatives.** Formerly President of Hoboken's largest nonprofit arts and crafts co-op, I was involved in forming "from scratch" this nonprofit co-op. More than 50 artists are now involved in the cooperative of which I am a former President and current board member. I am an expert at handling the start-up, administrative, and marketing matters which must be handled correctly if a co-op is to get off the ground. I have been successful at obtaining funding from the City of Hoboken and the Arts Council for this cooperative, and I would be able to guide others in obtaining funding for their cooperatives.
3. **Finally, I am an expert at many matters of home economics.** I would delight in teaching others my excellent dressmaking and alteration skills, and I would also enjoy teaching my cooking skills to others.

What I hope to do in Costa Rica specifically

I think of myself as an extrovert; therefore, I want to meet and visit with the people of Costa Rica in order to win their friendship, learn their ways of life, and show them methods of improving themselves. Helping them improve their lives will be the challenge I see for myself.

I look forward to working with the other Peace Corps volunteers and with individuals from other agencies in order to ensure the successful completion of each project. I believe working with numerous individuals from various agencies will require patience, flexibility, and adaptability on my part as well as the ability to listen carefully and communicate in an effective manner. I see myself as a tool to be used for accomplishing a wide variety of goals, and therefore I must remain as malleable as clay so that I can be molded and shaped precisely to the needs of each project. My experience as an artist and former business owner has helped me understand that I must remain flexible, and my background as President of the Artists' Co-op has helped

---

LETTER OF APPLICATION FOR THE PEACE CORPS

As a final assignment, candidates seeking to be chosen as a Peace Corps volunteer must write an essay or letter communicating the strengths and attributes they feel they could bring to the Peace Corps.

me gain the type of versatile leadership skills which I believe will be required as a Peace Corps volunteer.

I believe the Pre-Service Training will enable me to adapt to the culture of Costa Rica. Prior to my departure date, I am also seeking all the information on this culture which I can obtain. This information includes books which I am able to check out of the library, audio tapes on the Spanish language, and verbal communication with people who have experienced the Costa Rican culture. Even through conversations, I believe I can do much to acquaint myself with the customs and culture of the country to which I will be going. Like a sponge, I am absorbing everything I can about Costa Rica and its customs prior to Pre-Service Training. I am aware of how my behavior and conduct could be a positive influence on the Peace Corps image. I will do my best to respect the country's customs. I already have some knowledge of the Spanish language, and I am working hard to improve my vocabulary and refine my language skills even prior to the Pre-Service Training.

In terms of my personal and professional goals for Peace Corps service, I can handle all of the job description listed in the Volunteer Assignment Description for the Small Business Development area. I would be able to work on existing projects or on new ones, and I will do my best to help them be successful.

From 1995 through 1999, I have taken the initiative to develop and implement summer workshops for at-risk inner-city children who have been designated as "Youth at Risk." In the spring of 1995, for example, I sponsored eight African-American teenagers aged 15 and 16 who had dropped out of school. The purpose of the workshop was to raise their self-esteem through teaching them to access and utilize their natural creativity. With an extensive background as an artist, I was able to teach them skills in making a marketable object which they could choose to sell or keep after the class. Using my motivational and communication skills, I was able to motivate all students to come to my workshop class every day. My reward came in the fall of 1999, when all of those students who were former dropouts returned to school and stayed in school. Although I financed these workshops myself at first, I was successful in obtaining a grant for subsequent workshops, so that the 1999 workshop was sponsored by the Hoboken Community Foundation.

In summary, I feel have much leadership, vitality, and ability to offer the Peace Corps, and I am eager to put these to work for the accomplishment of the Peace Corps' aims.

LETTER OF APPLICATION FOR ADMISSION TO THE PEACE CORPS

Be deliberate about using the space in your essay to make the committee aware of your accomplishments, achievements, and track record of success in your field(s).

APPLICATION FOR MEDICAL SCHOOL

Kathryn Anne Davenport

LETTER OF APPLICATION TO MEDICAL SCHOOL

Choosing a career is often an emotional decision made because of deeply meaningful events or people in one's life. This applicant to medical school writes about the grandfather and his illness that inspired her to strive for a medical career.

I know a gentleman who suffers from cancer. Physically, he is a mere shadow of the man he once was. Mentally and emotionally, he is a giant. Because of the luminous qualities of his character, I can see through the cancer that weakens but does not rule him. Despite what the disease has taken, it has left in place his resilience and perseverance. When I look beyond his physical frailty, I see his strength of character. Perhaps defying science, he is determined to overcome great odds as he continues his fight. Therefore, what consumes my attention most is not the cancer but the qualities of his character which sustain him.

For years the mind and the body were treated as separate entities. I understand the patient's physical loss of control and the psychological ramifications, yet I fail to understand the disease itself. The body and spirit are inseparable and the study of one is incomplete without the study of the other. In essence, I began my journey toward medical school by initially earning a B.A. in Psychology. Now I am compelled to study the body so that I may offer to future patients a holistic evaluation of their physical health.

Many believe we are a product of our experiences. Having had nine years of extensive involvement in geriatrics and with the severely infirm, I have encountered everything from diabetes to AIDS. As an employee/volunteer at Medical Village, I provided care to the Alzheimers and AIDS patients, diabetics, quadriplegics, and paraplegics that comprised the 159-bed facility. I was trained in both the Restorative Feeding and Restorative Walking programs. Sensory stimulation as well as hand-eye coordination were integral parts of my patient contact. Through those experiences, I learned how to approach, communicate with, and care for patients suffering from Alzheimers and dementia. With the brain-stem injured, I performed range-of-motion exercises to prevent contraction of muscles and promote circulation. Evaluating and documenting patients' abilities and progress also comprised my duties.

For four years I volunteered at the Ronald McDonald House where I lent emotional support for critically ill children and their families. I continued my involvement with the infirm at Texas State Hospital and Dallas Medical Center. During that time, I was trained in the assessment of auditory deficiencies of premature infants. Outside of these medically related experiences, I acted as a soccer coach for Special Olympians and counselor for underprivileged children at a Christian camp.

At the age of 23, I look back over my brief life and see the faces I have encountered. I have responded to their physical needs with the compassion necessary to sustain their emotional health as well. However, the care I provided is miniscule compared to the wealth of knowledge I received from those patients. They have taught me that life is not simply a series of unrelated events. Rather, we are defined by our experiences and also by our choices. I made a choice in my youth to become involved in caring for the diseased and elderly, and that choice has shaped my aspirations. Involvement with the infirm has accelerated my maturity. Dedication to "my patients" has cemented a sense of responsibility toward my fellow man. I understand that our time here is crucial. I feel compelled to be productive and my experiences have convinced me that I belong in the medical field. When a patient needs care, no task is beneath me and no challenge is too great.

My decision to choose a medical career was made with intense consideration. The reality of facing grueling hours of clinical duties combined with taxing studies does not dampen my enthusiasm or lessen my desire. I can perceive of no other endeavor that would allow me to contribute so unselfishly to mankind. Physically, emotionally, and spiritually I would find any other profession less fulfilling and challenging.

As I embark upon a career in medicine, I am reminded of the cancer patient who captivated my attention. Long after he is gone, I will remember the part of his soul he allowed me to see. He exposed his fighting spirit and tenacious character and, in doing so, he helped me recognize and appreciate those same qualities in myself. That cancer patient is my grandfather. As for now, he continues to fight his battle. I desperately want to help win the war.

LETTER OF APPLICATION FOR ADMISSION TO MEDICAL SCHOOL

Compare this letter of application for medical school with the application on page 30. They are different, but both candidates allow the admissions committees to get an intimate and personal picture of who they are and why they have made their career choices.

Personal Statement and Biographical Sketch of James Allen Collins
North Georgia University School of Law

LETTER OF APPLICATION TO LAW SCHOOL

Often an essay is an opportunity to "explain" a reckless or irresponsible period in one's life. This individual is seeking admission to law school at middle age, and he provides an intensely personal glimpse into who he is, where he's been, why he's done some of the things he's done, and what he wants to do now.

I respectfully ask the admissions committee to consider the following factors when evaluating my undergraduate academic record. After graduation from high school, I was financially unable to enter college. I worked in a local factory while continuing to work on the family farm. I came from a family of eight children and grew up in rural eastern Georgia. Most of my life—through age 16—we were sharecroppers. During my sophomore year in high school, my father obtained an entry-level civil service job. We then moved to our own family farm which my parents had bought when my father returned from World War II. This was the first opportunity we had to farm our own land rather than to sharecrop. The income from my father's job and our farm still barely kept us above the poverty level. I'm not sure that it did.

I am the third oldest child and the oldest son. When my father began working in the public job, I took over the running of the family farm. My parents believed strongly in education and sacrificed a great deal to see that we were provided with quality education. We also sacrificed for each other. My oldest sister graduated from high school and went to work to help provide for us. When my next sister graduated, she was able to attend college a semester later. I enrolled at Georgia State University two years later with no outside financial aid. I worked part time and full time. I had six younger siblings who were still in school and who ranged in age from elementary through high school. I felt guilty, and my grades suffered. After dropping in and out of school several times, I decided to stay out of school and help the younger children. I knew that I would eventually return to college. In many respects, I'm glad that I made the decision to stay out of school and concentrate on helping support the family.

When my father died, my younger siblings needed my financial and moral support even more than before. Besides helping my family, I experienced a lot of personal growth during my absence from college. I completed the automotive mechanics course at the local community college and worked as a mechanic at a local dealership. I also repaired and serviced vehicles for many of the elderly and needy people in the community free of charge, because they needed the assistance. I still do some of this type of work when time permits.

After I entered military service, I experienced much of life that I never would have been able to experience otherwise. Besides serving my country, I also had the opportunity to provide for and help shape the lives of many individuals. I found a lifetime mate with like ideals and similar interests and who is also unselfish and dedicated to serving humanity. This time when I returned to college, I was able to work without the distractions of worrying about my family's basic needs. Five of the eight children in my family have earned bachelor's or advanced degrees and the other three have technical degrees and have done very well in their courses. I made the Dean's List each of my last four semesters even though I had a lot of earlier incompletes and failing grades to overcome. I am a hard worker and can excel in a rigorous curriculum.

My Professional Orientation

I have a passionate desire to work in the public service sector of criminal law. Though America is by far the greatest country in this world, we have a long way to go.

I know first hand that we don't all start out in life on an equal footing. As a minority I know that I have a responsibility to help level the field. I have experienced first hand the obstacles and road blocks that too often impede the pursuit of the basic rights of all humans. I know what it's like to be under-represented or not represented at all. I know what it's like to overcome adversity. I know that adversity builds character. It also makes one a better advocate. Unless you really understand what it's like to be in another's situation, you cannot be the best advocate. I grew up financially strapped, but I know that lack of funds does not necessarily hinder one's success. I was born with an eye condition that left me blind in one eye. It probably could have been corrected had we been able to afford proper treatment. Despite this setback, I overcame and often excelled.

There are many people with a lot to offer our society if given the slightest of opportunities. I began my military career as an enlisted man. I knew first hand what those at the lower ranks and pay grades must endure. When I became a non-commissioned officer and later a commissioned officer, I could better serve and lead because of understanding and being able to see all sides. Too many times I've been an "only" or "one of the few." I've been the "only" Black NCO in my section. I've been the "only" Black company commander in a battalion. I've been "one of the few" minority commissioned officers on a post. I've been the "only" Black profit center manager in a company I worked for, and later "one of the few" in each of these situations. I've tried to be a good advocate. I've personally helped many Blacks, whites, and other nationalities to succeed, despite the odds against them, and to realize their full potential—even though some of them would have been considered more "fortunate" than I. I've seen that many times some individuals in positions of authority place their personal agenda above the rights of others.

I want to be in a position to help insure "justice for all." I know that passion and commitment alone are not sufficient to do what I want to do. I need a legal education and a law degree to be equipped with the knowledge and credentials necessary for me to make a positive impact on our criminal justice system.

I am drawn to North Georgia School of Law because I know of its strong reputation in areas of advocacy. I personally know many North Georgia lawyers who set the standard for others to emulate. My personal lawyer is a North Georgia graduate. North Georgia is my undergraduate alma mater. I believe this fine institution's areas of expertise are an excellent fit for my goals.

LETTER OF APPLICATION FOR ADMISSION TO LAW SCHOOL

This essay is intended to convey his passion for and commitment to the area of law which he wishes to study.

TO: Selection Committee, Superintendent of Schools

FROM: Andrew James

DATE:

Dear Ladies and Gentlemen:

LETTER OF APPLICATION FOR A SUPERINTENDENT OF SCHOOLS POSITION

The final stage in the selection process for the top three candidates for a school superintendent position was this letter of application. Candidates were asked to answer the specific question, "What does it mean to be the educational leader of a school system, and how do you feel you have already provided leadership to a school system?"

I would like to place my name in application for the position of Superintendent of Schools of Wyett County, Pennsylvania. This letter is in response to your question directed at all applicants about what it means to be the educational leader of a school system and how I believe I have already provided leadership to a school system.

Strategic vision is necessary in order to lead a system into the future.
In order to lead a school system, I must have an overall understanding of the school setting. This encompasses an objective analysis of the present status of the organization followed by the development of a sense of mission. It is vital to discern where the system should be going and to identify necessary resources in order to move forward. Most importantly, it is my responsibility to motivate all stakeholders toward embracing a common vision that includes two principles which I consider fundamental:
1) <u>All</u> children <u>can</u> learn, and
2) In preparing our students, our focus is the provision of a nurturing and academically stimulating environment.

Aggressive and effective use of technology in our classrooms is a must.
When I was appointed Superintendent of Namath Falls, the School Board identified the need to upgrade our outdated facilities. When our school population increased due to the sudden influx of industry, it was necessary for me to mobilize all resources to secure building funds. Working with my staff and the community economic development forces, we thoroughly reviewed our enrollment, assessed our facilities, and lobbied throughout the community for the needed support. We have been able to secure over $14 million in school construction money though local bonds and federal funds.

Risk-taking and new initiatives are essential to maximize growth.
I have provided leadership for several initiatives designed to improve student achievement in this field. We implemented a district-wide technology program that provides each school with a computer lab and equips each homeroom teacher with a computer. The use of technology to enhance all curriculum areas is greatly encouraged. Extensive staff development activities have been conducted to support this program. Presently we have one computer for every four students, and our public school system has been praised at numerous educational conferences.

I am a master architect of effective personnel policies.
As the leader of any school district, I strongly believe I must support the teachers and assure that their voices are heard throughout the community. Our teachers are on the frontline in our teaching environments, and I always strive to maintain an open-door policy and a listening posture where my teachers are concerned.

Business Marketing Letters and Press Releases

Whether you have a small business or are part of a huge corporation, you always need marketing letters to communicate what you do to the outside world and to your customers in particular. In this section you will find examples of marketing letters used to promote an artist, to sell the services of a small business, and to try to interest the consumer in the service or product you are providing.

Marketing is a multifaceted function and is more a "mind set" within an organization than a specific action taken "every now and then." Many of the letters in this section were written for companies that "think marketing" all the time. There is no end to the types of letters that can be created to make the public aware of what you do as a business.

We hasten to say that this tiny section in the book can only "hit the highlights" of what we need to show you about business marketing, but you will find inside this section the following:

- A press release for an art gallery
- A press release for a new book
- A personal marketing letter
- A letter of introduction to be used in a mass mailing
- A letter of introduction used by a specialty steel company
- A letter expressing "thank you" to existing customers
- A letter saying "welcome" to new customers
- A business estimate used by a cleaning company in marketing its services
- A letter and resume used to market a mobile home repair business
- A letter marketing outplacement services

You will notice that all of these letters aim to "get to the point" rather quickly. The average person is bombarded by direct mail, and a marketing piece must usually be concise and attention-getting in order to have maximum "marketing power."

Use the ideas in this section to create your own marketing letters.

AMY'S HOME AND COMMERCIAL CLEANING SERVICE
(910) 483-6611
"No job too large or too small"

1110 Hay Street, Atlanta, GA 28305 • 910-483-6611 • preppub@aol.com

Date

BUSINESS ESTIMATE USED BY A CLEANING COMPANY IN MARKETING ITS SERVICES

Letters can be used as bids and business estimates. This letter could be used as a "model" so that the business needs to change only the specific names and pricing details each time the letter is sent.

To Whom It May Concern:

This letter is a formal estimate of work to be performed for Mr. and Mrs. Joe Beasley at their private residence in Atlanta, GA. The home has recently suffered smoke damage due to a fire in the back bedroom, and this estimate is being made available to both the insurance company and the Beasleys.

For the price of $50 an hour, Amy's Home and Commercial Cleaning Service will furnish all cleaning products needed to clean damage caused by grease and smoke and to complete all tasks including these:

- Clean all walls, woodwork, cabinets, doors, mantels, light fixtures, chandeliers, lamps, ceilings, fans, etc.

- Clean draperies, blinds, and windows in all rooms as well as all upholstered furniture, couches, antique chairs, needlepoint chairs, odd/miscellaneous chairs, the seats of 12 dining room chairs, bedspreads, mattresses, pillows, and accessories.

- Other items to be cleaned include a china closet filled with crystal and china as well as an Oriental curio cabinet filled with precious keepsakes, three completely furnished bedrooms, a TV, a stereo set, and VCR equipment.

- The home to be cleaned is elegantly decorated with pictures, mirrors, wall hangings, pedestals, Oriental statues, and vases as well as numerous crystal, porcelain, and wooden Oriental boxes and cabinets. The home will be dusted/cleaned.

- Other items covered in this agreement include trees and plants, silk floral arrangements, and Oriental coffee and end tables.

- The house is carpeted throughout and additionally contains Oriental rugs in the living room as well as other assorted rugs.

- Due to the large quantity of valuable and irreplaceable items contained in the house, it is impossible to list each piece separately. Considerable care will be taken to clean these valuable collectibles and keepsakes.

- We estimate it will take three people between 50-100 hours to complete this job.

Total for services rendered: 75 hours at $50 an hour — $3,750

PEOPLEFIND, INC.

1110 Hay Street, Houston, TX 28305
Telephone: (910) 483-6611
Fax: (910) 483-2439
http://www.prep-pub.com
e-mail: PREPPub@aol.com

To: Barry Wizardon
From: Dale Durgens

<u>Confidential</u>
Schedule of Fees for Outplacement Assistance
provided to Mainline Manufacturing

PEOPLEFIND, INC., is prepared to provide the finest quality resume-writing services and job-hunting planning assistance to Mainline Manufacturing employees. Services which could be provided include the following:

Group planning session: During this session which PEOPLEFIND would conduct at the Mainline Manufacturing site, PEOPLEFIND will provide expert guidance on job-hunting, introduce the Personal Review Form which is an essential tool used by PEOPLEFIND in the resume-writing process, and provide for an extensive question-and-answer session by the approximately 20 participants to be laid off by Mainline.

Cost: $1,500.00 (includes preparation time by PEOPLEFIND and materials for all participants).

Resume and Cover Letter Preparation:

Cost: $235.00 for each person for a professional resume with 15 copies and a model cover letter

<u>or</u> $243.00 for a professional resume with 15 copies, model cover letter, and both on a disk
<u>or</u> $250.00 for a resume (15 copies), cover letter, 15 sheets of stationery & 15 envelopes
<u>or</u> $258.00 for resume (15), cover letter, 15 sheets, 15 envelopes, and R/CL on a disk

Optional Group Follow-up Session with all participants on job-hunting tips and techniques and important strategies to use in getting in the door: Such a session could be provided which would allow for all participants to get together in a strategy formulation session with PEOPLEFIND to discuss the techniques in using their professional resume and cover letter to maximum effect.

Cost: $1,500.00 (includes preparation time by PEOPLEFIND and all materials to be distributed).

PEOPLEFIND'S services are prepaid. Satisfaction is always guaranteed.

BUSINESS PROPOSAL BY A RESUME-WRITING AND OUTPLACEMENT SERVICE

Like the letter on the facing page, this letter could be used as a template or model each time the company needs to prepare a business proposal tailored to specific customer needs.

PREMIUM SPECIALTY STEEL CO.
1110 Hay Street
Post Office Box 66
Worcester, MA 28302
910-483-6611
Pager: 910-483-6611
Fax: 910-483-2439

Date

Dear Exact Name:

With this letter, I would like to introduce you to the most reputable and most quality-conscious specialty steel fabricator in the business today. We have recently learned of your possible business interest in our region, and we want to put our considerable resources and know-how at your disposal.

Who we are
Premium Specialty Steel Company was founded in 1974, and it has grown from a fleet of three trucks into a 12-truck operation supported by a completely computerized batching system, state approved and fully compatible with all current regulations. Our highly professional staff consists of the following key individuals, all of whom have Your Total Satisfaction as our foremost goal:
- James Franklin, President
- Judith Franklin, Sales and On-Site Representative
- Amy Beasley, Dispatcher
- Donna Gaskins, Accounts Receivables Manager

Our goal: Your Total Satisfaction at all Times
Very simply, providing the best service possible at all times while guaranteeing a quality product is our number one goal. There is no other company in the specialty steel fabrication business that can come close to matching our Total Quality Management approach to product performance and customer service.

The next step
In the expectation that we will be able to "make you an offer you can't refuse," I would like to call you next week to introduce myself by telephone and verify a few details of your upcoming project in this area. I hope you will give me an opportunity to bid on the job you have coming up, because I can guarantee in advance **your total satisfaction** with our price, product, quality control, customer service, and follow-through. I hope you will welcome my call in a few days.

Yours sincerely,

Judith Franklin
Sales Representative

LETTER OF INTRODUCTION USED BY A SPECIALTY STEEL COMPANY

A letter can be a nice way to introduce your company to new business prospects. Here you see a letter used by a specialty steel business to make potential customers aware of its products and services. Notice in the last paragraph the reader is advised that a sales representative will be calling in a few days.

BOOK DESIGNERS, INC.
1110 Hay Street
Post Office Box 66
San Diego, CA 28302
910-483-6611
Pager: 910-483-6611
Fax: 910-483-2439

Date

Dear Exact Name:

In all the hustle-bustle of life, isn't it easy to forget to appreciate the people we value the most? That is why I'm writing you this letter. I want you to know how deeply appreciative I am to you for the business relationship we have enjoyed, and I want you to know that we are committed to helping you achieve your future business goals in whatever way we can. It is our company goal to be known as the most reputable and most quality-conscious bookbinding producer in the business today.

We've come a long way since 1989...

I think you already know that Book Designers, Inc. was founded in 1989 by Cayton Williams and has grown into a business that operates at the highest level of technical sophistication. Our highly professional staff now consists of the following key individuals, all of whom have Your Total Satisfaction as our foremost goal:
- Grace Williams, President
- Winston Turner, Sales Representative
- Caison Matthews, Office Manager

Our goal—Your Total Satisfaction at all times...

Providing the best service possible at all times while guaranteeing a quality product is our number one goal. We are committed to a Total Quality Management approach to product performance and customer service.

We're here when you need us...

If you have a potential project coming up and want some expert consulting and advice at an early stage, please call us and we'll make ourselves immediately available to provide advice or a bid. I personally guarantee your total satisfaction with our price, product, quality control, customer service, and follow-through. But, in the meantime, let me again just say "thank you" for the privilege of serving your business needs.

Yours sincerely,

Grace Williams
President

LETTER EXPRESSING "THANK YOU" TO EXISTING CUSTOMERS

A letter is also a nice way to tell customers that you appreciate their business and value them. This letter is sent to each customer from a book design and binding firm. In a competitive marketplace, customer retention is often a high priority, and this type of letter helps to keep customers coming back.

COMMERCIAL INDUSTRIES, INC.
1110 Hay Street, Columbia, SC 28302

Telephone: (910) 483-6611   Fax: (910) 483-2439

Date

LETTER OF WELCOME TO NEW CUSTOMERS

Getting off to a good start can be a critical factor in business relationships, and this letter is intended to welcome new customers while emphasizing the need for vigorous two-way communication.

Exact Name of Customer
Exact Title of Customer
Exact Name of Company
Address
City, state zip

Dear Exact Name of Customer:

It is my great pleasure to welcome you "on board" as a valued customer of Commercial Industries! You will see that we will be committed to your needs for rapid distribution of your products and to your business success, and we will attempt to serve your needs with an emphasis on Total Quality Management in every aspect. A permanent and long-lasting relationship with you is our goal, and we intend to achieve that goal by providing the finest service available for your needs.

Good communication is the key...
Commercial Industries was founded by Dillon Extasis in 1984, and there's one thing we have learned during those years when we've grown from a three (3)-warehouse operation into a twelve (12)-warehouse company. We have learned that **good communication is the key to satisfying you and making sure that you are completely happy with the quality product we intend to deliver.**

Please help us to serve you best by communicating freely with me about anything you may not be sure of as your business develops. I not only want our distribution services to be of outstanding quality, but I also want your experience to be an enjoyable one. We are committed to the highest quality standards in our customer service.

Let me close this brief letter by telling you again, **"Welcome!"** We appreciate your business, we will do our best to serve you, and we look forward to putting all of our resources and know-how at your disposal. Thank you for your confidence in Commercial Industries.

Yours sincerely,

Davida Smith
Manager,
Customer Relations

DUPLICATE ... DO NOT INNOVATE!

This letter is completely legal. Refer to Title 18, Section 1302, US Postal Service Regulations. This can be the most important communication you will ever receive if you can understand and ACT upon this incredible opportunity. My name is David Rhodes. In September 1987, my car was repossessed and bill collectors were hounding me like you wouldn't believe. I was laid off and my unemployment had run out. In January of 1988, I bought a new Cadillac, with cash, and I am now building a new home in Virginia and will never have to work again! In October 1987, I received this letter telling me how to earn $50,000 anytime I wanted to. Of course I was skeptical, but because I was desperate and had nothing to lose, I gave it a try. Today, I have all the money I want. You can too, but only if you act upon this opportunity ... I earned $200,000 the first year, and will be a millionaire soon. This money program WORKS PERFECTLY every time!

I have never earned less than $33,000 each time—IF YOU FOLLOW THE INSTRUCTIONS EXACTLY...It doesn't require you to sell anything or come into contact with people. The best thing is, you only have to mail this letter. If you always dreamed of getting that lucky break, YOU JUST GOT IT! So now it's up to you. If you follow these instructions exactly, in good faith, your dreams will come true...Follow these instructions, and in 20 to 60 days, you will receive more cash than you would believe, all in the mail.

1. Immediately mail out $1.00 (cash only) to each of the NAMES LISTED BELOW, with a note asking each one to add you to his/her mailing list. (wrap bill in note.)
2. Remove the FIRST NAME below, move the others UP and place YOUR name in the SIXTH position.
3. Make 100-150 copies of this letter, showing your name in the SIXTH POSITION.
4. ORDER YOUR LIST OF NAMES FROM: XYA Marketing Co., PO Box 66, Fayetteville, NC 28302 (100 names—$13.00; 200 names—$26.00; 500 names—$40.00). Phone 1-800-483-6611.
5. While you are waiting for your mailing list to arrive, place these letters in stamped envelopes.
6. Your mailing list will arrive in the form of GUMMED LABELS. Place the labels on the envelopes and mail them. WITHIN 60 DAYS, YOU WILL RECEIVE APPROXIMATELY $50,000 in cash. (This is a legal transaction.)

Note: As soon as you mail out the letters, you are automatically in the mail order business and people are sending you $1.00 bills asking to be placed on your mailing list. This is a way in which people help one another by working together without trying to sell something that no one needs. This service is PERFECTLY LEGAL. The system works – JUST DO IT!

1. Bill Smith, 20 Pam Drive, Shawnee, OK 74801
2. T.J. Maxx, 10 Rhawn Street, Apt. 2, New York, NY 10732
3. Howard Vianeck, 4132 Katella Avenue, Ste. 201, Grand Rapids, MI 45345
4. Scott Delph P.O. Box 5434, Boise, MT 43540
5. Daryl Johnson, P.O. Box 1044, Kettering, MI 83235
6. David Rhodes, 2250 Hollywood Boulevard, Charlotte, NC 27582

LETTER USED IN A CHAIN LETTER MAILING

This was a real letter used by a real person in a chain letter mailing. We are not recommending that anyone utilize this chain letter. We are showing it for purposes of illustration only.

For release: immediately
Date:
For further information: contact Kaley James, 910-483-6611

CARDIAN ZIGBUAWE OPENS NEW GALLERY

The Princess Hotel in Atlanta, GA, is pleased to announce the opening of a new gallery by Cardian Zigbuawe on December 15, 1999. Mr. Zigbuawe is a world-class authority on Asian sculpture and is recognized as a authority throughout the art world on period pieces from 1975-present.

Cardian Zigbuawe found his calling in 1968 when he opened his first gallery at the prestigious Beverly Hills Hotel in Beverly Hills, CA, with a focus on Asian sculpture. In 1969 he began his extensive collection of Chinese and Japanese art, acquiring a special expertise in jade works of art. It was at this time that Cardian started to display a special talent for discovery of important overlooked art.

Because of Cardian's knowledge and love for art, his gallery outgrew its original location enabling him to relocate to a larger space in the Beverly Hills. By this time his name was becoming so well known that insurance companies started to seek Cardian's opinion regarding evaluation of various jade works of art. Numerous complex insurance claims were subsequently settled as a result of his uncommon knowledge not only of jade and oriental art, but also of paintings and sculptures as well.

In 1975, Cardian and his two partners opened a gallery at a new location in the San Francisco Fairmont Hotel. As a result of a major purchase shortly thereafter from the Arcadia Museum in San Diego, CA, the business grew tremendously in the ensuing years. Throughout this period Cardian continued to broaden his art knowledge through extensive study of world history and its major religions. It is his love for research and his drive to find the hidden truth that makes him unique among peers. A classic example is a missing masterpiece by Turner, formerly owned by the king of Poland, which was overlooked by the famous auction house, Christies. Cardian bought out his partners in 1993.

Over the last 20 years his expertise has been sought by The Smithsonian Institute and Museum of Natural History, Washington; The Los Angeles County Museum; The Asian Art Museum, San Francisco; Oakland (CA) Museum; Internal Revenue Service; United States Postal Service; and the Federal Bureau of Investigation (re: stolen art).

PRESS RELEASE FOR AN ART GALLERY

Business marketing letters can take the form of standard press releases, too, since a press release and a business marketing letter have similar objectives. Both are intended to make the public aware of a product or service.

PREP PUBLISHING

Press Release

1110 1/2 Hay Street, Fayetteville, NC 28305 (910) 483-6611/Fax: (910) 483-2439

Publication Date: October 23, 1999

The book will be available from bookstores/libraries, from Seven Hills Book Distributor, or the publisher at 910-483-6611.

Title: *Back in Time*   **Author:** Patty Sleem

Price: $16.00
Publication Date: October 1999   **ISBN:** 1-885288-03-4
Size: 6" X 9"   **Pages:** 164 pages

For more info: Janet Abernethy, Publicist, 910-483-6611

Back in Time introduces a new mystery series featuring woman minister Maggie Dillitz. When Maggie trades in her Harvard M.B.A. and a lucrative career in the business world for a Yale Divinity School degree and a career in ministry, she expects relief from the competitive pressures of business and a life of satisfying service to her God and mankind.

What Maggie Dillitz encounters after graduating from divinity school are many subtle and other not-so-subtle forms of discrimination against women in ministry, especially against women in pulpit ministries. A single parent remarried to a former Harvard classmate with whom she is raising three children, Maggie finds her life turned upside down when a war in the Middle East claims the services of many of the senior ministers in the United Methodist Church. Maggie finds herself assigned on an interim basis to a large church in the South, and she enjoys the challenge of preaching in the modern church.

After preaching a sermon on the book of Amos, the prophet of "doom and gloom" who brought a message of correction from God to the Israelites twenty-seven centuries ago, Maggie finds herself in the middle of a hostile hornet's nest with her career on the line.

An unexpected turn of events brings an abrupt halt to the war in the Middle East along with the return of the senior minister to his post at Golgotha United Methodist Church. Protectively taking Maggie under his wing, senior minister Dr. William Farmer arranges for both him and Maggie to be involved in a mission project in Jamaica for two weeks in order to aid the homeless and hungry in the aftermath of a hurricane which devastated the island. During the mission project, Maggie must deal with the trauma of sexual discrimination in yet new forms. After Maggie preaches a funeral service for a friend dying at age forty of cancer, she finds herself at the center of a homicide investigation. The sequel is *Fall From Grace*, due in 2000.

PRESS RELEASE FOR A NEW BOOK

Written communication promoting a new product, such as a book, is often in the form of a press release rather than a standard letter.

Lightning Courier Service
325 Bladen Drive, Chicago, IL 28305

Office: (910) 483-6611   e-mail: preppub@aol.com

"For a quick trip, call Lightning"

Date

Dear Sir or Madam:

LETTER INTRODUCING A COURIER SERVICE

How does a new business get started? Often the marketing help can come in the form of a letter such as this one, which the new business can mail or distribute by hand to businesses which it has targeted as potential customers.

Do you have important documents and time-sensitive materials which require immediate delivery by a fast, reliable courier service with extensive experience and an outstanding reputation?

Locally owned and operated, Lightning Courier Service is positioning itself to serve the needs of Chicago's business, financial, and legal communities by providing fast, reliable, same-day delivery of your materials to any location within 200 miles.

Convenient hours, emergency availability

As a service business, our primary concern is to make ourselves available to meet the needs of our customers. We are available for "emergency" deliveries on Saturday, in addition to our regular hours of 8:00 A.M. to 5:00 P.M., Monday-Friday.

Experience in servicing commercial accounts

From 1979-1993, I ran Zip Courier Service in Vallejos, CA, servicing major accounts which included North American Title, Home Federal Savings & Loan, Bank of America, and Fidelity Savings & Loan, as well as AmeriMac Advent Mortgage and NMS Mortgage Service, Inc. These and other satisfied customers came to rely on our prompt, courteous, and dependable service. **In over fourteen years of business, we never missed a deadline or misplaced a package.** I can provide letters of recommendation from these customers, and I'm certain that any of our previous accounts would be more than happy to provide outstanding references upon request.

Integrity and dependability

When you choose a courier service to handle your most important, most sensitive documents, you want to ensure that you are dealing with someone you can trust. In more than twenty years of service to the Criminal Investigation Division of the U.S. Army, and in 30 years as a minister, pastor, and Christian education leader, I have proven time and time again that my integrity is beyond reproach.

It would be my pleasure to meet with you at your convenience to discuss your priority delivery needs and how Lightning Courier Service could meet them. To schedule an appointment, please call me at the numbers provided above, and I will be happy to provide a price quote on the services you require. Thank you for allowing us the opportunity to serve your needs in this area.

Yours sincerely,

William Jenkins, Owner

ALL-PURPOSE CLEANING AND REPAIR
Owners: Jan and Robert Abernethy
P.O. Box 87, St. Pauls, MN 90234
(910) 483-6611

Date

Mr. Michael Foster
Vice President
Nexus Construction Company
P.O. Drawer 9034
St. Pauls, MN 90234

Dear Mr. Foster:

I enjoyed talking with you in your office on March 18, and I am responding to your request for a formal expression of our desire to provide extensive cleaning services to Nexus Construction. Here is what I propose:

Services to be performed:
For a price of .09 (nine cents) a square foot, the following cleaning services could be provided:
  Cleaning of interior and exterior windows
  Cleaning of store fronts
  Cleaning of interior glass and frames
  Vacuuming of carpet
  Dustmop wood floors
  Mop vinyl floors
  Clean and mop bathrooms
  Dust and clean casework
  Clean food prep areas

For complex architectural building designs, we would reserve the right to provide a separate quote on a project basis.

As you know, we pride ourselves on our reliability and dependability, and you are aware of the quality services we have performed for you for various jobs on a project basis. It is our desire to handle as much of your cleaning business as possible, and I believe we can of valuable assistance to you in this area. We do take pride in our work, and you can certainly depend on our reliability at all times.

From our discussions I understand that you will be discussing this concept with your colleagues, and I will look forward to hearing from you.

Yours sincerely,

Robert Abernethy

LETTER FOLLOWING UP ON AN INITIAL VERBAL PROPOSAL

A business marketing letter often finalizes deals which have been discussed verbally or in concept. By putting in writing the details of a prior discussion, the company is committing to specific prices and terms and can "close the sale."

Date

Exact Name of Person
Title or Position
Name of Company
Address (number and street)
Address (city, state, and zip)

LETTER USED TO ACCOMPANY A BUSINESS RESUME

Sometimes a letter can be part of a marketing mailing. On these two pages you will see a letter and resume which were used as companion documents in a mailing sent to interest prospective customers in the services of a professional mobile home repair specialist.

Dear Exact Name of Person: (or Sir or Madam if answering a blind ad.)

With the enclosed resume, I would like to make you aware of my background as an experienced Mobile Home Repair Specialist and initiate the process of being considered for work as a contractor or subcontractor as your needs require.

As a self-employed Mobile Home Repair Specialist, I operate a company called Orion Mobile Home Repair in Warsaw, Wisconsin, and serve a variety of satisfied customers in neighboring towns. Satisfied customers include the following:
Social Services/Housing & Urban Development
Warsaw County Social Services Department
American Home Star Sales
Sterling Homes
Wilfred Thompson, Jr.

I offer more than 20 years of experience in performing electrical work, carpentry, and maintenance of all types. In addition to my experience as a Mobile Home Service Technician and Maintenance Technician, I have worked as a carpenter and once owned and managed a successful auto detail shop in Georgia. I am experienced in all types of cabinet work, and there is virtually no piece of equipment or fixture in mobile homes (as well as in apartments and houses) which I have not maintained, replaced, repaired, or installed. We have all the tools and equipment necessary to perform any phase of the setup, repair, and maintenance of mobile homes as well as for all types of general construction.

If you can use a reliable and honest subcontractor for your properties, please call me to discuss your needs. Our operation is highly mobile, and we can readily travel to your job site to meet your needs. I can provide excellent credit references as well as outstanding references from individuals and organizations who are acquainted with my work and professionalism.

I would enjoy the opportunity to discuss how I could be of service to you. Remember: *"Over 20 years of experience, and we do it all."*

Yours sincerely,

Orion Hamstead Pierce

ORION HAMSTEAD PIERCE
Mobile Home Repair Specialist
OVER 20 YEARS OF EXPERIENCE
"We Do It All"
Box 95, Warsaw, WI 28305
pager: 910-483-2439 ù cellular: 910-483-6611

OBJECTIVE	To serve the needs of organizations and individuals that can use a skilled mobile home repair specialist who offers an excellent personal reputation for reliability and honesty as well as proven skills in all aspects of mobile home repair, maintenance, and setup.
EXPERIENCE	**MOBILE HOME REPAIR SPECIALIST (Self-Employed).** Orion Mobile Home Repair, Warsaw, WI (1998-present). Am the owner and manager of Orion Mobile Home Repair, currently repair and/or replace floors, windows, doors, walls (interior and exterior), carpet, and vinyl; perform minor electrical and plumbing work.

Offer expertise in all aspects of mobile home repair: Handle jobs involving Kool Seal, skirting underpin, and remodeling.

Satisfaction Guaranteed/Excellent References: Guarantee satisfaction with all work performed, and can provide excellent references from these and other organizations whose mobile homes and apartments I service and maintain:

- Social Services/Housing & Urban Development
- Warsaw County Social Services Department
- American Home Star Sales
- Sterling Homes

SERVICE TECHNICIAN. Oakwood Mobile Homes, Warsaw, WI (1997-98). Was rehired by this company for which I worked previously, worked on the company's repossessions (Factory Certified Homes); repaired or replaced anything that was broken.
- Resigned under excellent circumstances to go into business for myself.

MAINTENANCE TECHNICIAN. Fulsome Acres Mobile Home Park, Warsaw, WI (1993-97). Repaired and rebuilt mobile homes in several parks which contained hundreds of trailers and apartments. Performed repairs and maintenance in both the mobile homes and the apartments.

SERVICE TECHNICIAN. Oakwood Mobile Homes (Freedom Mobile Home Sales), Warsaw, WI (1992-93). Repaired and/or replaced fixtures and equipment which was broken in existing homes and deficient in new homes.
- Selected for a special assignment to help set up a mobile home lot in FL.

MECHANIC. Craven Toyota, Warsaw, WI (1992). Managed the detail shop.

GENERAL MANAGER and **OWNER.** Scrub-A-Dub, Pensacola, FL (1988-91). Owned and managed a successful detail shop; closed the business and moved from FL to WI when my father became very ill.

CARPENTER. Quality Plus Construction, Sanford, NE (1986-88). Performed framing and did finishing work; became skilled in installing cabinets and cabinet tops. Handled inside and outside trim work.

BUSINESS RESUME

As mentioned on the preceding page, this business resume was introduced by the letter on the facing page, and the two documents were intended to introduce the services and reputation of an individual offering his services to private individuals and companies.

MASON FULBRIGHT

Landscaping - Cleaning - Tree Removal - Yard Work - Carpentry - Painting
Box 66, 1605 Morganton Road
Dallas, TX 89032

Phone: (910) 483-6611   Cell: (910) 483-2439

Company Background: Mason Fulbright Landscaping has been in business for 22 years.
Satisfaction Always Guaranteed

LETTER USED TO MARKET A LANDSCAPING SERVICE

This independent businessman maintains a batch of these letters in his car while he is on various jobs throughout Dallas. If he comes across an opportunity to market his services, he can simply pull out a letter, date and sign it, and fill in the amount he is bidding for the specific job. In this way, he can make a professional approach "on the spot" and he is ready to respond to each and every new prospecting opportunity.

Dear Sir or Madam:

This letter is a bid for services to be performed which consist of the following:

Trim shrubs
Edge yard
Cut grass
Pick up all trash

Once each week, I would perform the above services.

I would like to be paid every two weeks in the amount of _____.

A monthly payment schedule could also be arranged.

Our work is totally guaranteed, and we will redo any work which is not considered satisfactory.

Yours sincerely,

Mason Fulbright

Career-Changing Letters
(for people moving on to new fields or just moving up)

In this section, you will see examples of letters used to open doors in new industries and new fields. You will also see examples of letters used by people who were trying to "cash in" their experience in a specific field and find a better job at a higher level.

If you are changing careers or just thinking about doing so, you will find some helpful examples of letters which helped real people transition into jobs in radically different fields. If you are seeking further guidance on this subject, you can also use the following book by PREP Publishing: *Cover Letters That Blow Doors Open*.

Most people have at least three distinctly different careers in their working lifetimes. Sometimes the hard part of a career change is not performing in the new job once you find the work you want to do; it's establishing credibility in your job hunt and "getting in the door" for an interview.

The problem most people have when they try to write a "career-change" letter is that they wonder how much to write about experience in another field that is probably irrelevant to the job now being sought.

Understand this about potential employers to whom you are writing: They are "nosy" people who simply wonder why you are writing to them if your background has been in another field. **That's why the goal of the career-change cover letter is to be creative and help the employer "make sense" of you and your interest in that industry.**

You are trying to "sell" yourself in a career-change cover letter, **but the trick is to sell your potential** to do a job you've never done before instead of your experience. As you probably already know, it's easier to write a cover letter selling experience than to write one selling your potential!

While most people understand the importance of having a great resume, they fail to appreciate how important a cover letter can be. When you look at the cover letters in this section—and remember they were accompanied in every case by a resume—you will become aware of the fact that the cover letter is THE first impression of you and a great cover letter can blow a door open for you!

Date

Exact Name of Person
Title or Position
Address (number and street)
Address (city, state, and zip)

Dear Sir or Madam:

FROM DENTAL ASSISTING TO FLIGHT ATTENDANT

A cover letter is especially important in career changes. When your experience is in a different field from the one you are trying to enter, the cover letter can "make sense" of you and explain why you are sending your resume. In the case of this individual, the cover letter can explain why a dental assistant wants to become a flight attendant.

With the enclosed resume describing my considerable public relations and customer service experience, I would like to formally initiate the process of applying for employment as a Flight Attendant.

As you will see from my resume, I have worked as an Office Manager for a highly regarded dentist who is retiring from private practice shortly. Although I am highly regarded by this employer and can provide excellent references at the appropriate time, I have decided to change careers and aggressively pursue a dream I have had for some time: to become a Flight Attendant.

My experience in managing the private practice of a busy dentist gave me many skills which would be useful in airline situations. I am extremely poised when dealing with the public, and I am known for my ability to serve the public with tact and grace. I work well with people at all organizational levels, and I have become accustomed to putting others at ease when external events are in flux. While working for the doctor, I have become his trusted personal advisor and have handled numerous personal matters for him.

In other experience, I also excelled briefly as a Certified Nursing Assistant and Teacher's Assistant. My communication skills are excellent, and I genuinely enjoy working with people individually and in groups. I feel confident that my medical knowledge, certification in CPR, and proven ability to remain calm in crises could be assets in flight situations where a calm head and prudent thinking are needed in emergencies.

I hope you will contact me to suggest the next step I should take in making formal application for employment as a Flight Attendant. I can assure you in advance that I have an excellent reputation, and I am confident that I could be a valuable asset to your organization.

Sincerely,

Cynthia Drysdale

Date

Exact Name of Person
Title or Position
Address (number and street)
Address (city, state, and zip)

Dear Exact Name of Person: (or Dear Sir or Madam if answering a blind ad)

I would appreciate an opportunity to talk with you soon about how I could contribute to your organization through my education and experience in management as well as my strong communication skills and aggressive bottom-line orientation. Although I have been highly successful in grocery store management, it is my strong desire to transition into a career which will allow me to utilize my exceptionally strong sales and marketing abilities.

As you will see from my enclosed resume, I have been highly successful in all operational areas of store and customer service management with the Kroger grocery store chain. I am a highly respected management professional and winner of numerous awards for my expertise in developing employees, reducing shrinkage, increasing productivity and customer satisfaction, and increasing bottom-line profitability.

With a B.S.B.A. degree concentrating in Human Resources Management from the University of Pennsylvania, I possess an educational background which complements my 13-plus years of practical management experience. I have always enjoyed the challenge of training and guiding the professional development of others. I have trained dozens of Kroger managers and have produced highly effective professionals who are now some of Kroger's best managers. In company opinion polls conducted annually of employees, I am always described by employees as a fair yet firm supervisor who treats all people with respect. I believe attitude is one of the most important indicators of an employee's future success in a job, but I also believe that effective supervisory skills can shape attitudes, stimulate productivity, and minimize turnover.

I hope you will call or write me soon to arrange a brief meeting to discuss your current and future needs and how I might serve them. Thank you in advance for your time.

Sincerely,

Samantha Greystone

Alternate last paragraph:
I hope you will welcome my call soon when I try to arrange a time convenient for us to meet and discuss your current and future needs and how I might serve them. Thank you in advance for your time.

THE DIRECT APPROACH

What is the "direct approach?"
You need to master the technique of using the "direct approach" in your job hunt. By using the direct approach, you create an all-purpose letter, such as the one on this page, which you can send to numerous employers introducing yourself and your resume. The direct approach is a proactive, aggressive approach to a job campaign, and it sure beats waiting around until the "ideal job" appears in the newspaper (and 200 other people see it, too). Figure out the employers you wish to approach either (1) by geographical area or (2) by industry, and directly approach them expressing your interest in their company. Believe it or not, most people get their jobs through the direct approach!

Date

Exact Name of Person
Title or Position
Name of Company
Address (number and street)
Address (city, state, and zip)

ANSWERING BLIND ADS

What's the best way to answer a "blind ad?"

"To whom it may concern" or "Dear Sir or Madam" is the proper salutation for a letter responding to a "blind ad" or an ad which does not reveal the company name or the name of the person to whom you are writing. Sometimes companies don't put their name in the ad because they don't want their competitors to know they are hiring. Sometimes companies don't give their name because they think it might encourage telephone calls about the job.

To Whom It May Concern: (or Dear Sir or Madam)

I would appreciate an opportunity to talk with you soon about how I could contribute to your organization through my extensive expertise in the financial field including my recent experience as a Financial Consultant.

As you will see from my resume, I hold the Series 7, Series 63, Series 24, and Series 65 licenses and am a Registered Member of numerous exchanges and associations of securities dealers. In 1998 I left a Wall Street firm to relocate to the South, where my wife and her family live. Since 1998 I have been working for Merrill Lynch, and after my training and licensing, I established 364 accounts and produced $5 million in managed money in my first six-month period of production. Although I am excelling in my job and have been offered a branch management position in another state, I wish to remain in the Norfolk area. Since I am not under contract with Merrill Lynch, I am exploring suitable opportunities with area firms.

Much of my rapid success as a Financial Consultant stems from my background in nearly all aspects of finance, credit, and collections, in addition to my entrepreneurial experience. As Managing Director, I owned and managed a lead-based company for Dun & Bradstreet. Subsequent to that, I worked with Wall Street firms in New York City until I met my wife and she decided she wanted us to relocate to Norfolk to be near her family. I offer an extensive background in working with high net worth individuals.

I can provide outstanding personal and professional references, and I would be delighted to make myself available at your convenience for a personal interview. Thank you in advance for your professional courtesies and consideration.

Yours sincerely,

Elias Johnson III

Date

Ms. Myrtle McConnell
Clark Management, Inc.
Post Office Box 82
Virginia Beach, VA 34098

Dear Ms. McConnell:

I am writing to express my interest in the position of Manager of the Virginia Beach Resort and Tennis Club which was advertised in the *Virginia Beach Gazette* of Monday, December 18, 1999. With the enclosed resume, I would like to introduce you to my proven supervisory and guest services skills along with my track record of success as Owner/Operator and General Manager of a number of establishments.

In my most recent position in the hospitality industry, I purchased a 150-seat restaurant and 50-seat lounge from the O'Brien's chain. I changed the restaurant's name and developed a new, expanded menu while implementing higher levels of guest service. I directed the work of the front end, bar, and kitchen managers, overseeing a staff of 25 employees. In my previous position at Kasey's in Virginia Beach, we dealt with a large client base of repeat customers, arranging reservations at local golf courses as well as serving their dining needs.

For the past year, I have excelled as Business Manager of ABC Construction, helping my brother to set up his commercial contracting business. Now that his business is up and running, I am very interested in returning to the hospitality industry, and my wife and I are considering relocation to the Virginia Beach area. I feel that my strong management background and proven skills in customer service, staff development, and training would make me a valuable addition to your operation.

When we meet in person, you will see that I am a congenial professional and avid tennis player with extensive management experience that could make me an ideal candidate for this position. I offer an outstanding reputation in our industry and can provide excellent references at the appropriate time.

Yours sincerely,

Bill Adams

ANSWERING ADS THAT PROVIDE NAMES AND ADDRESSES

How do I respond to an ad that provides the name and address?
It's easy enough to reply to an ad when you have the name and address of the person you're writing to, but there's more to this question than meets the eye. Read the ad carefully and tailor your letter as precisely to the ad as possible. Notice the sentence in the last paragraph where Mr. Adams mentions that he's a tennis player. He is picking up on the fact that the ad is for a tennis resort and he is making his reader aware that he plays the game and understands the passion of the club's customers.

Date

P.O. Box 66
Dallas, TX 90345

ALL-PURPOSE COVER LETTERS

Seeking Management Trainee Position

Notice how this young professional emphasizes her management skills and versatility while pointing out that her experience has been in law enforcement and security. Even to employers outside the law enforcement and security field, this background tends to imply an honest and clean-cut individual and may inspire some confidence on the part of prospective employers.

To whom it may concern:

With the enclosed resume, I would like to respond to your advertisement in the *Dallas Chronicle* for a Management Trainee and make you aware of the considerable office, sales, and management abilities I could put to work for you.

As you will see from my resume, I am skilled in all aspects of office activities and am proficient with WordPerfect and the Windows 95 programs including Word, Excel, and Access. I am a very cheerful and adaptable person, as has been demonstrated by my ability to adapt rapidly and become quickly productive while working in long-term and short-term temporary assignments for major corporations, small businesses, and utility companies. I am skilled at operating a multiline switchboard system.

A resourceful and enthusiastic individual, I have always found ways to contribute to increased efficiency in all of my jobs. For example, in one job with an electrical supply company, I developed ideas which resulted in increased efficiency in supply parts ordering. In another job with a prominent retailer, I was named Sales Representative of the Month and was credited with playing a key role in increasing repeat business through my customer service and sales skills.

You will also see that I offer proven management skills and personal initiative. In one of my first professional positions, I was promoted rapidly by a children's entertainment company to responsibilities which involved traveling to conventions to book shows and negotiate contracts. The youngest person ever promoted to vice president, I am still a member of the Board of Directors of that company and am respected for my business insights and marketing instincts.

If you can use a versatile young professional known for an excellent attitude as well as superior work habits including reliability, dependability, and honesty, I hope you will contact me to suggest a time when we might meet to discuss your needs. I can assure you in advance that I could rapidly become an asset to your organization.

Sincerely,

Simone Guardado

Date

Mr. John Smith
XYZ Management Recruiters
Address (number and street)
Address (city, state, and zip)

Dear Mr. Smith:

After reviewing the materials you sent me regarding the Des Moines Public Schools Superintendency, I believe that my professional and personal attributes are complementary to the needs of the school system.

In my current position as Superintendent of Fort Leavenworth Schools, I am entrusted with serving 5,700 students and supervising a staff of 660. The challenges in this district serving military dependents have been many and varied. With the cooperation of the staff and the greater school community, we have been successful in securing outstanding financial support from both the Department of Defense and Congress. As a result, we were able to open a new elementary school and expand five existing schools.

As Superintendent in Huntsville, AL, and at Fort Leavenworth, I provided the impetus for expansion of technology in the instructional program. During this past year, one of Fort Leavenworth's elementary schools was chosen as a testbed site for President Clinton's Technology Initiative (PTI). This pilot project will afford our students and staff an opportunity to share innovative programs and instructional strategies.

Believing that mutual cooperation from internal and external sources is critical for success, I am known for my ability to forge strong alliances and partnerships with community organizations. While serving as Superintendent in Huntsville, I was instrumental in forming a regional school and business alliance (SABA) which developed partnerships with the business community. Serving as Director on several boards has also provided me with opportunities to gain community support for school programs. Indeed, any professional accomplishments I have achieved during my career have been attained through the combined efforts of many people. If I were to be selected as Superintendent, I would work diligently to gain local, state, and national support in order to move the Des Moines Public Schools forward.

Thank you for your interest in my qualifications, and I look forward to talking with you soon about the next step you suggest in my formally applying for the position as Superintendent of the Des Moines School System.

Yours sincerely,

Andrew J. Foster

RESPONDING TO RECRUITERS

How do I respond to a recruiter or headhunter who has approached me?
Don't take any shortcuts when responding to a recruiter who has approached you to see if you might be interested in a new situation. In Mr. Foster's case, he has been approached by a management recruiting firm handling the search for a school superintendent of a major school district. He makes sure the recruiter understands him professionally and philosophically by developing a cover letter
that fully markets his interest and background. As always, make sure your cover letter "sells" you!

Date

Exact Name of Person
Title or Position
Name of Company
Address (number and street)
Address (city, state, and zip)

ALL-PURPOSE COVER LETTERS

Background in Criminal Justice

Here's a tip: An all-purpose cover letter can be personalized to a specific company by mentioning the company name in the first and last paragraph of the letter. Or you could leave the body of the letter unchanged and simply address the letter to the person in the company who supervises people in the type of job you are seeking (e.g., Director of Security Services). So, with just a couple of changes in a standard letter which you can maintain in your computer, you will have a letter which seems personally prepared for each company you approach.

Dear Exact Name of Person: (or Sir or Madam if answering a blind ad.)

With the enclosed resume, I would like to make you aware of my background as an experienced professional who has excelled in managing human, fiscal, and material resources as well as in motivating, supervising, and instructing personnel.

As you will see, while my experience and education have been predominately in law enforcement and security, I have recently earned a bachelor's degree in Business Management. I earned this degree–and associate's degrees in Business Management and Criminal Justice Administration–while simultaneously excelling at meeting the demands of positions in the hectic and pressure-filled environment of military law enforcement and security. My time management and organizational skills have been refined as a Loss Prevention Associate for Simon's department store, and I have polished my communication skills teaching on a part-time basis as an instructor for the Basic Law Enforcement Training program at Smyrna Technical Community College, Atlanta, GA.

Throughout my career I have been handpicked for highly visible leadership roles and singled out to act in various capacities as an investigator, inspector and advisor, developer of training, and supervisor. I believe that my greatest strengths are the ability to motivate others and lead them to work together, along with my talent for being able to develop good working relations with people of all ages and skill levels.

If you can use an experienced and adaptable professional who offers sound judgment and decision-making skills, I hope you will contact me to suggest a time when we might meet to discuss your needs. I can assure you in advance that I could rapidly become an asset to your organization.

Sincerely,

Gerald Utley

Date

Exact Name of Person
Title or Position
Name of Company
Address (number and street)
Address (city, state, and zip)

Dear Exact Name of Person: (or Sir or Madam if answering a blind ad.)

Can you use an articulate, enthusiastic, and self-motivated young professional with a strong interest in entering the pharmaceutical sales field?

As you will see from my enclosed resume, I earned my B.S. in Biology from Michigan State University and maintained a 3.5 GPA. During my senior year I worked as many as 50 hours a week as a Research Assistant in the university's chemistry lab. I conducted research which resulted in a manual that was distributed at a national conference.

In my most recent job as a middle school science and math teacher, I refined communication, organizational, and time management skills while involved in numerous projects. I planned the school's first science fair as well as a Christmas play and a musical. My greatest accomplishment during this period was in taking a student who was working two grade levels below his classmates and developing an individualized plan to use while tutoring him. I spent four months working closely with him and brought him up to his proper grade level.

Earlier while serving for four years in the U.S. Army, I earned both an Army Commendation Medal and an Achievement Medal for my performance as a supervisor, dental office administrator, and assistant during dental surgery procedures. I quickly took the initiative for clearing up a logistics backlog and was also singled out for my role in producing well-trained and skilled X-ray technicians, surgical assistants, and clerical staff members.

I am confident that through my education, experience, and strengths in working with and communicating with others, I could rapidly become an asset to your organization. Please contact me to suggest a time when we might meet to discuss your needs.

Sincerely,

Julie M. Vogel

ALL-PURPOSE COVER LETTERS

Entering Pharmaceutical Sales Field

This all-purpose letter emphasizes the communication skills and versatility of a young professional with teaching experience as well as a distinguished military record. Lack of experience in a particular field is not a main reason why employers choose not to interview applicants. Employers are looking for a track record of accomplishment in whatever you have done so far.

Date

Exact Name of Person
Title or Position
Name of Company
Address (number and street)
Address (city, state, and zip)

ALL-PURPOSE COVER LETTERS

Sales and Accounting Skills
This all-purpose cover letter acquaints prospective employers with sales and accounting skills which could be utilized in versatile ways by a variety of employers in multiple industries. Notice how she emphasizes her strong personal qualities of initiative and congeniality while citing bottom-line accomplishments.
There is a tendency for employers to think, "If she did this for her previous employer, she could do this for me, too."

Dear Exact Name of Person: (or Sir or Madam if answering a blind ad.)

With the enclosed resume, I would like to make you aware of my strong desire to become employed in a role in which I could benefit your company through my computer knowledge, sales skills, and customer service experience.

As you will see from my resume, I am currently excelling as an Operations Clerk working for Advanced Technology in Miami, where I am employed in a temporary full-time position through Man Hours Temporary Service. In this job I am involved in a wide range of activities involving computer operations, customer service, and administrative support. I have become proficient in using Beyond Mail, in utilizing the LAN system, and in researching and coordinating service orders in the most efficient manner while applying my knowledge of internal telecommunications operations.

In my previous job in Orlando as an Administrative Aide, I became a valuable employee and was entrusted with many complex responsibilities because of my demonstrated initiative, intelligence, and customer service skills. Since I am bilingual in Spanish and English, I conducted new hires of employees in both Spanish and English and frequently translated communication between production workers and office personnel.

My computer skills are excellent, and I enjoy learning new software. While in my previous job I completed a major project in which I computerized data entry for all production workers' payroll. I am knowledgeable of software including Microsoft Word, Excel, Lotus 1-2-3, and PowerPoint.

Although I am excelling in my current position and can provide outstanding references at the appropriate time, I am seeking a permanent position with an employer that can make use of my strong communication, problem-solving, and decision-making skills. A highly motivated self-starter, I am confident of my ability to make significant improvements to your bottom line.

Sincerely,

Maria Sanchez

Date

Exact Name of Person
Title or Position
Name of Company
Address (number and street)
Address (city, state, and zip)

Dear Exact Name of Person: (or Sir or Madam if answering a blind ad.)

With the enclosed resume, I would like to make you aware of my interest in discussing the possibility of employment with your organization.

As you will see from my enclosed resume, I have been excelling in a track record of accomplishment while utilizing my skills in communication and customer service.

Both during the process of earning and after receiving my A.S. degree in Theater Arts from the University of New Mexico, I have distinguished myself in sales, public relations, customer service, and management roles.

As you will see from my resume, I offer a proven ability to work with and satisfy sophisticated customers of high-end products while also handling responsibilities related to collections, refunds, accounts payable and receivable, and other areas.

In my previous job as a Sales Manager in Beverly Hills, CA, I was responsible for hiring and training 19 sales associates in a store which catered to high-end customers of designer bridal gowns, evening wear, and lingerie. When I recruited sales professionals, I always looked for individuals with strong personalities who demonstrated a proven ability to be resourceful in customer service and problem solving while gaining the confidence of customers in a sales situation. Although I am only 23, I have succeeded in positions which often were filled by a much more senior individual because of my exceptionally strong communication skills, common sense, and ability to skillfully handle customers in any and all situations. On numerous occasions, my communication skills have enabled me to tactfully resolve difficult customer problems, find creative remedies to employee issues, as well as aggressively develop new business and new accounts.

Please give me every consideration for a position in your company where my superior customer service, sales, and public relations skills could benefit your organization. Thank you in advance for your time.

Yours sincerely,

Joy Van de Hoef

ALL-PURPOSE COVER LETTERS

Communication and Customer Service Skills
This all-purpose cover letter emphasizes strong communication and customer service skills. Most organizations can make good use of a young professional who has excelled in sales, public relations, customer service, and management roles.

Date

Exact Name of Person
Exact Name of Company
Exact Address
City, State Zip

ALL-PURPOSE COVER LETTERS

Sales Skills and Versatility

This all-purpose cover letter is from a young person who is emphasizing her positive attitude and customer service skills. There are many employers who will take a hard-working young person with a good attitude and train them, so don't think that you "have nothing" if you are young and lack extensive paid work experience. You are just the kind of "raw material" many employers are seeking!

Dear Sir or Madam:

With the enclosed resume, I would like to make you aware of my interest in joining your organization in some capacity which could use my strong background in sales and customer service as well as my solid training in accounting and bookkeeping.

Sales Distinctions

I am 24 years of age and have worked since I was 18 years old for Penney's. During that time I have excelled in every assignment and have received numerous cash bonuses as well as several Sales Recognition Awards (SRAs). I am proud to say that I have increased sales in every department in which I have worked, and while in Ft. Irwin, CA, I earned the distinction of the #1 camera sales representative in the U.S. while leading my department to a 25% sales increase.

Accounting and Bookkeeping Knowledge

In my spare time, I have nearly completed an Associate's degree in Accounting and Bookkeeping, and my degree program included coursework in financial reporting, accounts receivable and payables management, budget analysis, financial statement analysis, and other similar areas. I excelled academically while also performing with distinction in my full-time day job. My experience with Penney's includes accounting and bookkeeping, as I have handled responsibilities as a Head Teller and Cashier. In one assignment, I was responsible for balancing all money received daily from 16 cash registers, and it was my job to assure the correct balancing of more than $75,000.

I am a very well-organized individual with superior problem-solving abilities who rapidly masters new tasks and activities. I am certain that you would find me in person to be a congenial individual who would represent your company with poise and professionalism. I hope you will contact me soon to suggest a time when we could meet to discuss your needs and how I might be of service to you. I can provide outstanding personal and professional references at the appropriate time.

Yours sincerely,

Olivia N. Crosby

Date

Exact Name of Person
Exact Name of Company
Address
City, State Zip

Dear Sir or Madam:

Can you use a resourceful manager who offers proven skills in the area of automated information systems, financial management, and personnel administration?

While rising to the rank of Major in the U.S. Army, I had an opportunity to positively impact the lives of the many employees I supervised while also making significant contributions to organizational effectiveness.

In my most recent position, I was specially selected as Chief of a Budget Division which was in a critical transition phase. I managed a budget in excess of $160 million and supervised a 14-person staff while overseeing the strategic allocation of resources needed by 120 university ROTC programs and 490 junior ROTC programs.

In my previous position as a Division Chief, I expanded the number of ROTC programs in 16 states from 160 to more than 400 programs. Simultaneously I instituted Lotus and Excel spreadsheets to track variable and fixed expenses, and I created numerous efficiencies which permitted the purchase of computer equipment needed to set up a badly needed information system.

Prior to that I functioned as a top-level consultant and Quality Control Inspector. I reported to a Commanding General while organizing and supervising the work of inspectors conducting detailed analyses of the systems and procedures of a 10,000-person organization. I became an expert at the practical application of Total Quality Management principles.

I have excelled in "line" management positions, including Company Commander of a 100-person organization, and I have also served in "staff" roles. Once I served as a Project Officer on a top-level strategic planning task force responsible for designing the communications-electronics products and information systems of the future.

With an outstanding personal and professional reputation, I can provide excellent references at the appropriate time. If my background interests you, I hope you will contact me to suggest a time when we might meet in person to discuss your needs and how I might serve them. Thank you in advance for your time.

Yours sincerely,

Calvin P. Donatelli

ALL-PURPOSE COVER LETTERS

Military Professional in Transition
An all-purpose cover letter helped this military officer explore job opportunities in various industries. It is not always easy to decide what you want to do, and this accomplished individual with multiple talents wanted to use his resume and cover letter to "go fishing" in various fields and industries. His accomplishments in budgeting, programming, consulting, and management should interest numerous employers and introduce him as a multi-talented and versatile executive.

Date

Exact Name of Person
Exact Name of Company
Exact Address
City, State Zip

ALL-PURPOSE COVER LETTERS

Young professional emphasizing strong personal qualities

Young people lacking in extensive experience often make the best use of their cover letter by emphasizing their enthusiasm, versatility, and positive attitude.

Dear Sir or Madam:

With the enclosed resume, I would like to express my interest in working for your company and acquaint you with the experience and skills I have to offer.

Although I am only 20 years old, I have been working for the same employer since I was 16 years old and have earned a reputation as a versatile and valuable employee. On my own initiative and in my spare time, I have gained proficiency with several popular software programs and operating systems, and I am also taking courses in my spare time at Louisville Technical Community College to improve my knowledge and skills.

On numerous occasions, my employer has commended me for my sunny disposition and "willingness to go the extra mile" to provide outstanding customer service. I have proven my ability to excel as a team player as well as in handling total responsibility for a key activity. I have enthusiastically worked hard to help my employer in fund-raising efforts related to raising money for juvenile diabetes, muscular dystrophy, and March of Dimes.

Although I am highly regarded by my current employer and am being groomed for advancement into higher levels of responsibility, I would like to work in an office environment in which I can utilize and strengthen my administrative and computer operations skills. I am a quick learner and a self-starter and feel that I could rapidly become a valuable part of any organization.

If you can use a hard-working and dependable young person, please contact me to suggest a time convenient for you when we could meet. Thank you in advance for your time. I am a single (no children) and stable individual and can provide excellent references at the appropriate time.

Yours sincerely,

Mollie Poindexter

Date

Exact Name of Person
Exact Title
Exact Name of Company
Address
City, State, Zip

Dear Exact Name of Person (or Dear Sir or Madam if answering a blind ad):

With the enclosed resume, I would like to make you aware of my interest in exploring employment opportunities with your company and to acquaint you with my skills and talents.

As you will see from my resume, I have recently earned my B.S. degree in Political Science from Western Carolina University. Since this major requires extensive reading and writing, I have developed excellent analytical and communication skills.

In jobs which I held during the summers in order to finance my college education, I learned the importance of doing the small, behind-the-scenes jobs to the best of my ability because that is what often determines the customer's satisfaction. In all of my jobs, I played a key role in ensuring customer satisfaction. In a summer job at Applebee's Restaurant, I was selected to train new servers, and I was encouraged to join the company's management trainee program after college graduation.

In two of my summer jobs, I worked at prestigious country clubs and (in addition to improving my golf and tennis games!) was commended for my ability to graciously interact with executives, club members, and their guests. In another summer job, I operated a computer while performing customer service at a small business.

If you can use a highly motivated young professional with unlimited personal initiative as well as strong personal qualities of dependability and trustworthiness, I hope you will contact me to suggest a time when we might meet to discuss your needs. I can provide excellent personal and professional references, and I am eager to apply my strong customer service orientation and versatile skills to benefit an organization that can use a cheerful hard worker. Thank you in advance for your consideration.

Sincerely,

Brian Fenton

LAUNCHING A CAREER AFTER COLLEGE

College graduate seeks her first professional job
This letter introduces a young person with a newly minted B.S. degree. The letter is designed to help him explore opportunities in numerous fields. Notice how he emphasizes his strong personal qualities of initiative and reliability.

Date

Exact Name of Person
Title or Position
Name of Company
Address (number and street)
Address (city, state, and zip)

Dear Exact Name of Person: (or Sir or Madam if answering a blind ad.)

With the enclosed resume, I would like to make you aware of my strong interest in the position as Community Employment Specialist which you recently advertised.

As you will see from my resume, I am excelling in my current job in the profit-making private sector, but it is my desire to make a career change into the human services field. I am confident that my high-energy personality and sincere desire to help others could be of great benefit in the job you advertise. After reading your advertisement, I believe I satisfy all of the requirements you are seeking and in addition offer a sincere desire to be of service to the developmentally disabled population.

In my current job, I am highly respected for my ability to establish and maintain smooth working relationships. I am certain I could excel in identifying and developing job training and placement sites in local businesses, and I believe my business experience would be an asset in that regard.

I can provide excellent personal and professional references at the appropriate time, but I would prefer that you not contact my current employer until after we have a chance to talk.

I hope my versatile talents and experience will interest you, and I am confident I could become a productive and caring member of your professional team at Maryland Community Services at Annapolis. Thank you in advance for your time.

Yours sincerely,

Michelle Chan

CAREER-CHANGE COVER LETTERS

From profit making to human services

Changing careers can be easier if you make sure your cover letter is specially designed to help you accomplish that purpose. This individual is changing from profit-making activities to the human services field. Notice how her cover letter helps her potential employer understand why someone with her background is applying for the Community Employment Specialist job. Remember, you are trying to get in the door for an interview, so the employer must be persuaded in the cover letter that it is worth his or her time to interview someone outside the field.

Date

Exact Name of Person
Title or Position
Name of Company
Address (number and street)
Address (city, state, and zip)

Dear Exact Name of Person: (or Sir or Madam if answering a blind ad.)

With the enclosed resume, I would like to formally make you aware of my interest in your organization.

As you will see from my resume, I have excelled in jobs which required originality and creativity in prospecting for new clients, business savvy and financial prudence in establishing new ventures, as well as relentless follow-through and attention to detail in implementing ambitious goals.

I was recruited for my current job when the company decided that it wanted to set up a new commercial division and needed someone with proven entrepreneurial skills and a make-it-happen style. Under my leadership we have set up a new commercial division which has targeted the healthcare and pharmaceutical industry as a primary customer base in addition to major financial institutions and large corporations. Although I now manage several individuals, I personally prospected for the initial accounts and I discovered that my extensive training and background related to chemicals and microbiology was of great value in interacting with healthcare industry decision makers.

Although I can provide outstanding personal and professional references and am being groomed for further promotion within my company, I have decided that I wish to transfer my skills and knowledge to the healthcare industry. You will notice from my resume that I have been a successful entrepreneur and previously started a company which I sold to a larger industry firm. I succeeded as an entrepreneur largely because of my ability to communicate ideas to others, my strong problem-solving skills, and my naturally outgoing and self-confident nature. I am certain I could excel in the healthcare industry in any role which requires extraordinary sales, marketing, and relationship-building abilities.

If my background interests you, and if you feel there is a suitable position in your organization in which you could make use of my sales and marketing strengths, I hope you will contact me to suggest a time when we might meet to discuss your goals and how I might help you achieve them. Thank you in advance for your consideration and professional courtesies.

Yours sincerely,

Douglas Schlegel

CAREER-CHANGE COVER LETTERS

From commercial sales to healthcare

In this letter, a talented individual is attempting to change from commercial sales to the healthcare industry. His cover letter points out that he has excelled in jobs which require creativity and a highly disciplined nature, and those qualities could also be critical to success in the field he is trying to enter.

Date

Director of Human Resources
Charlotte Community College
2200 Airport Road
Charlotte, NC 28374

Dear Sir or Madam:

With the enclosed resume describing my qualifications and experience, I would like to formally respond to your advertisement for a Civil Engineering Technology Instructor.

As you will see from my resume, I offer skills and experience that would be of great value to your students. After earning a B.S. in Civil Engineering and then completing one year of graduate studies, I served as a U.S. Army Engineer Officer. After military service, I excelled as the Chief of the Master Planning Branch at Fort Bragg. Since 1998, I have excelled as a Staff Engineer with the City of Charlotte. Although I am held in high regard by my colleagues and am considered a valuable asset of the city, I enjoy teaching and would relish the opportunity to share my vast experience with students at the beginning of their careers.

You will also see from my resume that my teaching credentials are top-notch. Since 1995, I have served as an adjunct instructor with Charlotte Technical Community College and have taught courses including Surveying, Topographic Surveying and Aerial Photography, Astronomical Calculations and State Plane Coordinates, Highway Surveying, and Construction Staking and Layout.

I am current with the latest thinking in my field as continuous professional development has been a routine with me throughout my career. Indeed, my current job requires that I remain current in environmental issues such as wetlands and erosion control. I have attended numerous review courses offered by North Carolina State University, Clemson, and the University of North Carolina's Institute for Technology Transfer. In addition to teaching at adjunct colleges since 1995, I also excelled as a Senior Engineer Instructor while serving as an Army officer.

You would find me in person to be a congenial individual who takes much pleasure in sharing my technical knowledge with younger colleagues. It would certainly be a pleasure to talk with you in person to discuss how my unique background could benefit your academic program and enhance the Civil Engineering career path of your undergraduates.

I hope you will contact me to suggest a time when we might meet in person to discuss your needs and how I might serve them. Thank you in advance for your time.

Yours sincerely,

Jason Bessemer

CAREER-CHANGE COVER LETTERS

From government to academia

In this letter, a city engineer is attempting to make a career change from government to the academic environment. He has some part-time teaching experience in addition to experience in training others as a military officer. Every employer knows that attitude is a critical factor in job performance, so this individual is stressing his strong desire to share his vast experience and technical knowledge with others in what for him will be a second career.

Date

Exact Name of Person
Exact Title of Person
Exact Name of Organization
Address
City, State zip

Dear Exact Name: (or Dear Sir or Madam if answering a blind ad)

With the enclosed resume, I would like to make you aware of my interest in utilizing my outstanding sales, marketing, communication, and management skills for the benefit of your organization.

Although I most recently have been working in the aviation industry field and am excelling in my current position, I have decided to embark on a radical career change. I have a strong desire to work in a professional position in which I can combine my extroverted personality and "natural" sales ability with my customer relations and problem-solving ability.

My recent experience in airport management, air traffic control, and in piloting advanced attack aircraft may not appear relevant to your needs, but my stable work history also includes several jobs which, I believe, illustrate my versatility. In one job I excelled as a Juvenile Counselor and thoroughly enjoyed the experience of providing a strong role model for troubled youth who had essentially been kicked out of their homes and labeled as "uncontrollable." In another job in California, I was part of the movie-making industry as I worked as a double for Mel Gibson. I also worked previously as a professional model. A wine expert and gourmet cook, I grew up in an Italian family which was in the restaurant business so I learned customer service at a young age!

In my current job involved in managing people and key areas related to airport management at one of the military's busiest airlift centers, I am continually using my problem-solving and decision-making skills. I am confident that my management ability, resourcefulness, and ability to relate effectively to others are qualities which could transfer to any field. In one of my jobs in the aviation industry, I managed a $3.5 million budget with outstanding results, and I offer a strong bottom-line orientation.

If you can use a highly motivated self-starter known for unlimited personal initiative and a creative problem-solving style, I hope you will contact me to suggest a time when we might meet to discuss your needs. I am single and would relocate and travel extensively as your needs require, and I can provide outstanding references at the appropriate time. Thank you in advance for your consideration.

Yours sincerely,

Mason Jensen

CAREER-CHANGE COVER LETTERS

From aviation to sales
In this letter, an Air Traffic Controller is seeking to change fields and move from aviation into an industry which can utilize his strong sales, marketing, and communication skills. Notice how he tries to make the employer understand why someone with his specialized technical background is approaching companies that need generalists and communicators. In a career change, experienced professionals often must sell their personality and potential more than their actual work experience in order to "blow the door open."

Date

Exact Name of Person
Exact Title of Person
Exact Address
City, State zip

CAREER-CHANGE COVER LETTERS

From Food Industry to Accounting and Finance

In this letter, a young person completing his bachelor's degree reaches out to employers in various fields. He emphasizes his track record of accomplishment with his current employer. Although this is an all-purpose cover letter, Mr. Ferdinand is mostly interested in accounting, financial, or management activities, so there is a subtle emphasis on his skills and interest in those functional areas within this all-purpose framework.

Dear Sir or Madam:

With the enclosed resume, I would like to acquaint you with the considerable accounting, financial, and management skills I could put to work for your organization.

As you can see from the enclosed resume, I am continuing to excel in a "track record" of promotion with a food industry corporation. I began with the company as an assistant manager, was promoted to store manager, and advanced to my present position as supervisor overseeing the operations of 11 stores in five cities.

While utilizing my strong communication and problem-solving skills in guiding store managers at 11 locations throughout New Hampshire, I am continuously involved in financial analysis and budget preparation. You will see from my resume that I hold an A.A.S. degree in Accounting and am currently pursuing completion of my Bachelor's degree. I have acquired practical work experience as well as formal course work in areas including management and program analysis, auditing, budget preparation, and quantitative analysis.

My computer operation skills are highly refined. I offer proficiency with numerous popular software products including Lotus 1-2-3 and offer the ability to troubleshoot and repair various types of equipment problems. While previously serving my country for two years in the U.S. Army, I received extensive training in computer operations and telecommunications operations/repair.

You would find me in person to be a dynamic young professional who prides myself on my ability to rapidly become a contributing member of any team. I can provide outstanding personal and professional references at the appropriate time, and I hope I will have the opportunity to meet with you in person to discuss your needs and how I might meet them.

Sincerely,

Terrell A. Ferdinand

Date

Exact Name of Person
Title or Position
Name of Company
Address (number and street)
Address (city, state, and zip)

Dear Exact Name of Person: (or Sir or Madam if answering a blind ad.)

With the enclosed resume, I would like to make you aware of my interest in putting my considerable management and communication skills to work for your organization.

As you will see from my resume, I am pursuing a Master's in Public Administration (M.P.A.) degree at the University of Texas at San Antonio while excelling in my full-time job as an executive with Parke-Davis Pharmaceutical Division. It is my strong desire to transfer my considerable skills into the public sector, and I feel I can make major contributions to a government organization through my strategic thinking skills and management ability, as well as my highly effective approach in training, developing, and managing other employees.

You will notice that I have thus far excelled in a track record of achievement as a sales and marketing executive. I am certain that the planning, organizing, problem-solving, decision-making, and negotiating skills which I utilize daily in my job could be effectively applied in the public sector. In my prior position with Smith Boyle, Inc., I worked extensively with government officials while servicing up to 700 commercial and government accounts in Utah cities. I am well acquainted with government purchasing procedures and with the steps involved in government decision making.

I can provide outstanding personal and professional references at the appropriate time, and I can assure you that you would find me in person to be a poised communicator who would take pride in contributing to your organizational goals. I hope you will contact me if you feel my considerable management and communication skills could be helpful to you.

Thank you in advance for your time.

Sincerely,

Danny Flanders

CAREER-CHANGE COVER LETTERS

From Private to Public Sector
In this letter, an accomplished sales professional is attempting to transfer his management abilities and communication skills into the public sector. He adds to his credibility by pursuing a degree in public administration, but he has not finished the degree yet. Notice that he points out his familiarity with the government planning process through his experience in servicing government accounts.

Date

Exact Name of Person
Exact Title
Exact Name of Company
Address
City, State, Zip

Dear Exact Name of Person (or Dear Sir or Madam if answering a blind ad):

With the enclosed resume, I would like to make you aware of the considerable skills I feel I could offer your organization.

As you will see from my resume, I have excelled for ten years in a track record of advancement with the Macy's organization, where I started as a management trainee and advanced into a senior management position in charge of 25 individuals. After earning my undergraduate degree in Business Administration with a minor in Economics, I was attracted to the Macy's organization because of its tradition of regarding its managers as profit centers and treating them essentially as entrepreneurs. While hiring and supervising personnel, I handled general management responsibilities including preparing business plans four times a year, reviewing progress monthly toward goals, and performing extensive community relations and public relations. For example, I worked annually with the Boys & Girls Club to coordinate a special function for "Kid of the Year," and I was active in the Chamber of Commerce.

Although I was excelling in my job and held in high regard, I made the recent decision to resign from Macy's for two reasons: first, I wanted to spend a few weeks caring full-time for my widowed mother, who had undergone a serious operation, and second, I had decided that I wished to pursue a career outside retailing. I left on excellent terms and can provide outstanding personal and professional references within the Macy's organization including from my immediate supervisor, Martin Wurtheim, who would gladly welcome me back at any time.

I feel certain that I could make valuable contributions to your organization through the diversified management experience I have gained as a Senior Manager at Macy's. Although I am only 34 years old, I have controlled buying decisions of more than $5 million annually while refining my skills in prospecting, customer service, public relations, financial forecasting and financial analysis, and budgeting.

I am single and would cheerfully travel as your needs require. If you feel that my skills and background might be of interest to you, I hope you will contact me to suggest a time when we might meet in person to discuss your needs.

Sincerely yours,

Christopher Jarvis

CAREER-CHANGE COVER LETTERS

From retail to retail-related

This letter holds the key to this individual's intense desire to become employed in a sector other than retail. Although he has a background as an accomplished retail manager, he desires a change. Remember that in a career-change situation, your approach simply has to "make sense" to prospective employers and they must feel that you are genuinely interested in leaving the industry you know best—not just "having a bad day."

Date

Exact Name of Person
Title or Position
Name of Company
Address (number and street)
Address (city, state, and zip)

Dear Exact Name of Person: (or Dear Sir or Madam if answering a blind ad.)

    I would appreciate an opportunity to talk with you soon about how I could contribute to your organization through my education in finance as well as through my reputation as a hard-working, knowledgeable, and dedicated professional.

    As you will see from my enclosed resume, I recently received my Bachelor of Business Administration (B.B.A.) degree with a concentration in Finance from The University of Colorado at Boulder. I personally financed my college education by working full time. I am especially proud of the fact that I accomplished this despite having to commute to classes while I was simultaneously advancing in jobs which required expertise in managing human and material resources as well as time.

    The majority of my experience with the retail giant Buy Mart since 1997 has been in inventory control and support activities, but I have been given opportunities to apply my education and knowledge. Selected for a six-month assignment as a Billing and Data Processing Supervisor, I have also been involved in completing reports and audits which required financial skills.

    Although I have built a track record of accomplishments and have held supervisory positions since the age of 20 with this national retailer, I am ready for a career change which will allow more opportunity to apply my education in finance.

    If you can use a self-confident and self-motivated individual who is persistent and assertive, I hope you will contact me to suggest a time when we might meet to discuss your needs and how I might help you. Thank you in advance for your time.

Sincerely,

Gisela Myshka

Alternate last paragraph:
    I hope you will welcome my call soon when I try to arrange a brief meeting to discuss your current and future needs and how I might serve them. Thank you in advance for your time.

CAREER-CHANGE COVER LETTERS

From Managing People to Managing Money
In this letter, an individual with a newly-minted degree in Finance is attempting to move away from responsibilities for managing people to responsibilities for managing finances. With this letter, she will be able to approach Controllers of large companies while also exploring financial planning and financial consulting careers with organizations such as Solomon Smith Barney. She may also approach nonprofit organizations since they often like their top managers to be skilled in financial management.

Date

Exact Name of Person
Title or Position
Name of Company
Address (number and street)
Address (city, state, and zip)

CAREER-CHANGE COVER LETTERS

From the Grocery Industry to a Career in Human Resources
In this letter, a grocery store manager is seeking to transfer her strong bottom-line orientation and impressive accomplishments in boosting sales and profit into a new industry. She is primarily interested in the pharmaceutical industry, and the letter is designed to acquaint pharmaceutical companies with her knowledge of the territory she would be covering as well as with her fine personal and professional reputation. She is hoping that the company will be willing to train a highly motivated producer who has excelled in another industry.

Dear Exact Name of Person: (or Dear Sir or Madam if answering a blind ad.)

I would appreciate an opportunity to talk with you soon about how I could contribute to your organization through my excellent sales, communication, and customer service skills. I am responding to your advertisement for a Pharmaceutical Sales Representative. I am very knowledgeable of the Dallas, TX, area and offer an outstanding personal and professional reputation in the community.

As you will see from my enclosed resume, I have been highly successful in sales and operations management with a major corporation. Beginning as a Customer Service Manager, I was promoted to manage stores with increasing sales volumes of $7 million, $8.5 million, and $11.5 million annually. In my current position, I have raised total sales by 20% and profit levels by 25% through my aggressive sales orientation.

Although I am held in high regard by my employer and can provide outstanding references at the appropriate time, I have decided that I would like to apply my sales, customer service, and communication skills within the pharmaceutical sales field. I am certain that my sales ability and strong bottom-line orientation would be ideally suited to pharmaceutical sales.

As a store manager, I have become very familiar with a wide range of pharmaceutical products as I have provided oversight of store merchandising, vendor relations, and product mix. I frequently interact with pharmacists and other health care professionals with regard to pharmaceutical products carried by the store.

With a B.S.B.A. degree, I possess an educational background which complements my sales and management experience. My highly-developed communication skills, assertive personality, and time-management ability have allowed me to effectively manage as many as 100 employees. I offer a reputation as a forceful yet tactful salesperson who is able to present ideas as well as products in a powerful and convincing fashion.

I can assure you that this is a very serious attempt on my part to transition into the pharmaceutical sales field, and I hope you will call or write me soon to arrange a brief meeting to discuss your current and future needs and how I might serve them. Thank you in advance for your time.

Sincerely,

Gloria Pena

Date

Exact Name of Person
Exact Title
Exact Name of Company
Address
City, State zip

Dear Sir or Madam:

With the enclosed resume describing my qualifications and experience, I would like to initiate the process of applying for a position as a travel attendant.

First Aid Knowledge
As you will see from my resume, I am knowledgeable of first aid procedures through my medical and scientific training in the area of anesthesiology.

Fluency in French
An American citizen, I am fluent in French. I have traveled extensively throughout the U.S. as well as in Germany, Greece, France, and the Caribbean. Although I became an American citizen at age 13, I was raised in the South of France in Gandrage.

Modeling Background
During my junior and senior years of high school, I was a part-time model for both a department store and for a meat packing plant which featured me on television commercials. After high school, the Wilhemina Agency in New York recommended me for a runway modeling job in Paris because of my modeling ability and fluency in French.

Customer Relations and Management Experience
Most recently I have excelled as a small business manager, and I am skilled in dealing with the public, resolving problems in a gracious manner, and managing my time for maximum efficiency and profitability. I have developed my customer base through word of mouth because of excellent service and public relations.

Experience as a Waitress and Hostess
You will see from my resume that I previously worked as a hostess and waitress in the Hilton Hotel in Chicago, where I frequently served celebrity customers in an upscale restaurant/bar which specialized in catering to the affluent.

Please send me any formal application materials I need to complete in order to be considered for a flight attendant position with your airline, and I would be delighted to make myself available for a personal interview at the appropriate time. I can provide excellent personal and professional references.

Yours sincerely,

Angela Hapsburg

CAREER-CHANGE COVER LETTERS

From Small Business Management to Flight Attendant
A change from a small business environment into a major airline company often requires a career-change cover letter. In this case, a talented person with experience in numerous functional areas is expressing her desire to become an airline attendant, and she projects herself as a well-traveled individual who could deal with the public with poise and charm. She'll have to "sell herself" in an interview, but she needs a cover letter that will "blow the door open."

Date

Exact Name of Person
Exact Title
Exact Name of Company
Address
City, State, Zip

Dear

CAREER-CHANGE COVER LETTERS

From Social Services to Academic Administration

Changing careers from social services to academic administration is the purpose of this cover letter. Although Ms. Bustier has enjoyed her work in human services, she is interested in obtaining her Ph.D. and feels that she would be better able to pursue this goal if she were transplanted to an academic institution. What she is marketing to academic institutions is her managerial resourcefulness and expertise in staff development.

With the enclosed resume, I would like to make you aware of the background in program management and staff development which I could put to work for your organization.

While excelling in the track record of advancement which you will see summarized on my resume, I have applied my strong organizational skills in implementing new programs, organizing conferences and seminars, training and counseling professional-level employees, and transforming ideas into operational realities. On numerous occasions, I have developed effective formats for grants, reports, documents, and quality assurance protocol which have been described as "models."

In my current position, I have served as a Program Manager for the state of South Carolina while spearheading the development of new housing options and employment opportunities for the developmentally disabled and mentally impaired. With a reputation as a vibrant and persuasive communicator, I routinely interface with legislators, state and federal officials, as well as with local program managers. It has often been my responsibility to take a new law and make sure it is efficiently and resourcefully implemented at the local level while assuring compliance with federal and state guidelines. I am continuously involved in teaching and training others, not only the professionals whom I directly supervise but also professionals regionally and locally who turn to me for advice and assistance in problem solving.

I feel confident that my resourceful leadership, expertise in staff training and staff development, and pragmatic approach to operations management and service operations delivery could be valuable to your organization.

If you feel you could use my considerable experience in initiating new programs, making existing programs work better, and establishing effective working relationships, I hope you will contact me to suggest a time when we might meet to discuss your needs and how I might serve them. I can provide outstanding personal and professional references at the appropriate time.

Yours sincerely,

Elaine Bustier

Date

Director of Personnel
City of Chesterfield
Grayson Hall, Suite 123
Chesterfield, VT 98231

Dear Sir or Madam:

With the enclosed resume, I would like to formally initiate the process of becoming considered for a job as a Fireman within your organization.

As you will see when you read my resume, I have excelled in every job I have ever taken on. Currently I am a member of the management team for one of the area's largest and oldest furniture stores, and I have become skilled at problem solving and decision making. I began with the company in a part-time job, was hired full-time after one week, and have been promoted to increasing responsibilities because of my proven ability to make sound decisions under pressure.

While serving my country in the U.S. Army, I was promoted ahead of my peers to a job as Telecommunications Center Operator and earned numerous commendations for my management ability and technical skills. I was praised on numerous occasions for my ability to "think on my feet" and to remain calm and make prudent decisions under stressful circumstances. I was entrusted with a Secret NAC security clearance.

Throughout my life, I have been known as a highly motivated self-starter with a strong drive to excel in all I do. Even in high school, I was on the All-Star baseball team and was elected Captain of the football team in my senior year.

I am sending you my resume because it is my strong desire to make a career in the firefighting field, and I am willing to start in an entry-level position and prove myself. I am always seeking new ways in which to improve my skills and increase my knowledge; for example, I am learning Spanish in my spare time because I feel Spanish language skills will be an asset in any field with our growing Hispanic population. I can assure you that I would bring that same level of self motivation to firefighting as a career field, and I hope you will give me an opportunity to show you in person that I am a dependable young individual who could become a valuable part of your organization.

I hope you will contact me to suggest a time when we might meet to discuss your needs and how I might serve them. I can provide outstanding references. Thank you in advance for whatever consideration and time you can give me in my goal of becoming a professional firefighter.

Sincerely,

Jorge Perez

CAREER-CHANGE COVER LETTERS

From Store Manager to Fireman

From store manager to fireman? It's possible if the cover letter can "blow the door open." Notice how this young person goes back to his high school years to cite a few of his accomplishments and to market his strong drive to excel in all he does. Prospective employers want to feel that you have the kind of passion for a new field that will see you through the rocky period of intense training and learning.

Date

Exact Name of Person
Title or Position
Name of Company
Address (no., street)
Address (city, state, zip)

COVER LETTERS FOR ENTREPRENEURS

Entrepreneur Seeking a New Industry

On this page you will see a cover letter of an entrepreneur seeking a career change after transitioning his business to new management. Although he has been in the antiques and oriental rugs business, he cites his accomplishments in founding profitable entities as the "fish bait" which he hopes will capture the attention of prospective employers in numerous industries. What employer can't use a savvy individual who could come in and triple sales?

Dear Exact Name of Person: (or Dear Sir or Madam if answering a blind ad.)

I would appreciate an opportunity to talk with you soon about how I could contribute to your organization through my business management, sales, and communication skills.

As you will see from my resume, I have founded successful businesses, tripled the sales volume of an existing company, and directed projects which required someone who could take a concept and turn it into an operating reality. While excelling as a retailer and importer of products that included oriental rugs and English antiques, I have become accustomed to working with a discriminating customer base of people regionally who trust my taste and character. In addition to a proven "track record" of producing a profit, I have earned a reputation for honesty and reliability. I believe there is no substitute in business for a good reputation.

I am ready for a new challenge, and that is why I have, in the last several months, closed two of my business locations and turned over the management of the third operation to a family member. I want to apply my seasoned business judgement, along with my problem-solving and opportunity-finding skills, to new areas.

If you can use the expertise of a savvy and creative professional who is skilled at handling every aspect of business management, from sales and marketing to personnel and finance, I would enjoy talking with you about your needs and goals. A flexible and adaptable person who feels comfortable stepping into new situations, I am able to "size up" problems and opportunities quickly through the "lens" of experience. I pride myself on my ability to deal tactfully and effectively with everyone.

I hope you will welcome my call soon to arrange a brief meeting at your convenience to discuss your current and future needs and how I might serve them. Thank you in advance for your time.

Sincerely yours,

Desmond Vaughn

Alternate last paragraph:
I hope you will call or write me soon to suggest a time convenient for us to meet and discuss your current and future needs and how I might serve them. Thank you in advance for your time.

Date

Exact Name of Person
Title or Position
Name of Company
Address (number and street)
Address (city, state, and zip)

Dear Exact Name of Person: (or Sir or Madam if answering a blind ad.)

With the enclosed resume, I would like to make you aware of my interest in contributing to your organization through my considerable management experience as well as my proven motivational, sales, and organizational skills.

Although most of my business savvy has come from "real-world" experience, I do hold an M.S. degree in Business Administration, a Master's degree in Guidance and Counseling, and a B.S. degree. After earning my college degree, I worked for several years as a High School Guidance Counselor, and economics forced me to seek a simultaneous part-time job as a Salesman for used and new cars with a prominent automobile dealership. That part-time job opened my eyes to my talent for selling cars and motivating others, and thus began an impressive career in the automotive industry.

After attending Chevrolet's two-year Dealer Trainee Program, I became General Manager of a Chevrolet dealership in Indianapolis, IN. I was successful in turning around that dealership which had experienced multimillion-dollar losses in three previous years, and I led it to show a profit of $500,000—its first profit in four years. Subsequently, I served as a consultant to start-up dealerships and to mature dealerships in need of a strong manager to resolve sales and profitability problems.

My first job in the Kansas City, MO market was as General Sales Manager of Cross Roads Chevrolet, where I played a key role in increasing market penetration by 60%. I was then recruited by to serve as President and General Manager of Twin City Chevrolet. I led the company to achieve gross sales of $32 million a year along with a $1 million profit-before-tax income for three consecutive years. We received the Outstanding Dealer's Award from Chevrolet three years in a row and were recognized as a five-star dealer—the ultimate achievement in customer service—for two years. Most recently, I have managed a successful start-up of a used car dealership which became a major force in the market in less than two years.

I am a dynamic individual with an outstanding reputation within the industry along with an aggressive bottom-line orientation and a results-oriented style of interacting with others. I hope you will welcome my call soon when I try to speak with you briefly about your needs and whether my background might be useful to you.

Sincerely,

J.C. Longenecker

COVER LETTERS FOR ENTREPRENEURS

Entrepreneur Seeking a New Challenge in Automotive Industry
This successful entrepreneur is not seeking to change fields or industries but to find a new challenge in the industry in which he has excelled. His cover letter is intended to capture the attention of top automobile executives who may be seeking a proven profit producer with the ability to function in a management or consulting/troubleshooting role. Like most entrepreneurs, this talented individual is looking for a new challenge.

Date

Exact Name of Person
Title or Position
Name of Company
Address (number and street)
Address (city, state, and zip)

COVER LETTERS FOR ENTREPRENEURS

Entrepreneur Returning to a Previous Field

This successful entrepreneur is seeking to return to a career field he was in more than 10 years ago. At middle age, he went back to college to earn his B.S. degree and now wishes to resume a career as a Golf Course Superintendent.

Dear Exact Name of Person: (or Sir or Madam if answering a blind ad.)

I would appreciate an opportunity to talk with you soon about how I could contribute to your organization through my experience as a golf course superintendent with a reputation as a creative and innovative manager of resources.

As you will see from my enclosed resume, I offer a strong history as a golf course superintendent with more than 15 years of experience at several successful and heavily played courses in the California area. I was highly effective in taking on the challenge of renovating and refurbishing courses which were in need of improvements. For 150-acre courses located in residential developments and one private club, I brought about significant changes which transformed struggling facilities. While rebuilding these facilities, I applied abilities in areas which included hiring and training personnel, coordinating the renovation of capital equipment, planning for long-range success, and completing design projects for sprinkler layout, drainage, and reconstruction of greens, tees, and fairways. I also oversaw the design and installation of water reservoirs for irrigation, including a 110-acre reservoir at Rolling Hill Golf Course in San Diego, California.

My organizational and time management skills have been displayed more recently while attending college full-time, excelling academically, and simultaneously creating a successful residential landscape design business. Building on my earlier A.A. degree in Agronomy and Turf Production and golf course experience, I recently earned a B.S. in Agribusiness and Environmental Resources.

I would like to point out that I have relocated permanently to the Pittsburgh area to be near family members. If you can use an experienced golf course superintendent with a broad base of experience and well-developed abilities, I hope you will contact me to suggest a time when we might meet to discuss your needs. I can assure you in advance that I could rapidly become an asset to your organization.

Sincerely,

Reynold W. Krueger, Jr.

Date

Exact Name of Person
Title or Position
Name of Company
Address (number and street)
Address (city, state, and zip)

Dear Exact Name of Person: (or Sir or Madam if answering a blind ad.)

With the enclosed resume, I would like to initiate the process of being considered for employment within your organization. I am a May graduate of Dartmouth University with an excellent scientific education along with superior technical writing skills, experience in laboratory analysis and instrumental analysis, as well as some knowledge of medicinal chemistry.

While earning my B.S. in Chemistry, I excelled in courses including Medicinal Chemistry, which focused on modern pharmaceuticals, and Instrumental Analysis. I am skilled in operating equipment and devices including fluorescence spectrometers, atomic mass spectrometers, UV/VIS molecular absorption spectrometers, high performance liquid chromatography (HPLC), Gas chromatography (GC), as well as IR/Raman spectrometers, NMR, and FTIR.

At Dartmouth, I was a popular tutor of Chemistry and Calculus, and I acted as a Mentor for 11 Engineering and Science students. During the summers while earning my college degree, I worked in technical environments which taught me much about teamwork. For example, in a summer job with Monsanto, I worked on an assembly line assembling, inspecting, and packing electrical control panels. Another summer I worked as a Procedure Writer for B&R Company, where I developed and revised Defense Waste Processing Operations Procedures with special emphasis on chemical processing procedures. In another summer job, I worked as a Production Assistant for Westinghouse.

I feel confident that you would find me in person to be a warm and congenial individual who relates well to others and who offers strong communication skills. While mentoring other Engineering and Science students at Dartmouth, I frequently mediated disputes and trained students to utilize conflict management techniques.

If you can use a sharp and astute young chemistry graduate who offers excellent analytical and communication skills, I hope you will contact me to suggest a time when we might meet in person. I am flexible and able to relocate according to your needs. Thank you in advance for your time.

Yours sincerely,

Chester Bartholomew

SEEKING FIRST JOB IN FIELD

First job in Chemisty Field
Chemistry graduate seeks first job in his field with a cover letter that emphasizes his tutoring experience and summer jobs. Students without experience in their field need to remember that their past work experience is relevant to prospective employers because it still shows the development of good work habits. Notice that this student mentions his unpaid work experience in mentoring students at Dartmouth.

Date

Exact Name of Person
Title or Position
Name of Company
Address (number and street)
Address (city, state, and zip)

Dear Exact Name of Person: (or Sir or Madam if answering a blind ad.)

With the enclosed resume, I would like to make you aware of my background as a versatile and experienced professional with a history of success in areas which include computer operations, logistics and supply, production control, and employee training and supervision.

As you will see, I have completed requirements for my bachelor's degree in Computer Science from Devry College. I am proud of my accomplishment in completing this course of study while simultaneously meeting the demands of a career in the U.S. Army. In my current military assignment as a Technical Inspector at Ft. Carson, CO, I ensure the airworthiness of aircraft utilized by the 18th Airborne Corps which is required to relocate anywhere in the world on extremely short notice in response to crisis situations.

Throughout my years of military service I have been singled out for jobs which have required the ability to quickly make sound decisions and have continually maximized resources while exceeding expected standards and performance guidelines. I have been responsible for certifying multimillion-dollar aircraft for flight service, training and supervising employees who have been highly productive and successful in their own careers, and applying technical computer knowledge in innovative ways which have further increased efficiency and productivity.

I offer a combination of technical, managerial, and supervisory skills which will allow me to quickly achieve outstanding results in anything I attempt. Known for my energy and enthusiasm, I am a creative and talented professional with a strong desire to make a difference in whatever setting and environment I find myself.

I hope you will contact me to suggest a time when we might meet to discuss your needs. I can assure you in advance that I could rapidly become an asset to your organization.

Sincerely,

Rob Harrell

SEEKING FIRST JOB IN FIELD

First Job in Computer Science

Computer Science graduate emphasizes his maturity and work experience which he hopes will distinguish him from other recent Computer Science graduates. Remember when you are marketing anything, including yourself in a job hunt, you are trying to market what is unique about the product (or you). In Mr. Harrell's case, he is hoping that employers will be impressed that he completed his degree while excelling in a demanding full-time job.

Date

Exact Name of Person
Title or Position
Name of Company
Address (number and street)
Address (city, state, and zip)

Dear Exact Name of Person: (or Sir or Madam if answering a blind ad.)

With the enclosed resume, I would like to initiate the process of being considered for employment within your organization.

As you will see from my resume, I will receive on May 10 a Bachelor of Arts degree in English with a minor in French and Writing, and I have excelled academically. I have worked as a Staff Writer for my college newspaper, and I have become skilled at composing copy that requires little editing and in meeting tight deadlines. I have also tutored students in both English and French.

In an internship as an Advertising Copywriter with a respected and award-winning advertising agency, I created copy for the agency's web page, wrote a 12-month newsletter aimed at children, and compiled a portfolio of sample ads which was received quite favorably by my supervisor.

In a summer job with a magazine in Arizona, I worked in the distribution and circulation part of the business and became a valuable part of the magazine's staff within a short period of time.

Although I have limited hands-on experience simply because I am 20 years old, I can assure you that I am an accomplished writer. I have been published in Tapestries and in The National Book of Poetry. My life experiences have been quite diverse as I have traveled extensively worldwide including in Europe and Africa as well as South America. One summer I lived and worked in Suriname.

I can provide outstanding personal and professional references at the appropriate time, and I can assure you that you would find me to be a hard-working, congenial individual who prides myself on always doing my best. If you can use a hard worker who could become a valuable part of your organization through my creativity and language skills, I hope you will contact me to suggest a time when I can make myself available for a personal interview at your convenience. Thank you in advance for your time.

Sincerely,

Madeline A. Pereira

SEEKING FIRST JOB IN FIELD

First Job in Publishing or Advertising

English major is seeking job in publishing or advertising. You will see that she emphasizes her summer work experience, publishing credits, and extensive international travel. She is trying to project herself as an ambitious and talented young professional who has demonstrated a deep and abiding interest in the writing field.

Date

Exact Name of Person
Exact Title
Exact Name of Company
Exact Address
City, state zip

SEEKING FIRST JOB IN FIELD

First Job Utilizing History Degree

History graduate emphasizes that the company he worked for during college had offered him a full-time job upon college graduation. Employers are looking for people who are highly regarded by other employers, because they generally feel that if your current employer thinks highly of you, it is because of your good attitude and excellent work.

Dear Sir or Madam:

With the enclosed resume, I would like to make you aware of my interest in your organization and to acquaint you with the considerable talents and skills I could put to work for you.

As you will see from my resume, I recently earned my B.A. degree in History from North Carolina State University, and I was offered a full-time management position immediately upon graduation with the company for which I had worked throughout college. In my current position, I manage a wide range of functional areas for a large cinema complex. My responsibilities include training and hiring employees, overseeing cash control and assuring accurate financial management, auditing a wide range of activities, and assuring outstanding public relations and customer service. While working for the company on weekends and during summers and other breaks throughout college, I was named Employee of the Month five times and I earned a reputation as a hard worker known for the highest standards of reliability, integrity, and initiative.

Although I am held in high regard in my current position and am being groomed for further promotion by the company's owners, I am interested in applying my management skills in a more traditional business environment. I can provide excellent personal and professional references at the appropriate time.

Since the cinema business is generally an afternoon and night time business, I am usually at work between 5 p.m. to 12 midnight, so you would be able to reach me at home most mornings. Thursday is my regular day off, so I could make myself available to meet with you personally on any Thursday or perhaps on another day if arrangements were made well in advance. I feel certain that you will find me to be a dynamic young professional whose abilities could enhance your organization.

Sincerely,

James Ray Watkins

Date

Exact Name of Person
Title or Position
Name of Company
Address (number and street)
Address (city, state, and zip)

Dear Exact Name of Person: (or Sir or Madam if answering a blind ad.)

I would appreciate an opportunity to talk with you soon about how I could contribute to WKRG TV-3 as a Salesperson.

As you will see from my enclosed resume, I am an experienced retail salesperson with a college background in Media Journalism and English. Although I have no previous experience in broadcast sales, I feel that my intelligence, educational background, and exceptional written and verbal communication skills would more than make up for any lack of practical experience.

I have a strong history of success in leadership roles and in environments where I have excelled in selling my ideas and concepts to others. Beginning with my days as student body president of my high school, on through college volunteer activities requiring negotiating and communication skills, I have always been highly effective in getting my views across to others in a persuasive and effective manner while still displaying tact and an understanding of their views.

One area that I did not mention on my resume but would like to point out now is that while I was in college, I was given an opportunity to write public service announcements and then represent a writing class by presenting them on the air on a new campus radio station.

I believe that I have high levels of raw talent, enthusiasm, and energy that would translate into successful sales for your station and allow me to become a productive member of your sales force. I hope you will welcome my call soon to arrange a brief meeting at your convenience to discuss WKRG TV-3's present and future needs and how I might serve them. Thank you in advance for your time.

Sincerely yours,

Rainey L. Crocker

SEEKING FIRST JOB IN FIELD

First Job in Media Journalism and English
Media Journalism and English major is emphasizing his natural sales ability and leadership skills. Especially in sales, employers will frequently offer employment to a young person with "the right stuff" in terms of personality and the "true grit" for sales success. This young professional is "selling" his raw talent, enthusiasm, and energy in addition to his intense desire to enter the media sales field.

Date

Exact Name of Person
Title or Position
Name of Company
Address (number and street)
Address (city, state, and zip)

SEEKING FIRST JOB IN FIELD

First Job in Nursing Field
Nursing graduate emphasizes her externships and clinical rotations. In general, the rule about whether to put a Grade Point Average (G.P.A.) on your resume is this: If your G.P.A. is 3.5 or above, it is probably in your best interest to reveal it on your resume and in your cover letter because many employers believe that if you worked hard and excelled in school, you will work hard and excel in your job.

Dear Exact Name of Person: (or Dear Sir or Madam if answering a blind ad.)

With the enclosed resume, I would like to make you aware of my interest in employment with your organization and acquaint you with the considerable experience and skills I could offer you.

As a Candidate for a B.S. in Nursing, I am maintaining a 3.7 GPA in my Nursing Program at Duke University in NC. I also hold a B.A. in Political Science from Emory University in Atlanta. After volunteering at Emory Medical Center I knew I wanted to pursue a nursing career and I transfered to Duke after two years at Emory.

You will see from my resume that I am currently working as a Nurse's Aide II in the Surgical ICU at University of North Carolina at Chapel Hill Medical Center. I was offered this job after excelling in my summer externship in Surgical ICU at UNC-CH Medical Center. I have tremendously enjoyed my work in Surgical ICU and can provide outstanding professional references from those who have observed or supervised my enthusiastic, caring, and professional approach to caring for ICU patients.

I have also performed seven-week clinical rotations in orthopedic, pediatric, psychiatric, OB/GYN, community health, and surgical ICU environments at Duke Hospitals, Durham County Hospital, Raleigh Health Clinic, and Chapel Hill Medical Center. For two semesters at Emory in 1997, I was privileged to be able to work with a pediatric hematologist/oncologist in setting up a database for patients with neutropenia. After we set up this database, patients with the condition were able to receive very expensive treatment, G-CSF, at no cost while the pharmaceutical company providing the drug conducted research on the condition and the drug's effects. I have also worked in jobs as a bank teller and student assistant during the summers and school years.

Please give me every consideration for employment, as I can assure you that you would be taking on a dedicated young professional who offers a true commitment to the nursing profession. I would be delighted to make myself available for personal interviews at your convenience. Thank you very much for your consideration of my talents, skills, and experience.

Yours sincerely,

Faith A. Staszewski

Date

Exact Name of Person
Title or Position
Name of Company
Address (number and street)
Address (city, state, and zip)

Dear Exact Name of Person: (or Sir or Madam if answering a blind ad.)

With the enclosed resume, I would like to make you aware of my interest in being considered for employment within your organization in any capacity in which you could utilize my versatile knowledge related to human resources and human services as well as my communication skills, management abilities, and computer operations knowledge.

Since graduation I have been excelling in a job as a Management Trainee but I am seeking a position in which I can utilize my education in sociology and social work. You will see from my resume that I completed a Social Work Internship at Walker Senior High School where I earned a reputation as a highly motivated individual who was most effective in working with at-risk juveniles. Indeed, as an upperclassman during my junior and senior years at Michigan State University, I served as a Peer Mentor helping incoming freshmen transition into college life. Through my experience as a Peer Mentor and as a Social Work Intern, I gained insights into the particular problems faced by first-generation college students and by low-income students.

In a part-time job while earning my degree, I refined my counseling and interviewing skills as an M.A.S. Administrator at the V.A. Medical Center, where I interviewed Persian Gulf and Vietnam veterans.

While in college I had several field experiences relevant to social work and sociology. In one situation I functioned as a Home Assistant, working with Thomas A (mentally challenged) adults and assisted those consumers in acquiring more independence and mastery of their everyday activities. In another situation as an Autism Therapist, I worked with an autistic child in a private home.

I hope you will give me an opportunity to talk with you in person because I am sure that my personal qualities and professional skills could enhance your organization's goals. Thank you in advance for your consideration.

Sincerely,

Leo Martelli

SEEKING FIRST JOB IN FIELD

First Job in Social Services Field
Sociology and Social Work graduate emphasizes his internship and peer mentor experience. Although this individual is in a Management Trainee position (notice he omits mentioning the industry in which he is currently working), he is yearning to obtain a position in the field for which he obtained a college degree. He is trying to come across as a young professional committed to making a difference in his chosen field, not just making a living in any type of work.

Date

Exact Name of Person
Exact Title
Exact Name of Company
Address
City, State, Zip

SEEKING TO ADVANCE IN RETAIL

Moving onward and upward
A corporate reorganization has caused the elimination of one office along with a proliferation of jobs in another city. This young, single professional is interviewing for jobs within her current organization, but she is also ready to "see what's out there" in other companies

Dear Exact Name of Person: (or Dear Sir or Madam in answering a blind ad):

With the enclosed resume, I would like to make you aware of my extensive sales, merchandising, and management skills as well as my interest in exploring the possibility of utilizing my experience to benefit your organization.

After earning a B.S. degree (cum laude) from Ohio State University, I was recruited by the Belk organization as an Associate Buyer in 1995. I achieved unusually rapid advancement to Buyer after only one year and four months, and since 1997 I have excelled in handling a $10 million volume while buying for 22 stores. The buying function had been handled in New York City for the previous five years, and I instituted a major reorganization which led to increased sales.

My sales and gross margin results have been consistently superior, and I have never received anything less than "above average" on annual performance evaluations of my business, sales, marketing, merchandise planning, and inventory control skills. I am well known for my ability to establish and maintain effective working relationships with people at all levels, from top-level buying and merchandising experts in New York City to store managers and vendors. I pride myself on my ability to react quickly to emerging trends and to respond decisively in averting problems before they happen.

If you can use a dynamic and results-oriented individual with excellent communication skills, I hope you will contact me to suggest a time when we can meet to discuss your goals and needs and how I might help you. I can provide excellent references.

Thank you in advance for your time and professional courtesies.

Yours sincerely,

Amy Stanfield

Date

Exact Name of Person
Exact Title
Exact Name of Company
Address
City, State, Zip

Dear Exact Name of Person: (or Dear Sir or Madam if answering a blind ad):

With the enclosed resume, I would like to make you aware of my interest in your organization and introduce you to my considerable financial management skills. I am interested in making a career change from financial management in the retail world to financial management in the financial services field, and I have much to offer.

After earning my college degree, I began working for the Sears organization and have excelled in an unusually rapid track record of advancement to Buyer. I am responsible for a $10 million sales volume, and what I do is similar to managing a portfolio of commercial accounts. In 1998, I increased volume by over 4% while also increasing profit margin dollars, and in 1999 so far, I am showing a 26% increase in sales.

While handling multimillion-dollar responsibility related to 14 departments in 22 stores, I travel extensively with an average of 15 trips annually to New York to negotiate with vendors, six trips to the corporate office in Charlotte, and numerous trips to stores throughout eastern NC. In handling my financial responsibilities, I work extensively with financial software. I am highly proficient with Lotus 1-2-3 and use it on a daily basis to analyze data for stores, vendors, and product lines.

I believe the primary reason for my success has been my communication skills and my ability to establish and maintain excellent working relationships. Each time I have been reassigned responsibility for a new area within Sears, I have been enthusiastically welcomed by store managers who had heard "through the grapevine" that I am a true professional who delivers outstanding bottom-line results.

Although I could remain with the Sears organization and am held in high regard, I have decided that I wish to make a change into the financial services industry. I thrive on the fast pace and highly competitive nature of retailing, and I am certain I would thrive on the fast pace, aggressive sales orientation, and highly competitive environment of the financial services industry. With my strong communication, sales, and financial management skills, I feel certain I could make valuable contributions, and I would hope to rise into the ranks of management someday. I hope you will contact me to suggest a time when we might meet in person to discuss your needs.

Sincerely,

Candi Melrose

SEEKING A CAREER CHANGE FROM RETAIL

Moving to a new industry
Although she has enjoyed the glamour of retailing buying, she is ready for a slower pace in anticipation of the demands of motherhood. This young professional accentuated her financial management skills on the resume which accompanied this career-change cover letter.

Date

Exact Name of Person
Exact Title
Exact Name of Company
Address
City, State, Zip

SEEKING TO RETURN TO THE PUBLIC HEALTH FIELD OR TO UNIVERSITY TEACHING

This individual has had an exciting career, but she has spent a few years out of the country working for an international construction firm and is seeking to return to a university setting or to a public health role. She is attempting to use this all-purpose cover letter to apply for positions within the academic community as well as within health care organizations.

Dear Exact Name of Person: (or Dear Sir or Madam if answering a blind ad):

With the enclosed resume, I would like to make you aware of my strong background in public health, biochemistry, environmental health, scientific research, and laboratory technology.

Prior to earning my Master of Public Health with an emphasis on International Health from Princeton University, I was honored by being named a Hubert Humphrey Fellow by the U.S. Government. I had also completed extensive post-graduate education at the University of South Carolina and the University of the West Indies, where I served as a tenured faculty member and as Dean of Health Sciences.

Experience in public health in a corporate setting

In 1990 an international construction company aggressively recruited me away from my tenured faculty position, and I took on a key management role within that company. In an essentially entrepreneurial role, I established the company's environmental and public health programs, and I am proud of the results of the employee education programs which we instituted. Through my leadership, the company was able to dramatically reduce the incidence of malaria and other communicable diseases and increase awareness of methods of preventing AIDS and sexually transmitted diseases. I also provided technical expertise on proper environmental practices to ensure that mining operations were in compliance with stipulated regulations.

Experience in university teaching and administration

As a tenured university professor at the University of the West Indies, I lectured in subjects which included Epidemiology, Public Health, Biochemistry, Pharmacology, Pharmaceutical Chemistry, and Environmental Health. I achieved tenured status in an unusually short time, and I earned a reputation as a popular teacher who could "translate" complex scientific concepts into easily understood language. As Dean of Health Sciences, I planned and implemented programs in Medicine, Environmental Health, Pharmacy, Radiography, and Medical Laboratory Technology. In addition to developing numerous budgets for the faculty, I coordinated the Accreditation Program for Registered Pharmacists including establishment of clinical rotations.

I can provide outstanding personal and professional references at the appropriate time, and I would be delighted to make myself available for a personal interview at your convenience.

Sincerely,

Jannine Oxford

Collections Letters

Unfortunately, most people in business encounter customers who try to avoid payment. The letters in this section are used by a personnel service providing permanent placement services.

If you are writing collections letters, be sure to examine the laws in your state to assure that the language of your letters is in compliance with collections laws.

You will see that the letters vary in tone. Often companies have an inventory of collections letters which they use in the process of collecting money owed and debts outstanding, and they choose the letter they send based on the particular customer situation.

PEOPLEFIND, Inc.
1110 Hay Street, Dallas, TX 28305
Telephone: (910) 483-6611
Fax: (910) 483-2439
http://www.prep-pub.com
e-mail: preppub@aol.com

Date

COLLECTIONS LETTER #1

The collections process actually begins with the first letter acquainting the customer with his or her financial obligation.

Dear Exact Name of Person:

Congratulations on your new job!

We have sincerely enjoyed working with you to help you find your job. Many employers in the community use PEOPLEFIND exclusively as their means of finding qualified employees, and we were happy to help you find the "fit" you were looking for with an area employer.

According to the terms of the contract you signed with PEOPLEFIND, you are now legally required to take care of your financial obligation to PEOPLEFIND. Come by our office immediately so that we can settle the terms of payment. You do not need an appointment.

We are sure you want to begin your new job with the added satisfaction of knowing you have taken care of your financial responsibilities to PEOPLEFIND.

Sincerely,

Chris Penguin
Office Manager

PEOPLEFIND, Inc.
1110 Hay Street, Dallas, TX 28305
Telephone: (910) 483-6611
Fax: (910) 483-2439
http://www.prep-pub.com
e-mail: preppub@aol.com

Date

Dear Exact Name of Person:

Our records reflect that you are delinquent in your payment schedule with PEOPLEFIND Personnel Service.

When we set up your payment schedule for our fee, we did so while taking the greatest care to ensure that our fees would become due after you had had time to be paid and to deposit your checks.

Although it is PEOPLEFIND's policy to stress the different methods of payment to each applicant, I shall now reiterate that you may either make your fee payments in person, send them in check form to the address noted above, or drop them in our drop box prior to our office hours.

You now owe PEOPLEFIND $623.00. Please settle this payment problem promptly so that we are not forced by corporate policy to initiate formal legal collections action.

Sincerely,

Chris Penguin
Office Manager

COLLECTIONS LETTER #2

This is the mildest letter in the collections series you will see displayed in this book.

PEOPLEFIND, Inc.
1110 Hay Street, Dallas, TX 28305
Telephone: (910) 483-6611
Fax: (910) 483-2439
http://www.prep-pub.com
e-mail: preppub@aol.com

Date

COLLECTIONS LETTER #3

Each letter in the collections series gets progressively more aggressive.

Dear Exact Name of Person:

We have contacted you with little success on a number of occasions regarding your **legally enforceable financial obligation** to PEOPLEFIND.

Our records show that you have an outstanding balance with PEOPLEFIND of $XXX.XX. Your promissory note is legally binding and you will be required to pay to PEOPLEFIND your entire balance, plus late charges and interest accrued on late payments, as well as court costs, if this matter becomes a formal collections activity and you force us to obtain a court judgment against you. Such a judgment can be extended for many years and would drastically affect your credit and financial dealings.

Please contact our office immediately to settle this payment problem so that we are not forced by corporate policy to initiate formal legal collections action.

Sincerely,

Chris Penguin
Office Manager

PEOPLEFIND, Inc.
1110 Hay Street, Dallas, TX 28305
Telephone: (910) 483-6611
Fax: (910) 483-2439
http://www.prep-pub.com
e-mail: preppub@aol.com

Date

Dear Exact Name of Person:

As you are well aware, your account with PEOPLEFIND Personnel Service is delinquent, and repeated telephone calls and letters have not succeeded in motivating you to honor your legal obligation.

As a result, it is now our intention to take action in small claims court which will lead to the complete payment of your account. We have been in the personnel business for 16 years, and in all cases when we have been to small claims court, **our contract has been upheld**, and **a judgment has been awarded** for the amount owed to PEOPLEFIND plus court costs. If you do not show up in court on the date summoned, a judgment can still be rendered against you and a 10-year blight on your credit record will result.

A small claims court decision in PEOPLEFIND's favor will result in a judgment against you that will tarnish your credit reputation and credit record. Upon the decision of the magistrate in our favor, we will take the necessary legal action to see that your financial delinquency is reported to the credit bureau and legal authorities. You will find that you will be:

- **unable** to obtain a loan for a car, television, or consumer product for 10 years.
- **unable to work** in any company or institution where credit checks are required: banking and other similar industries are the most apparent, but many other types of jobs require that an employee be bonded so checks of your character and credit will be conducted. Most employers believe that your credit history is a direct reflection of your character and honesty.

By (MONTH, DAY, YEAR), your account must be brought up to date, or you must have signed authorization from the owner that other arrangements have been made. If you have special hardships which you wish to discuss with the owner, Anne Gregory, you may call and make an appointment Monday-Friday, 9-6 p.m. As the formal paperwork which you signed in our office (which will be presented in court) shows clearly, you were quite aware that our service was not free when you asked us to find a job for you. We intend to collect the total amount you owe us plus court costs if you have not brought your account up to date by (MONTH, DAY, YEAR).

Sincerely,

Chris Penguin
Office Manager

COLLECTIONS LETTER #4

Each letter in this series tries to appeal to a different sentiment or present different arguments for doing the right thing.

PEOPLEFIND, Inc.

1110 Hay Street, Dallas, TX 28305
Telephone: (910) 483-6611
Fax: (910) 483-2439
http://www.prep-pub.com
e-mail: preppub@aol.com

Date

COLLECTIONS LETTER #5

This letter clarifies that a court action is imminent.

Dear Exact Name of Person:

Despite repeated attempts on our part to work with you on the **legal financial obligation** you have to PEOPLEFIND, you continue to show absolutely no intention of doing the right thing.

You therefore leave us with no option but to **file legal action** against you to collect what is rightfully and legally ours. Please understand that you bring this on yourself.

Be assured that because of the time that you have wasted and because of your total disregard of the law, I shall ensure that the **maximum** placement fee amount **plus** maximum interest **plus** all court costs **plus** attorney fees will be paid to us by you upon our receipt of a legal judgment against you.

It is indeed unfortunate that you choose to have your **credit rating** and **personal reputation** severely damaged, and all for nothing. Because when we receive judgment, you will be **required** to pay us immediately all that you owe.

By the time you read this, the papers will already have been filed with the magistrate. If you do, however, make payment to PEOPLEFIND before the sheriff delivers your summons, and pay our filing costs, I may still be able to cancel your court appearance. Don't let yourself down.

Sincerely,

Anne Gregory
Owner/Operator
PEOPLEFIND Personnel

PEOPLEFIND, Inc.
1110 Hay Street, Dallas, TX 28305
Telephone: (910) 483-6611
Fax: (910) 483-2439
http://www.prep-pub.com
e-mail: preppub@aol.com

Date

Dear Exact Name of Person:

Not only have you shown no concern for your legally binding payment obligation to PEOPLEFIND, but you also have been a tremendous personal disappointment to me, especially since I have gone so much out of my own way to help you.

Well, time is up! You have until 5:00 p.m. this Thursday to bring payment to PEOPLEFIND. At that point the matter will be completely out of my hands. If we don't see you by then, company policy requires me to see you in court, from which there will be only one result. You will be ordered to immediately pay your total balance owed to PEOPLEFIND, and the court won't care whether or not you can pay or how you're going to do it.

Again, I am more disappointed than anything else. When somebody takes her time to show she cares about you and to help you, which I have done, it doesn't take much for you to show a little consideration in return. Why don't you do the right thing and save us both some time and spare yourself a lot of expense?

Sincerely,

Chris Penguin
Office Manager

COLLECTIONS LETTER #6

It's understandable that writers of collections letters often want to express their personal disappointment with the individual who owes money, because there have usually been many promises made and broken by this point.

Letters of Complaint
(also see Letters of Appeal)

Sometimes it's necessary to write a letter of complaint if you feel you encountered a situation in which you were shortchanged. The letters in this section show effective approaches in communicating about products, services, or situations which did not meet your expectations or provide the value you sought.

Giving the details is important

As with an appeals letter, a main thing to keep in mind when writing an complaint letter is that you need to give as many details, dates, specific names, and so forth as possible so that the individual reading your letter of complaint will clearly follow your train of thought and be persuaded by your point of view. If the facts are on your side, make sure you give the facts in very detailed and explicit ways. It's O.K. to show your emotion in such a letter but make sure you don't substitute emotion for factual information.

Make sure your reader understands "how to make it better"

Usually you have an ideal outcome in mind which could occur as a result of the complaint letter you are writing. As with appeals letters, you must persuade your reader to do what you want him or her to do in a complaint letter.

State your request or recommendation clearly

Before you write a letter of complaint, write down the result you hope will be achieved by the letter you are writing, and state very clearly for your busy reader the action you hope he or she will take. If your reader is confused after reading your letter of complaint, he or she may do nothing. A good way to test whether or not your letter "makes sense" is to read it out loud to someone else and see if that person understands your point of view and would be persuaded to take the action you desire.

Date

Mr. Vance McGowan
Vice President of Agency for Georgia
Northeast Mutual Life Insurance
200 Mutual Boulevard
Atlanta, GA 78909

Dear Mr. McGowan:

With the enclosed resume, I would like to make you aware of my desire to become a Northeast Mutual Insurance Agent and to own my own insurance agency. It is my goal to take over the agency of Melton Edwards when he retires or be considered for an agency position, and I hope Northeast Mutual will give me the opportunity to do so. There is a technical problem which prevents this from occurring, and the reason I am writing this letter is to ask your help in resolving the problem so that I can remain with the Northeast Mutual "family" rather than be forced to join a competitor.

As you will see from my resume, since 1982 I have been the Office Manager of Melton Edwards's Northeast Mutual Insurance Office in Macon, GA. During that time, I have earned my Bachelor of Science degree and have become a Licensed Insurance Agent with the state of Georgia. I am licensed to sell auto, life and health, and the full range of fire insurance products.

While working for Melton Edwards, I have played a key role in helping this agent become a Million Dollar Roundtable Agent on multiple occasions, and I have become knowledgeable of all aspects of managing an insurance agency for maximum profitability. We continually re-underwrite our book of business to remain profitable, and we maintain vigilant quality control of our multiline single-agency business in order to maintain a quality book of business. Although Melton Edwards is my father as well as my employer, I am not viewed by our clients as "the boss's daughter" anymore! I have been told by many of our clients that I am the reason they now remain with Northeast Mutual, and they appreciate the manner in which I maintain good relationships with them and look out for their well being.

According to current regulations, I am prevented (1) from becoming a Northeast Mutual Agent in Macon and taking over my father's agency when he retires and from (2) being considered for an agency position because I am not considered "a Northeast Mutual employee." I want to live and work in Macon, where I grew up and where my strongest personal and professional relationships exist. I feel very loyal to Northeast Mutual and have a strong desire to take over my father's agency someday, and I am confident that this would be very beneficial for Northeast Mutual as well as for me. I am writing this letter because of the highest regard I have for Northeast Mutual products, and it is my deep desire to represent them professionally throughout my working life.

Sincerely,

Dorothy Stincilmeyer

SEEKING AGENCY OWNERSHIP

Seeking Ownership of Insurance Agency

This letter could have been shown in the Letters of Appeals section also. She is presenting an argument related to why she feels she is the best candidate to take over her father's insurance agency, even though company policies essentially prohibit it. She is hoping they will make an exception to the policy and review the unique circumstances of her case.

Date

Stewart, Martin, Smith, and Franklin, Attorneys
ATTN: Mr. Walton Stewart
P. O. Drawer 85
San Antonio, TX 29856

LETTERS OF COMPLAINT

Sometimes a one-page letter expressing the details of our complaint is just not enough. This writer hotly contests his lawyer's performance in his divorce case, and in real life this letter saved him more than $7,000 in legal fees.

Dear Mr. Stewart:

In reference to your request for settlement of my account with you and your firm, please find enclosed my check # 5678, to fulfill my obligation to you concerning the matter in which you represented me. There are several points I wish to bring forward regarding these proceedings which will, I believe, justify the difference between my check of $750 and your stated invoice amount of $7,500.

(A) Contract between Walton Stewart and David McKinney

There was no written contract, but an oral contract between the above mentioned parties. I requested legal assistance concerning the matter of settlement of Property Distribution as well as Defense against Alimony and Attorneys' Fees. Throughout the proceedings you continuously represented yourself as being the most capable attorney to represent my interests by stating various cases you had or were handling and to the satisfactory judgments your legal abilities had gained for your clients. You made reference to your handling of cases before the Supreme Court and to the limited number of local attorneys skilled in making such presentations. You made reference to your busy schedule, including numerous speaking engagements before various legal gatherings, and you inspired confidence through the prominent display of your several degrees and legal attainments, for which I agree that you should be proud, as they are most impressive.

I agreed to compensate you at the hourly rate of $150 per hour for the services you would be providing and which you represented that I would be receiving.

I in no way took the above-stated representations as any type of guarantee of the outcome of my case. I did, however, take your self promotions as a guarantee of the professional competency of you as an attorney and as to your competence in the handling of all aspects pertaining to the protocol and handling of a trial or hearing.

My actual experience in having you handle my case, however, was bitterly disappointing and revealed an attitude of professional apathy on your part as well as, on occasion, reckless disregard for my case and circumstances. I believe some of the following facts will illustrate what I am talking about.

1. **Car values**: [See Exhibit A from judgment] You took the highest Blue Book value for my car, a 1998 BMW [$15,900.00], yet you never placed a value on my ex-wife's 1995 BMW ($9,596).

2. **Certain items** Judge Clamath awarded to me for the Property Settlement never appeared on any list submitted during the trial.

(B) Alimony Hearing:

1. As we discussed in our meeting on (date), in my Affidavit of Financial Standing [See D. E. #4], I had an additional error, because of my not being familiar with the form that you asked me to use. When I offered you this form, I requested that you double check my math, as I myself had done with all the forms I had supplied to you. Your staff waited until the day of the hearing to type this form and request my signature. You and your staff completely ignored my request to double check my math on this form, which gave the Defendant [my ex-wife] a decided mathematical advantage.

2. [See D. F. Exhibit 1]. In my ex-wife's Financial Standing Statement, specifically, Gross Monthly Income [shown as both monthly and yearly amount], I had repeatedly enquired as to when you were going to have my ex-wife furnish Financial Accountability. Your standard response was always: "It will be furnished, don't worry;" After the hearing your excuse was that you had been "denied by Judge Clamath." I had to produce my financial history before a deposition taken on (date) [see Defendant Exhibit 12]. This, as you will remember, was even before our Hearing for Property Settlement. You never requested a Deposition for any Financial Accountability before our Alimony Hearing, and you relied on my ex-wife's attorney to furnish said records [which on many occasions you said yourself could not be trusted for accurate information.]

3. I would like to address our meeting on (date). You had repeatedly stated that I would only have to "pay token alimony of maybe $200/month to $300/month for no more than one [1] year." I will remind you that during this meeting you first brought up the figure of $750/month and my reaction was that that was an outrageous figure.

I will also remind you of a statement you made during this meeting, which I will never forget: "I have to be careful how I handle your case, because of how it might impact my next case in front of Judge Clamath." If for one minute I thought your being careful would cost me $750/month for four [4] years, I would have dismissed you on the spot.

(C) We will now visit our meeting of (date).

I presented my documentation of my ex-wife's yearly earnings, which were substantially higher than had been represented by you or her attorney in our Alimony Hearing. These figures I obtained quite easily and legally from the Medical Board [see my Exhibit #1]. At this meeting you had one of your legal colleagues in attendance, not only as an observer, because you repeatedly requested her input into the proceedings. This was the only meeting we had during which you felt compelled to have your own counsel present, without offering me the same courtesy, and I want you to know that this was a very intimidating situation—two seasoned attorneys versus a client with no legal experience. You will recall that during this meeting I was able to defend my actions in securing evidence that you would not secure, that could only have benefited my case in the Alimony Hearing. The materials which I presented to you were materials which I had repeatedly asked you about—actually not asked, but in reality begged you to secure—and yet you made me defend my actions in securing them. The result of this meeting was your <u>finally</u> filing a First Request For Production of Documents on (date), five [5] months after the Alimony Hearing and over one [1] year after the Property

Settlement. My question in hindsight is this: Why did you bother? **The horse was out of the barn and long gone.** The damage was done!!

This meeting also prompted you to seek the only Deposition taken from my ex-wife on (date) [Exhibits #6,7,8]. All of the above substantiated my findings which I presented to you on (date), six [6] months after the Alimony Hearing.

Mr. Stewart, you were able to obtain information six [6] months after the trial, information which would have had a significant bearing on the outcome of my hearing had you obtained this information prior to the hearing. You obtained this information easily and without hindrance, even though you had stated that you had been prevented from obtaining this evidence before the Alimony Hearing.

Do you as a lawyer under oath not have an ethical obligation, if not also a moral obligation, to inform a client that you are not willing to secure evidence that would be paramount to that client's case? I will take this opportunity to refute an objection which I am certain you are sure to make: namely, that this new evidence would not have made a difference. One can only speculate on that. We will never know for sure because you were negligent in performing your duties, and that has resulted in great financial hardship for me.

(D) Attorney Fee Hearing:
Once again during our preparation meeting for this hearing you stated, "I have to be careful how I handle your case, because I will want to be awarded fees in upcoming hearings." **Mr. Stewart, were you $3,485.00 careful? That is what I have calculated.**

(E) Miscellaneous:
1. I will bring to your attention billing to my account. Please remember that during our first meeting I showed you a handwritten account by my previous attorney, and you assured me of your firm's billing protocol. Yet the first three checks I wrote were never posted to my account! When I questioned this, however, I was assured everything was "in order." I will further point to invoices received from your office beginning (date) running through (date). I was billed nine [9] times for the same service [See Exhibit #4]. I have another occurrence of being billed for preparation of hearing, $175.00, when no date of hearing had been established. I will ask: **Can we draw a correlation between the slipshod way this case was pursued and handled and the slipshod billing practices which were utilized by your firm?**

2. Repeatedly you referred to the fact Mr. Allen [my ex-wife's attorney] was a favorite of Judge Clamath and how she was inclined to bend over backward to accommodate his wishes. Meanwhile I was being bled to the tune of a total of $43,544.00 [extraordinary number of continuances granted].

3. Speaking of accountability, during the Lawyer Fee Hearing, Mr. Allen was never once asked by you to support his allegation of hours worked on my ex-wife's case. I will ask you, sir: How many blank/open invoices are **you** in the habit of paying? I must remember that you were being careful and would not want to offend Mr. Allen and certainly not Judge Clamath.

In closing, Mr. Stewart, if for one moment I thought I had received the type of defense which I had been promised, and which I was led to believe I would receive by your aggressive self-promotion, I would gladly pay your stated fee. But I did not receive what I was promised or what was self-promoted. Instead I am paying $2,000/month in related costs and have had to endure much hardship and mental anguish. Whatever implied contract we might have had was long ago broken by you, by the careless way in which you ignored my interests and mishandled this case.

The Alimony Hearing has been reviewed by another attorney, and I am assured that I had every right to an appeal [see my exhibit # 2]. I will tell you that the assessment of your performance by several attorneys I have spoken with regarding this case has been less than flattering to you.

When I first met you and for a period of time afterward, you had my sincerest respect and trust. Now that respect has ended and the trust has been shattered. Instead of making a friend for life out of me, you have done your best to make an enemy.

Before the encounter between Mr. Allen and yourself, I also had a great deal of respect for the legal profession. That respect has also been greatly eroded as I have witnessed the spectacle of lawyers ignoring their client's best interests in order to curry the favor of judges in future cases.

Mr. Stewart, these proceedings have exhausted all of my available funds. I am offering you my check #2194 in the amount of $750 to settle this account. I have no other funds and am unable to borrow additional funds [see my exhibit #3]. I realize you may feel this is only a token payment, but you led me to believe for two years that all my alimony payments would be was a "token payment" [$36,000 is not a "token payment" to me]. Mr. Stewart, I truly believe I don't owe any further amount for the services I received, and if you were the man you had made yourself out to be, you would return all monies I had paid you, because you said you would not charge a client for services not provided.

If you will not accept this settlement and take further action, I will have no choice but to seek legal counsel, make this paper public knowledge, and defend my actions to the furthest extent the law will allow.

I have had this paper reviewed by another attorney and he feels there would be no grounds for any type of libel suit for the statements made herewith.

Sincerely,

David McKinney

Date

Senator Jesse Helms
403 Dirksen Senate Office Building
Washington, DC 20510

LETTERS OF COMPLAINT

It can frequently be a good idea to involve one of your senators or congressman in a dispute you are having. Quite often the office of the elected official will look into the matter and write their own letters of enquiry further investigating your problem.

Dear Senator Helms:

I am writing to ask for your assistance with a problem with the Veterans Administration medical care system which concerns a disputed claim regarding the service-connected disability of my late father, James P. Knox, Social Security Number 000-00-0000.

Due to medical problems suffered by my mother—confusion and some memory loss suffered as a result of surgical procedures she has undergone and language barriers—she could not possibly give an accurate and complete account of my father's medical history. I believe that my father's medical records were not reviewed thoroughly, that we did not receive a complete and thorough hearing, and that the VA representative was not knowledgeable of my father's case and did not give us fair representation. According to the VA, my mother must wait for 18 months to two years for the VA in Washington to review the case. I do not believe it is fair that she is penalized because of someone else's incompetence and refusal to give the case a fair hearing.

My father applied for a service-connected disability in 1995 on the basis of hypertension and arteriosclerosis heart disease with angina. The claim was denied. That decision was based on the records which did not document such disease until the 1990s. But in fact, the medical records clearly indicate otherwise. This leads me to believe that the records were not completely, accurately, and thoroughly reviewed.

The question is whether or not my mother is entitled to Dependency and Indemnity Compensation (DIC) on the basis of my father's medical condition being service connected. My father served on active duty with the U.S. Army for 24 years and retired in 1976. He completed tours of duty in Vietnam and Korea. He had constant chest pain documented as far back as 1954 and did not retire until 1976. He died in August 1996. He was on record as having chest pains and numbness in his arm as well as general malaise of an undetermined cause for the last five years he was on active duty. After episodes in 1978 of dizziness, a 130/90 blood pressure reading, and one year of impotence, an enlarged thyroid was noticed by a medical student. After over a year of burning chest pain, an EKG was done, and the provisional diagnosis of arteriosclerosis was made by a cardiologist. A 1974 physical showed chest pains and infectious hepatitis for which he was treated in 1963.

My mother, sister and I arrived at 9:15 a.m. at the Federal Building, Room 5423, in Charlotte, NC, for the 11 a.m. hearing on January 27, 1997, to meet our assigned representative and discuss our testimony and the evidence. Mr. Flake came to the waiting area and introduced himself as our representative, and he told us he was going to talk with the hearing officer and see if the hearing could be set up for earlier because another hearing had been canceled. He was informed that my sister and I were representing our mother because of her emotional state of mind. He stated that he could not discuss the case with us until she signed a release form. My mother then did sign two release forms.

When the meeting continued Mr. Flake stated that we were not going to like what he had to say because he had reviewed the records and found no new documentation. He then informed us that the hearing officer had not changed his position and that the claim would be denied. When I tried to explain, he stated that he understood; *he then unbuttoned his shirt to show us the scars from his heart surgery!* I felt that his actions and remarks were tasteless and insensitive. He stated that the hearing officer had already made the decision to turn down the claim. I said that since both he and the hearing officer worked for the VA and had already decided the case without hearing all the facts, how were we supposed to get fair representation? He became very offensive at this point. Mr. Flake stated that the hearing was just a formality. When I realized a decision had been made and the hearing was basically a farce, I asked what our options were. The issue of the case going on to the VA in Washington was discussed.

Since the hearing I have obtained partial copies of active duty medical files and records which go back to 1954 and which substantiate that, as early as 1954, complaints of chest pain were made and documented. On February 4, 1954, slight pain in the heart area and a heart murmur were diagnosed. Chest pains were documented on November 6, 10, and 14, 1958, with cardiac asthemia (burning pain in the heart area).

At issue is the timing of my father's illnesses and of various diagnoses. From the period 1971 to 1981, my father made complaints of chest pain, dizziness, impotency, and fatigue and the cause was always undetermined. An enlarged thyroid was detected and testing was done and again no cause or treatment was made. Eventually in 1981, heart disease was diagnosed. High blood pressure readings were recorded at least as far back as February 1975 and his inpatient records show that he was treated for hypertension for the last 18 years.

I request that the VA thoroughly review my father's case and examine his medical records in more detail. My mother was very distressed and disbelieving that the VA would turn down this claim. I feel very strongly that she is owed an apology from the VA and that she does not deserve to be forced to wait another two years for this to be resolved when this matter can be settled at the Winston-Salem VA Regional Office. I hope that there is some way for you to help us get a fair hearing from the VA without having to wait so long. Thank you for any assistance or any advice you can give.

Sincerely,

Thelma G. Guin

Date

LETTERS OF COMPLAINT

Sometimes you have to make proper authorities aware of invasions of your privacy or infringements of your rights. Make sure your reader knows what you want him or her to do. In the case of this writer, Mr. Atkins wants an investigation by the Department of Transportation.

Mr. James Foster
Chief of Operations
Department of Transportation
Highway Division
P.O. Box 9200
Atlanta, GA 90376

Dear Mr. Foster:

With this letter, I wish to make a formal complaint and request that you investigate the charges which I make herein, perform your own analysis, and provide me with a written opinion as to observations I wish to make.

I have sufficient reason to believe that Mr. Jim Smith (in concert with Mr. David Jones) ordered and/or participated in an unauthorized entry onto and survey of my property at 236 Cain Road, Lot 23, in Spring Town on December 15, 1999. D.O.T. employees entered my property without permission, drove down stakes, and performed a survey to gather and manufacture data to be used against me in a lawsuit by a third party. Mr. Smith is also listed as the chief witness in the case.

The use of this information by the witness directly engages D.O.T. This is a clear infraction of my rights as a property owner.

I feel that this issue is worthy of investigation by D.O.T. or the Attorney General's Office because it raises the question of legality. The Department of Transportation is a taxpayer-funded public service agency and not a for-hire private enterprise.

In my opinion, this incident is part of an attempt to bully me into signing documents for D.O.T.—and I refuse to do so.

Please reply. Thank you in advance for your time.

Sincerely,

D.W. Atkins, Jr.

CC: Attorney General, State of GA

Letters in Confidence

Not only in job hunting but in numerous other situations in life, you may want to make your reader aware that you wish your letter to be held in the strictest confidence.

On the following page, you will see an example of a letter used in job hunting which expresses the desire for confidentiality on the part of the recipient of the letter.

Confidential letters should usually be addressed to a specific person by name. In that way you will know exactly who will be reading your letter and you will know that your letter will not be passed through many hands before getting to the right person.

Sometimes it simply takes a phone call to find out the correct name of the person to whom you should write. For example, let's assume that a job hunter discovered through an article in the *"Wall Street Journal"* that the Sears Company was planning on making a major push into fashion merchandising. Let's further assume that the newspaper article named the executive who had been hired to handle the new venture being undertaken by Sears. Since the job hunter is in an executive position with a major competitor, she does not wish her interest in Sears to become widely known or to be gossiped about in retailing circles. What the job hunter should do is call the Sears organization and ask for the mailing address of the person named in the article so that she can address the letter confidentially to that person. See the letter on page 120 to see an example of how to write this type of letter.

In confidential matters, be sure to mark the outside of the envelope "confidential" so your letter won't get opened by someone other than the person to whom you have addressed the letter.

Date

Exact Name of Person
Title or Position
Name of Company
Address (number and street)
Address (city, state, and zip)

LETTER EXPRESSING INTEREST IN EMPLOYMENT

How do I make it clear I want my interest to be confidential?

It's okay to ask a prospective employer to keep confidential your expression of interest in the company.

Dear Exact Name of Person: (or Sir or Madam if answering a blind ad.)

With the enclosed resume, I would like to <u>confidentially</u> make you aware of my interest in exploring employment opportunities within your organization.

As you will see from my resume, I have excelled in a track record of promotion within the agricultural industry and farm management. I earned my degree in General Agriculture at New Mexico State University and was awarded a Moorhead scholarship based on my high entrance exam scores. In my first job out of college, I was general manager of a small farm with two full-time workers, 15 seasonal workers, as well as a variety of crops, beef cattle, and sows.

Most recently I have been promoted to Assistant Manager supervising nine people on a 1,000-head sow farm, and I am in charge of all aspects of production as well as personnel problems and employee issues.

With a reputation as a resourceful problem solver, I have become experienced at taking care of all farm financial matters including payroll, loan procurement, accounts payable, and accounts receivable. I am also skilled at managing people and have frequently managed a staff of employees who were all Spanish speaking.

Although I am highly regarded in my current position and am being groomed for further rapid promotion, I am aware of your company's fine reputation and am expressing my interest in exploring ways in which you could utilize my expert technical knowledge as well as my proven management abilities. I have an excellent reputation throughout the industry, and I can provide outstanding personal and professional references at the appropriate time.

If you can use a highly motivated professional with a proven ability to make significant contributions to the bottom line, I hope you will contact me to suggest a time when we could meet in person to discuss how my experience and knowledge could be put to work for you.

Thank you in advance for your time.

Yours sincerely,

Doug Gascho

Date

Exact Name of Person
Title or Position
Name of Company
Address (number and street)
Address (city, state, and zip)

Dear Exact Name of Person: (or Sir or Madam if answering a blind ad.)

With the enclosed resume, I would like to make you aware of my interest in the possibility of putting my strong management, production operations, and sales background to work for your company. Please treat my inquiry as highly confidential at this point. Although I can provide outstanding personal and professional references at the appropriate time, I do not wish my current employer to be aware of my interest in your company.

As you will see from my enclosed resume, I have been in the multipurpose concrete applications business my entire working life. I began in entry-level positions with Fabrico Concrete in New Orleans and was promoted to Plant Manager and Sales Manager. Then I joined Alfred Wright and Son, Inc., in Lafayette, LA, where I tripled production and transformed that company into an attractive acquisition candidate which caught the attention of Handy Concrete. When Handy Concrete Company bought Alfred Wright in 1996, I became a Division Manager and recently was promoted to Regional Manager.

In my current position I manage operations at 10 divisions while supervising three Division Managers and overseeing activities of 85 people at 10 locations. I also supervise four sales and customer service professionals in addition to preparing budgets for each of the 10 divisions.

If you can use a versatile professional with a thorough understanding of all facets of the concrete applications business, I hope you will contact me to suggest a time when we might meet. Should you have ambitious goals in either the production management or sales area, I feel certain my extensive industry knowledge and contacts could be useful.

Sincerely,

Eugene H. Dubois, Jr.

LETTER EXPRESSING INTEREST IN EMPLOYMENT

Here's another example of the wording to use when you want to stress that you wish your approach to be confidential.

Date

Exact Name of Person
Title or Position
Name of Company
Address (number and street)
Address (city, state, and zip)

Dear Exact Name of Person: (or Sir or Madam if answering a blind ad.)

I would like to make you aware of my strong interest in the position of Training and Development Manager advertised in the *Houston Chronicle*. As you will see, I have a track record of success as an experienced instructor and training program developer as well as proven skills in employee supervision, staff development, and production management.

As you will see, I have excelled as an instructor, course developer, and technical writer. Training development, overseeing the professional development of assigned personnel, and providing counseling and guidance for more junior personnel have always been key areas of responsibility.

With a versatile background which includes experience in the telecommunications field as well as aircraft and vehicle maintenance, I have been involved in most areas of operations to include logistics, planning and scheduling, and safety as well as in heavy equipment operations. I offer a reputation as a skilled communicator who has been especially effective in providing instruction in individual and group situations. I am especially proud of the associate's degree I earned while excelling in my full-time job.

With regard to my salary requirements, I would be delighted to discuss the private details of my salary history with you in person, and I can assure you that I can provide excellent references at the appropriate time.

If you can use an experienced professional who is dedicated to setting and achieving high standards in all areas of performance, I hope you will contact me to suggest a time when we might meet to discuss your needs. I am confident that I could become an asset to Dickinson Associates.

Sincerely,

Chico Flores, Jr.

WHEN THEY ASK FOR SALARY REQUIREMENTS

What if they ask for salary requirements?

It's usually not in your best interests to provide your salary requirements in response to an ad. It's better to discuss that subject in person with the employer, and always let the employer bring the subject up. If the employer initiates a discussion of salary, he or she is probably interested in you and you'll be able to negotiate your best package. See the fourth paragraph for the exact wording in handling this delicate matter if the ad to which you are responding asks for salary requirements.

Date

Exact Name of Person
Title or Position
Name of Company
Address (number and street)
Address (city, state, and zip)

Dear Exact Name of Person: (or Sir or Madam if answering a blind ad.)

I would like to take this opportunity to thank you for considering me for the job on June 4 as a Sales Representative for Proctor & Gamble, Inc.

I enjoyed meeting with you and learning more about the company. I believe that Proctor & Gamble has a quality product line and I would be honored to represent these products.

I would also like to thank you for considering my busy schedule as a Account Representative and allowing me to come back for the second interview in the same afternoon. I am an extremely reliable and dependable professional, and I appreciated your professional courtesies in requiring me to be away from my current job as little as possible.

In response to your question about my salary history, I am currently making in the neighborhood of $35,000 with a raise anticipated within two months that could take me to close to $40,000. I enjoy a full benefits package with my current employer.

I am very interested in the position we discussed, and I can provide exceptionally strong personal and professional references at the appropriate time. Thank you for talking with me and helping me learn more about your fine company, and I hope to hear from you soon.

Sincerely,

Courtney Chaing

Alternate fourth paragraph:
In response to your question about salary history, I have enjoyed a compensation package in the range of $60,000-$80,000 in my most recent positions, which were structured as base plus commission. I realize that the Account Executive position you advertised may not involve compensation at that level, but I wish you to know that I am a hard charger who is accustomed to being compensated based on my results and contributions to the bottom line. I am confident of my ability to achieve and exceed ambitious sales goals, and I would very much enjoy an opportunity to talk with you again about the position you are seeking to fill.

WHEN THEY ASK FOR SALARY HISTORY

What if they ask about salary history?
You may be asked to provide your salary history in writing, but be sure to add in everything so that the prospective employer receives a fair picture of your total compensation. You could always tell the employer that you would be "delighted to discuss the private details of my salary history with you in person."
On the other hand, see the alternate fourth paragraph below. This paragraph was developed for a professional who had earned a lot of money in previous positions but knew the job for which she was applying wasn't paying in the range to which she had been accustomed. She nevertheless wanted the employer to know she was interested.

<u>Confidential</u>
Date

Mr. Wilson James
Vice President
Sears, Inc.
556 Decipher Falls
New Winston, PA 17898

Dear Mr. Wilson:

Through an article in the *Wall Street Journal* on December 19, 1999, I have become aware of your appointment as Vice President of Sears with the specific responsibility of creating a new fashion merchandising division. Congratulations!

With the enclosed resume, I would like to make you aware of my interest in confidentially exploring the possibility of joining your management team. Although I am held in the highest regard within my current organization, I am excited about your company's strategic initiatives, and I wish to confidentially express my interest in becoming part of this exciting new venture.

From my enclosed resume you will see that I am excelling in handling responsibilities equivalent to those of a General Merchandise Manager for Macy's Department Store. I supervise a 29-store operation and manage a staff of buyers and assistant buyers while handling responsibility for sales and gross margin, merchandise mix, and advertising. In my previous retail management experience, I enjoyed a track record of promotion with Penney's Department Store, where I began as a Department Manager, was promoted to Assistant Buyer and then to Buyer, directed the company's strategic moves as its Public Relations Director, and became Divisional Sales Manager. I was subsequently recruited by Macy's and have been in my current job since 1993.

Although I am held in high regard by the Macy's organization and can provide excellent references at the appropriate time, I am aware of your company's fine reputation and feel that my impeccable retailing credentials could be a valuable addition to your organization. My experience at Penney's and Macy's has taught me many truths about business and retailing including these:

- Doing an average job in retailing will put you out of business.
- Innovative marketing, creative problem solving, and aggressive merchandising are the keys to outperforming your competitors.
- Determine what your customers want and give them more of it.

If you can use a successful retailing executive who could bring added strengths and creativity to your strategic initiatives, I hope you will contact me to suggest a time when we could talk about your needs. I would certainly enjoy the opportunity to meet you in person.

Yours sincerely

Alexandra Simons

USING THE DIRECT APPROACH IN CONFIDENTIALLY EXPRESSING YOUR INTEREST IN A COMPETITOR

Let's take the example we imagined on page 115 when we visualized a retailing executive learning from a *Wall Street Journal* article about a new venture by Sears and the executive recruited to head up the new venture. The writer of this letter called Sears to find out the mailing address of the executive named in the WSJ article and then wrote this letter expressing her interest in joining the Sears executive team working on that venture. It is important to the writer of this letter, however, that her approach be kept in confidence.

Letters as Bids

Often a great, down-to-earth letter can work wonders when it comes to making a bid for a job or trying to get your company's name placed on a list for future bidding opportunities.

On the following pages, you will see examples of letters used to communicate the desire of businesses to bid on future or current jobs. Letters such as the ones on the following pages are often a formality but a necessary one in order to be considered as a subcontractor in future business dealings.

The tone of these letters will vary depending on whether or not you know the individuals involved. However, here's a tip: even if you know the individuals to whom you are writing and generally call them by their first names in informal business situations or in social settings, it's never wrong to address someone formally as "Mr." or "Mrs." or "Ms." in a formal business letter. This type of letter often gets passed around to other people in the company when a business decision is being made about subcontractors, and you might hurt your chances of getting the job if you come across as too familiar and not professional enough.

Clayton T. Powers
1110 1/2 Hay Street
Tempe, AZ 28305
(910) 483-6611

Date

LETTERS AS BIDS

This is a letter written in the style of the direct approach. Clayton Powers is approaching companies in major cities in Arizona to make them aware of his interest in being placed on their list of bidders.

Request for Bids
Department of Veterans Affairs
Property Management Section
587 Braden Mall, Suite 34
Tempe, AZ 45687

Dear Sir or Madam:

    I am a building contractor located in Tempe, AZ. I cover all areas of home improvement, roofing, dry wall, carpentry, painting, carpet, window and door installation and related areas.

    I am interested in expanding my work base to all counties of Arizona. I am requesting to be placed on your list of bidders. Please send any forms or information that I may need to submit. A recent reference will be Mr. Ralph Jensen, who may be contacted at (910) 483-6611. I can provide additional references upon request.

    Thank you for your consideration, and I look forward to hearing from you soon.

Sincerely yours,

Clayton Powers

PROFESSIONAL SIGNS, INC.

Kevin Staples, Owner
1110 1/2 Hay Street
Virginia Beach, VA 28305
Phone with voice mail: (910) 483-6611
Mobile: (910) 483-2439

Date

TO: Reed Townsend by fax at (910) 483-7778
FROM: Kevin Staples
RE: Proposal

This is a formal proposal related to the sanding and repainting of two steel beams at Framington Steel.

We propose to sand and repaint the two steel beams for $400 and restore them to their original condition.

I can provide excellent personal and professional references and have a reputation for quality work and reliable personal work habits. Thank you for the opportunity to submit this proposal.

Yours sincerely,

Kevin Staples

LETTERS AS BIDS

Sometimes a formal bid in writing must be sent to follow up on a verbal discussion in which a proposed price has been discussed.

Letters Related To Consumer Credit And Finance

There are many situations in life which require that you write letters pertaining to your credit situation or a financial matter. You may find yourself in a situation in which your credit cards get stolen, and you may need to write letters to the major credit bureaus to communicate information about fraudulent charges appearing on your credit file. You may have to write a letter disputing a bill.

Usually resolving consumer credit or financial problems takes some time, but it is vital that you put your information in writing rather than relying on verbal communication.

In this section you will see an example of a letter which was written to resolve a problem in an individual's credit file, and you will see a letter written to advise an organization of the circumstances which led to late payments.

These are not the most creative and imaginative letters you will be required to write in your life, but the point of these letters is that you must communicate in writing about such matters so that there will be a record of your circumstances or situation.

Date

Urgent Message to all Credit Bureaus:
Experian
PO Box 2106
Allen, TX 75013-2106

Trans Union
PO Box 6790
Fullerton, CA 92834-6790

Equifax Credit Information Services
PO Box 105069
Atlanta, GA 30348

Dear Sir or Madam:

I wish to provide the latest information pertaining to my credit activity. I wish you to know that I have been a victim of fraud in that my credit cards and checkbook were stolen in July 1999.

Please do not show 45 Roper Road, Atlanta, GA 85234 as a previous address of mine!!! This has never been an address of mine, and I have reason to believe that two young women who stole my credit cards and checkbook in July 1999 use that address as their residence.

The J.C. Penney's charge on my credit report is false, and I have obtained evidence from Penney's that shows clearly that someone named Sherry Johnson signed the purchase receipt using my Penney's credit card. I want you to remove that charge from my credit file.

Please place a Fraud Alert on my file if that is what you do when someone's credit cards have been stolen.

A copy of a recent utility bill, my letter to Penney's, and a copy of the police report are attached.

Please feel free to call me to verify any information. I am a business woman and need to make sure that my credit reputation is not tarnished by the two young thieves who stole my cards and checkbook.

Sincerely,

Your Name
Your Address
Your Phone Number

LETTER TO CREDIT BUREAUS REQUESTING FRAUD ALERT ON YOUR CREDIT FILE AFTER A ROBBERY

It's not fun to have your credit cards stolen, but if it happens, you will have numerous letters to write. One of those letters is a letter to the credit bureaus which are often asked to provide information about your creditworthiness to individuals or businesses enquiring about you.

Date

Trans Union Consumer Relations
PO Box 403
Springfield, PA 19064-0403

LETTER TO TRANS UNION CREDIT BUREAU

This letter is an attempt to explain an aberrant payment history which occurred in the aftermath of a husband's death and a period of grief which left this widow in a disorganized state of shock.

CONSUMER STATEMENT
From Marcy Wilson

Dear Sir:

My husband, Timothy Wilson, passed away and, in closing the estate and suffering from shock, I was late with some of my financial obligations.

I have since paid everything but, in doing this, I was slow with some of my other obligations. However, each time they were due, if I could not pay them off at that time, I would ask for and receive an extension. **I paid all of these accounts off in full by the maturity date of the note. I have a zero balance on everything except Bellweather Bank, where I owe $7,000, and it is current.**

World Bank shows a charge off for a vehicle. This is absolutely incorrect! I carried a copy of this credit report to World Bank where the loan was paid off before the final date of the contract. The bank said that it was incorrectly reported because it was not a charge off and that they would make the necessary corrections. They apologized.

American Express was paid at the time of my husband's death. I sent them the receipt and they informed me that they must have credited the wrong account and assured me that they would get it straight. This they have not yet done!

I am enclosing a money order for the Craven Regional Hospital for $93. I did not know that I owed them anything. When we received their bill I thought that it included everything. Please, please correct and send me a copy of my credit report.

Thank you very much.

Sincerely,

Marcy Wilson
SSN: 000-00-0000

Follow-up Letters

The best way to "close the sale" after an interview is to send a follow-up letter expressing your sincere interest in the job for which you interviewed.

A letter written after an interview allows you the opportunity to be more friendly and personal since you are writing to a person with whom you have held a conversation.

In job-hunting matters, employers are often left to decide between two strong candidates for a job. Sometimes the two candidates seem equally qualified. You can tip the scales in your favor after an interview by writing a skillful follow-up letter.

As you will see in the nine examples of follow-up letters in this section, this type of letter gives you many opportunities.

- **A follow-up letter is an excellent medium for transmitting your expenses.** You often need to send an invoice for mileage and other expenses incurred while attending an interview, and you will see the low-key and gracious fashion in which this is handled in one of the follow-up letters.

- **A follow-up letter gives you a chance to express yourself more elegantly and precisely on a specific subject than you did in an interview.** Most of us leave an interview feeling that we didn't handle a certain question very well. The follow-up letter gives you an opportunity to make it clear that, yes, you would be delighted to relocate and would welcome the opportunity to travel as the job requires.

- **The follow-up letter gives you an opportunity to show your "style" and personality to the interviewer.** You can strike a friendly tone in this letter.

Even if you got onto a first-name basis with your interviewer, it's often polite to greet him or her as "Mr." or "Mrs." in the follow-up letter. The letter you write to your interviewer may get shown to others, and you can't go wrong by going for a businesslike approach in addressing the individual. The concept here is that you are writing to someone because of his or her title or position in the organization, and you defer to that title or position in a rather formal way when you address the individual in the follow-up letter.

Date

Mrs. Diana Carver
Executive Vice President
Maytel Fashions
110 Hay Street
Dallas, TX 45678

FOLLOW-UP LETTER

How do you write a follow-up letter after an initial telephone interview but before the face-to-face meeting?

When you write a follow-up letter, try something different! Remember you are trying to come across as a unique and intriguing individual. Especially in the highly creative world of retailing, striking a creative posture in the cover letter can increase an employer's interest in you.

Dear Mrs. Carver:

I very much enjoyed our conversation this week and am looking forward to personally meeting some of your former colleagues at Maytel Fashions.

Prior to this, I would like to take the opportunity to respond more specifically to several of the areas we discussed.

1. **My fashion background**: I want to share with you an article which appeared in *Merchandising Today* entitled "Filene's turns its eye toward fashion in textiles" which contains photographs of me and my domestics buyer. The article credits me with putting Atlanta on the fashion map right along with Paris, Milan, and New York because of my aggressive—and highly profitable for Filene's—fashion orientation. I will not bother giving you a summary of the article since you can read it for yourself. Let me simply emphasize that I have an exceptionally strong fashion background and a proven ability to identify and cater to the customer's fashion tastes.

2. **My numbers skills**: As you will see from my enclosed resume, which you have already seen, I offer much more sophisticated financial skills than most retailing executives generally possess. In part, my financial expertise derives from my four years as the Operations Director with Sears. With both Filene's and Sears Department Store, I have aggressively assumed profit-and-loss responsibility. At Filene's, I am handling financial responsibilities generally assigned to a General Merchandise Manager while supervising a 15-store operation.

3. **Ability to track weekly financial progress**: Since financial control is such a critical ingredient in retailing success, it is an absolute requirement that executives at my level track weekly financial progress. I am accustomed to this discipline and would bring a style of rigorous financial management to Maytel. I'm a "numbers man," I can assure you of that.

Thank you very much for introducing me to Maytel.

Sincerely,

James Lawrence

Date

Exact Name of Person
Exact Title of Person
Exact Name of Organization
Address
City, State zip

Dear Exact Name:

Thank you for the time that you spent with me on Monday. I enjoyed our conversation and I enjoyed your insights about Quantas, Florida.

You suggested that I think about some of the key challenges that Quality Plus offers, and I have done so. Since we met and spoke at length, my thoughts have focused on two main areas.

1. I am enthusiastic about the performance-driven organizational climate at Quality Plus. This is the type of organization I am seeking, and I am confident that I could excel in any environment where initiative, creativity, and personal drive are encouraged. I am a results-oriented merchandiser who is continuously focused on priorities, and I possess the successful merchandiser's "sense of urgency." I believe I am, however, one of those unique hard chargers whom others regard as a congenial colleague and who prides myself on my ability to develop, motivate, and work effectively with others at all organizational levels.

2. I am excited about the creative challenge of joining a highly structured organization that is experiencing very rapid growth. I strongly believe that, especially in a growth mode, organizations need structure as well as disciplined executives to guide and harness that growth in the most productive fashion. I believe that creativity is best expressed in an environment where there is sufficient structure to ensure consistency and reliability in all operational areas.

I want you to know straightforwardly that I am very interested in joining your impressive team, and I am confident that I could make valuable contributions to Quality Plus through my experience, creativity, proven executive abilities, and highly motivated nature. I certainly appreciated all your courtesies to me, and I hope we shall be talking again soon.

Yours sincerely,

Your Name

FOLLOW-UP LETTER

Follow-up letter after an interview
If you are really interested in the job for which you interviewed, you should aggressively say so in the follow-up letter. Employers want you to court them.

Date

Exact Name of Person
Title or Position
Name of Company
Address (number and street)
Address (city, state, and zip)

FOLLOW-UP LETTER

Dear Exact Name of Person: (or Sir or Madam if answering a blind ad.)

How do I write a follow-up letter after an interview?
A picture is worth a thousand words. This follow-up letter after an effective interview "closed the sale" and helped a young restaurateur move into the financial accounting arena.

I am writing to express my appreciation for the time you spent with me on 9 December, and I want to let you know that I am sincerely interested in the position of Controller which you described.

I feel confident that I could skillfully interact with your 60-person work force in order to obtain the information we need to assure expert controllership of your diversified interests, and I would cheerfully travel as your needs require. I want you to know, too, that I would not consider relocating to Salt Lake City to be a hardship! It is certainly one of the most beautiful areas I have ever seen.

As you described to me what you are looking for in a controller, I had a sense of "déjà vu" because my current boss was in a similar position when I went to work for him. He needed someone to come in and be his "right arm" and take on an increasing amount of his management responsibilities so that he could be freed up to do other things. I have played a key role in the growth and profitability of his multiunit business, and he has come to depend on my sound financial and business advice as much as my day-to-day management skills. Since Christmas is the busiest time of the year in the restaurant business, I feel that I could not leave him during that time. I could certainly make myself available by mid-January.

If you felt you needed me to work with you during my vacation from the 26th until I go back to handle the New Year's business on the 29th, I would be happy to work with you as you close the books and handle end-of-year matters. Please note that I will be out of town from Saturday the 19th until Monday the 22nd visiting relatives.

It would be a pleasure to work for a successful individual such as yourself, and I feel I could contribute significantly to your business not only through my accounting and business background but also through my strong personal qualities of loyalty, reliability, and trustworthiness. I am confident that I could learn Quick Books rapidly, and I would welcome being trained to do things your way.

I send best wishes for the holidays, and I'd like to send a special compliment to your wife for the delicious cookies she baked!

Yours sincerely,

Jacob Evangelisto

Date

Exact Name of Person
Title or Position
Name of Company
Address (number and street)
Address (city, state, and zip)

Dear Exact Name of Person: (or Sir or Madam if answering a blind ad.)

I want you to know how much I enjoyed talking with you in Sioux Falls on Friday, December 12.

I fully understand the concept of developing retail applications in the convenience store industry. I believe you are aware that I performed essentially that job for the construction industry in a previous position. With Prime Computer Systems, I rose from System Programmer to Director of Development as I transformed a failing operation into an efficient and profitable business. The Building Material System product which I reengineered became the #1 product in the industry and is still one of the leading industry products.

As you are aware, I have developed expert knowledge of the convenience store industry in my current job. As Vice President of Management Information Systems (MIS), I was credited with making many major contributions to Scotchman, a 70-store convenience store chain, which made it an acquisition target of Texaco. Now that we are a part of the 1,100-store convenience store chain of Texaco, I am directing network systems development for this vastly larger organization. I understand Texaco's growth goals, as you explained them to me, and I feel I could become a valuable member of your management team in the strategic planning and implementation process.

One of my strengths at this point in my career is that I have a vast knowledge of many different areas, ranging from accounting systems and accounting development, to user interface, to putting together specifications, to the continual troubleshooting of problems and refinement of systems. It has been my responsibility to sit with technical experts in all functional areas and be able to assure the attainment of specific goals in their area of operation. I believe you already know much about my background, but I do want to reiterate that I offer expert knowledge of the convenience store industry from the user point of view, knowledge of the MMS product and system, along with expertise related to UNIX, NT, and programming.

Thank you for giving me so much of your time and letting me become better acquainted with your needs. I enclose a copy of my mileage statement and hotel statement. I believe I could become a valuable member of your management team.

Sincerely,

David R. Shelton

FOLLOW-UP LETTER

Follow-up letter after an interview which transmits expenses associated with the trip
Notice the last paragraph. A follow-up letter is an excellent opportunity to send your requests for reimbursement for any out-of-pocket expenses you incurred in connection with the interview.

Date

Exact Name of Person
Exact Title of Person
Exact Name of Organization
Address
City, State Zip

FOLLOW-UP LETTER

Follow-up letter after an interview
Employers find the interviewing process to be as draining and "plastic" as job hunters find it to be. That's why employers depend on follow-up letters to give them an indication of who really wants the job.

Dear Exact Name:

Thank you for the time you spent with me on Thursday and for arranging my subsequent meetings with other members of the Merck organization. My entire visit was handled in a most exemplary manner and inspired my confidence in the organization.

I was favorably impressed with everyone whom I met. They were all competent, intelligent, well prepared, and thorough during my meetings with them, which is evidence of Merck high standards. I have sent a separate letter to Patricia Simmons in order to follow up on several points that were raised during our discussion. I am sending you a blind copy of the letter.

I have a genuine interest in pursuing the opportunity at Merck. I feel that my highly motivated nature, disciplined work ethic, executive abilities, sales experience, and medical knowledge would combine very effectively with the dedicated professionals I met. I have enclosed my expense report along with appropriate receipts.

Thanks for your help.

Sincerely,

Your Name

Date

Exact Name of Person
Exact Title of Person
Exact Name of Organization
Address
City, State Zip

Dear Exact Name:

It was truly an honor for me to meet in person the brains behind the product and the system which I have come to know as XYA. I am even more aware now than I was before my visit that XYA is managed by extremely capable individuals most of whom, I learned, are solidly grounded in the accounting discipline.

Corrine and I both liked Loredo very much. We're partial to small towns and to the strong family values usually emphasized in such towns. After our visit, we could see ourselves living in Loredo and enjoying the special benefits of small town life.

I believe you already know much about my background, but I do want to reiterate that I offer expert knowledge of the industry from the user point of view, knowledge of the XYA product and system, along with expertise related to UNIX, NT, and programming. I am an extremely versatile professional who adapts easily to new projects and varied consulting assignments. I derive much satisfaction out of helping business people solve their problems, and I am skilled at establishing and maintaining effective working relationships at all organizational levels.

If you would like to add to your outstanding management team a highly creative problem-solver with a head full of common sense and expert knowledge of how your system works at the user level, I would like to express my interest in XYA. I think I could become a valuable addition to your already-outstanding team.

Thank you very much for giving me so much of your time and for letting me become better acquainted with the key decision makers and strategic thinkers at XYA.

Sincerely,

Your Name

FOLLOW-UP LETTER

Follow-up letter after an interview
Show a sincere interest in the company, in the town where the company is located, and in the nature of the employer's business. Employers are looking to find someone who would really like the job and enjoy the work.

Date

Exact Name of Person
Exact Title
Exact Name of Company
Address
City, State Zip

FOLLOW-UP LETTER

There's no one formula for a follow-up letter. Just be genuine, speak from the heart, and aggressively indicate that you feel you are the best person for the job, if that's what you think. A major executive position just came open in the company for which this individual has worked for more than 30 years, and he is responding within hours of his interview with a great follow-up letter expressing his strong interest in the position.

Dear Exact Name of Person: (or Dear Sir or Madam if answering a blind ad):

I enjoyed meeting with you yesterday, and after our discussion I am even more certain that I am the executive you are seeking as a Divisional Merchandising Manager of the Ready to Wear Division.

As you are aware, I offer a track record of achievements with Sears Department Stores, where I began working after high school. While excelling in numerous professional development and executive training programs, I feel as though I have earned my "Ph.D. in retailing" in my more than 30 years of experience with Sears.

I am proud of the significant contributions I have made to Sears' bottom line over the years, and I am known for my strong financial control and meticulous attention to detail. I am also known for my aggressive emphasis on team building and relationship building among the buying team, between the buyers and stores, and with vendors. Through the years, I have acquired the know-how which enables me to foster a results-oriented environment while providing the kind of supervision which buyers thrive on. I have come to believe that buyers are very unusual individuals, and I excel in mentoring, coaching, interacting with, motivating, supervising, and inspiring buyers of different experience levels.

You will see from my resume that I have utilized my personal initiative and expert knowledge of the shoe business to produce valuable bottom-line results. I am a youthful, energetic, and highly computer-proficient manager who could certainly continue to produce valuable bottom-line results as a Divisional Merchandise Manager, and I would cheerfully relocate as your needs require.

I believe in the intrinsic vitality of the Sears organization, and I want to continue to "make it happen" in Ladies' Ready to Wear.

Sincerely,

Michael Knight

Date

Exact Name of Person
Exact Title of Person
Exact Name of Organization
Address
City, State Zip

Dear Exact Name:

It was certainly a pleasure talking with you about the opportunity to work for Davis Enterprises, and I appreciated your providing me with extensive detail about what would be involved.

As I believe you know, I am highly regarded in my current position and have only started investigating other opportunities because, after over 15 years with Ignatius, I feel that I would like to tackle a different kind of challenge. The job you described is of great interest to me and is one in which I feel I could excel.

As you expand into different retail markets, I have experience and skills that could be of enormous value to you. With a reputation as a fast learner and resourceful problem solver, I have often been specially selected to play a key role in opening new stores, getting employees trained, and making sure that the new operation is established in the most efficient manner. Solving problems—and trying to view them as opportunities—is second nature to me now, as my management position at Food Lion requires me to solve a wide variety of problems all day long.

At the end of the day, of course, profitability and efficiency are what we all are seeking and measuring, and I offer a strong bottom-line orientation which would complement your fine management team. From what I know so far about the company, I believe Thadeus, Inc., would offer the congenial colleagues and aggressive strategic corporate goals which I am seeking in an employer.

If you feel, as I do, that I could play a valuable role in your expansion plans, I hope you will contact me to suggest the next step in this process. Again, it was surely a pleasure meeting you, and I appreciated your professional courtesies toward me.

Sincerely,

Your Name

FOLLOW-UP LETTER

Employers often wonder why a senior executive wants to change jobs. You may want to anticipate that curiosity and give the employer some insight into the reason for your desire to make a change.

Date

Exact Name of Person
Exact Title of Person
Exact Name of Organization
Address
City, State Zip

FOLLOW-UP LETTER

When you are changing fields, it is especially important to write a follow-up letter after an interview to cement your credibility. Employers don't want to train someone who will be with them only a few months, so you can emphasize your strong interest in the position in the letter you write after the interview.

Dear Exact Name:

I would like to take this opportunity to thank you for considering me for the interview on August 16, 1999 as an Account Executive for Bayer Consumer Products. I enjoyed meeting with you and being able to learn more about the company. I believe that Bayer Consumer Products has a quality product line, and I would be honored to represent these products.

Thank you very much for considering my busy schedule as a State Parole Officer and allowing me to come back for the second interview in the same afternoon. I am an extremely reliable and dependable professional, and I appreciated your professional courtesies in helping me be away from my current job as little as possible.

Please be assured of my deep commitment to changing careers from the law enforcement field to sales and marketing. As we discussed during the interview, I was recruited aggressively after college graduation by my current employer, and I was attracted to the parole field because of my interest in helping others. Although I have excelled professionally, I have decided to channel my highly ambitious nature and strong bottom-line orientation into a career in sales.

I am very excited about the position we discussed, and I am confident I could excel in both the training and in the job itself. I am known for my excellent ability to establish and maintain strong working relationships. I can provide exceptionally strong personal and professional references at the appropriate time. Thank you for talking with me and helping me learn more about your fine company, and I hope to hear from you soon.

Sincerely,

Your Name

Last Will and Testament:
Letters That Express Your Final Wishes

It is not the purpose of this book to provide legal advice, but we do feel we must include in such a book a letter which serves as one's parting wishes in life.

The Last Will and Testament was written for a man of modest means who simply wanted to put on paper and have a record of his thoughts regarding the disposition of his earthly assets.

Like any letter which you write to record your thoughts and express your opinions and instructions, writing your Last Will and Testament can be a comfort to you and provide peace of mind.

Please seek appropriate legal advice in this area and read the example which follows as merely a simple and brief example of a document or letter that all of us need to write at some time.

LAST WILL AND TESTAMENT

OF

CHANDLER McDOOGAL, JR.

I, Chandler McDoogal, Jr., currently residing at 5990 Fortitude Avenue, Austin, TX 78325, being of sound mind and demonstrating sound memory and understanding, do hereby make and publish and do declare this to be my Last Will and Testament, published on December 30, 1999, and hereby revoking and making null and void any and all papers of a similar nature by me at any time heretofore.

First: I order and direct that my executors herein named shall pay all my just debts and funeral expenses, as soon after my demise as may conveniently be done.

Second: All of my clothing, tools, pictures, and jewelry, except my wedding ring, I bequeath to my co-executor Chandler McDoogal III, my son.

Third: All other property, insurance, checking account, and retirement funds will go to my wife and Chief Executor Mable McDoogal. No Executrix appointed under this Will will need post a Bond Surety or other security in this or any other jurisdiction. I, Chandler McDoogal, Jr., the Testatrix whose name is signed to the attached or foregoing instrument, having been duly qualified according to law, do hereby acknowledge that I signed the executed instrument as my Law Will and that I signed it willingly as my free and voluntary act for the purposes therein expressed.

Signature: _____

Chandler McDoogal, Jr.

Date: _____

EXPRESSING YOUR FINAL WISHES

Of course there are many ways to make your wishes known regarding your estate. Numerous professionals can help you. On this page is a very simple last will and testament, just to give you an idea of what a very simple last will looks like.

Legal Letters and Notices

Quite often you find it necessary to prepare letters related to some legal issue. Instead of presenting legal letters related to a wide variety of legal matters, we have chosen to show samples of letters written to support one individual's point of view in a bitter custody battle between a husband and a wife.

If you must ever write a letter of support for a friend who is engaged in a legal struggle such as child custody, or if you find it necessary to communicate your opinion related to legal situations, these letters may be helpful to you.

You will find legal letters in other sections of this book, too, so consult the Table of Contents. For example, you might want to consult other sections including Letters of Appeal, Collections Letters, Letters of Support, and Letters of Understanding and Intent.

Child Custody Proposal prepared by Alice Warner for David Warner:

CHILD CUSTODY PROPOSAL PREPARED BY A WIFE IN A CUSTODY SETTLEMENT

Many matters need to be put in writing in the course of a divorce settlement, and this letter shows the basic content of a child custody proposal.

I, Alice Warner, would like to be awarded primary custody of our son, David Warner, Jr., born October 5, 1989. I propose that I be given primary physical custody of David during the week and that his father, Michael Warner, be awarded visitation rights giving him physical custody of David every other weekend. Visitation would begin at 7:00 P.M. on Friday and end at 7:00 P.M. on Sunday. I agree to additional weekend visitations above those in this proposal, as mutually agreed on by Michael and me.

In regard to major holidays, in order to ensure fairness, I feel that we should alternate custody on major holidays. David would spend Mother's Day with me, and he would spend Father's Day with Michael. Christmas, Halloween, New Years, Thanksgiving, and David's birthday, we would alternate. I would also agree to allow Michael to have custody of David for 45 days every summer. Although Angela Hastings is not the biological daughter of Michael Warner and the court has awarded no custody rights to him, Michael Warner has raised her since she was 2½ years old. He is Dad to her, and as such, I agree to allow him visitation of Angela at the same times as he has visitation to David. The only limitation to this portion of the proposal is that I feel Angela should have the right to decide whether or not she wants to go with him for a particular visitation, as she is a young lady now and does not always wish to be with her parents when she can be with her friends. Michael would be welcome to see Angela as often as he would like to exercise that privilege and it is agreeable with her.

The purpose of proposing that custody be handled in this manner is to cause as little change in the children's lives as possible. I would like for them to be together throughout the week, as they have always been together on school days and are used to living in the same household. The children are close, and it would be wrong to separate them.

I would like to retain possession of our home at 1110 Hay Street. The children and I need a place to reside and it would only be right to give them back the only home they have known for the last seven years. I would like to retain possession of my 1997 Subaru, as it was purchased as my source of transportation when we traded in my previous automobile. I need the car in order to have a reliable source of transportation for the children and myself. I would like to have the animals, which include two Dalmatians, one snake, one ferret, and two cats.

I plan to attend school full-time in order to learn the skills I need to take up a profession in which I can earn enough to support the children and myself in the lifestyle to which we are accustomed. I agree to keep Michael fully informed of the children's progress at school, make sure that he has copies of report cards, and is informed of all special events at school in order to give him the opportunity to participate as fully as possible in the children's lives. Michael will be provided with a phone number and a pager number so that he can reach me at all times. I will agree to Michael's participating in any of the children's school and sports activities regardless of his visitation times.

Sincerely,

Alice Warner

Letter of Support and Affidavit by Casey Jones for Marcia Foster:

I have known Marcia Foster for 11 years—we met through a mutual friend. Upon meeting her, we became instant close friends. I had been diagnosed with Hodgkin's Disease—a cancer of the lymph nodes; at the time, she was very sympathetic and concerned about what I was going through. She was one of very few friends who chose to become involved, rather than disappear from my life. We even became roommates, and she took it upon herself to see that I made my medical appointments.

During a particularly difficult time, I quit taking chemotherapy, as I was finding the side effects virtually impossible to deal with. She found a different doctor to consult with me and directed me to University Medical Center. Upon my arrival there, I was told by oncologists that I had less than six months to live unless a new variety of chemotherapy worked for me. They implemented a last-resort protocol that I could better deal with, yet also, amazingly, cured my cancer. My white blood-cell count was dangerously low on several occasions due to my inefficient immune system. On these occasions, she literally forced me into the hospital; once, I was told that had I not been admitted, I would not have lived through the night. At that time, dealing with my medical problems was a full-time job for me—and for her, as she was my primary support system. Despite her enormous commitment of time and energy to helping me in this time of difficulty, she still found time to be a devoted mother to her daughter.

Shortly after this time, she married Peter Foster. After a very difficult pregnancy and an even more difficult delivery, she gave birth to a son. I've never seen a mother more protective, proud, and attentive to her children. Her daughter and son worship her like children rarely do these days—I've interacted with the three of them more than enough to know. She has functioned as a single mother in spite of the fact that she was married. With her husband away most of the time, she has had to play both mother and father roles. As long as I've known her, her children have never failed to come first and foremost. I never have, nor could I ever, imagine Marcia Foster endangering her children in any possible way.

I have been free of cancer now for eight years. I am happily married, gainfully employed, and have been able to see my own daughter reach the age of almost thirteen. I'm very lucky to have had the opportunity to have Marcia in my life—I might not be here, otherwise. I feel that her children deserve the same opportunity.

Sincerely,

Name

Date

Sworn before me _____ Signature _____

Traverse County, TX

Notary _____

My commission expires _____

LETTER OF SUPPORT AND AFFIDAVIT

During a divorce proceeding, friends are often asked to provide supporting documentation. Here is an example of a letter of reference provided by a friend.

STATE OF SOUTH CAROLINA, COUNTY OF DADE
AGREEMENT

LEGAL FINANCIAL AGREEMENT

In a divorce settlement, lots of decisions have to be made about property and debts. Here is an agreement prepared by divorcing spouses outlining their respective financial responsibilities and obligations.

   WHEREAS, Martha Reasford Giltz and Barry Smilingford were married on or about 10 September, 1985; and

   WHEREAS, they purchased certain real property described as 1605 Morganton Road and borrowed money from First Citizens Banking & Trust in the principal amount of $84,800.00; and

   WHEREAS, they are both jointly and severally liable for this debt, with monthly payments in the amount of $662.00; and

   WHEREAS, the parties have now separated and Barry Smilingford has agreed to retain possession of this real property and assume responsibility for all payments due under the Note to First Citizens, as well as all obligations including but not limited to taxes, insurance, maintenance and upkeep on the above referenced property; and

   WHEREAS, Martha Reasford Giltz has agreed to vacate the property so long as Barry Smilingford assumes responsibility for payments as set forth above.

   NOW THEREFORE, know all men by these presents for and in consideration of the mutual covenants and conditions contained herein, the parties do agree as follows:

   1) Barry Smilingford shall reside in the home located at 1605 Morganton Road, and shall assume responsibility for all payments and obligations under that certain Note to First Citizens as set forth above. Barry Smilingford shall also be responsible for the payment of all taxes, insurance, maintenance, repair, and any and all funds due in relation to the above property. Barry Smilingford further agrees to indemnify and hold harmless Martha Reasford Giltz for any and all claims against her for any of the payments hereinafter assumed by Barry Smilingford.

   2) Martha Reasford Giltz agrees to vacate the premises and reside elsewhere so long as Barry Smilingford fulfills his obligations under this agreement.

   IN WITNESS WHEREOF, the parties hereunto set their hands and seals this 30 day of December, 1999.

_____

_____

Witness   Barry Smilingford

_____

_____

Witness   Martha Reasford Giltz

Date

Mr. Stan Miller
Miller Realty & Appraisal
312 E. University Street
P.O. Box 875
San Francisco, CA 90234

Dear Stan:

Reference: Extasis Property

I am writing in reference to your phone conversations with me on August 31st and September 1st of this week regarding the Extasis Property and also in reference to the extension of time through September 4, 1999, expiring on the Extasis Property Option Agreement.

The Extasis family and I assume that you have no further interest. We consider your Option Agreement null and expired.

It has been a pleasure meeting and working with you, and I send my best regards.

Yours truly,

Bill Tucker, President
Bill Tucker Realty

CC: Stephanos Extasis

LETTER OF NOTICE REGARDING AN OPTION AGREEMENT

Real estate transactions often require letters at strategic stages in the purchasing process. This letter provided written notification that an Option Agreement is null and expired.

Letters of Apology

Sometimes we find ourselves in a situation in which we must apologize for something we have done or for a problem we may have caused. In this section, you will find a letter of apology written by a businessperson to another businessperson.

As with any apology we make in life, the problem for which we must apologize is frequently not our fault, or certainly not entirely our fault. Sometimes we apologize because we want to make the other party feel that we do take seriously the difficulties which have occurred.

The letter of apology in this section was written by a business in an attempt to salvage good will and maintain a working relationship with the other party.

Date

Mr. Wilson Price
Price, Jones, and Wilson
1110 Hay Street
Austin, TX 28307

Dear Mr. Wilson:

I am writing this letter to apologize most sincerely for the distress you have been caused by the actions of Dingbat Stephens, former employee of PEOPLEFIND Personnel, who was terminated for professional misconduct on November 19, 1999. I was not aware until nearly a week after her termination, when Simona Said's probation officer called our office at 4 P.M. on November 25 to ask for Dingbat Stephens, that Mrs. Stephens had placed someone in your office who had a criminal record. Because of Dingbat Stephens's poor attitude, crude manner, and unprofessional conduct, I terminated her employment with PEOPLEFIND for cause. She walked out of my office cursing in front of customers and, when she left, she still was in possession of the keys to my office and to my post office box. On November 19 between 10 A.M. and 3 P.M., I had Jackson Locksmith come to my office to change the locks on all my office doors.

When your administrative assistant Shirley Mason called me today, I was shocked to learn that one of my employees had knowingly placed a felon in your firm without notifying you. Mrs. Mason also informed me that you terminated the employment of Simona Said and then changed all the locks on your office building after terminating her. Shirley Mason called today to say that you thought it would be fair for PEOPLEFIND Personnel to pay for the costs associated with your having your office locks changed. I suggested to her that your law firm and PEOPLEFIND Personnel team up to take Mrs. Stephens to Small Claims Court to recover the expenses you incurred because of Dingbat Stephens.

I called your office again this afternoon to ask Mrs. Mason how much you have paid to have your locks changed, but she was not in. My thrifty Scottish-Irish nature does not allow me to say that I will pay for something until I know what the cost is. I left a message for Mrs. Mason to please call me with information about the exact amount that you have paid to have your locks changed. **I am asking that you provide me with a copy of your locksmith's bill along with a letter stating that you feel you had to change your locks because of the actions of Dingbat Stephens.** I intend to take Dingbat Stephens to Small Claims Court to recover the money, and I wish to use that letter in Small Claims Court.

I do not take lightly what happened as a result of Dingbat Stephens's unprofessional behavior. Please send me the locksmith's bill and the brief note I asked for and I will try to see that proper action is taken.

Sincerely,

Christine Ysi

LETTER OF APOLOGY

Businesspeople as well as individuals sometimes have to make apologies. Here you see a letter of apology written from one business to another regarding an incident caused by a derelict employee.

Letters Of Appreciation

Sometimes we find ourselves in a situation in which we must write a letter of praise or appreciation to an individual or about an individual.

Letters of appreciation can be highly valued by the people receiving them, and it is sometimes easier to express our gratitude in writing than verbally.

Letters of appreciation can be used to express an employer's feelings about a job well done by an employee. In the military, formal Letters of Commendation are awarded to individuals in recognition of exemplary performance.

Letters of appreciation can also be written to show a consumer's thanks for special treatment he received as a customer. In the example in this section, you see a letter written as a compliment to an employee.

Victoria Secret
1110 Hay Street
DeLimits, Missouri 89324

Date

To Whom It May Concern:

My name is Victoria Secret. I would like to let you know how well we were treated at State Line Games in McColl, South Carolina. Our group has been going there for the last two weeks. We generally have a group of six to ten of us when we go. We used to go to South of the Border, but we were treated so graciously at State Line that we always go there now.

The girls in the rooms are very nice, and so is the young fellow they call Tony—he goes out of his way to do everything for our group, to make sure we are happy. Then there is the man they call "Mr. Vince." He is a real gentleman. He is always kidding with everyone in the place—everyone talks about how nice he is to everyone.

The atmosphere in your place is just beautiful, and the decorations are very attractive and create the feeling that your customers are "at home." We love State Line Games and you can count on us to be your steady customers.

Thanks,

Victoria Secret

LETTER OF APPRECIATION

It's nice to take the time to thank someone for a job well done, and this customer felt so well treated that she took the time to write a letter complimenting the employees of a frequently visited entertainment spot.

Letters Of Introduction

There are situations in which it is appropriate to write a letter of introduction.

If you are seeking a new job, you will find sample letters to use in the "Changing Careers" Section. Usually a letter that accompanies a resume is called a "cover letter" or "letter of interest." A cover letter is a letter introducing a resume and introducing any special circumstances (i.e., your desire to change fields or your decision to relocate) not mentioned in the resume which might cause the potential employer to think favorably of you.

In this section you will find a letter of introduction used by a consultant to introduce his services to potential client corporations.

The second example you will see in this section is the letter of introduction and fact sheet used by a business to introduce its services to the public. You will find letters of introduction in other sections of this book, too. For example, in the Business Marketing Letters and Press Releases section, you will find numerous letters of introduction including a letter of introduction from a specialty steel company and a letter of introduction used in a mass mailing.

ROY PARKER, Jr.
525 Country Club Drive
Livingstone, AL 85324
(910) 483-6611

Date

Exact Name
Chief Executive Officer
Exact Company Name
Address
City, state zip

Dear

With this letter, I would like to introduce the diversified consulting expertise which I could put to work for your company. I am single and available for worldwide relocation, and I would cheerfully travel as extensively as your needs require.

Extensive knowledge of styrenic polymers and polystyrenes

In 1998 I assumed the Technology Development Group in FASTNER Co., a producer of styrenic polymers and in particular polystyrenes for major appliances. I came into the company on an 18-month project and assumed responsibility for the following:
- Market development programs
- ISO-9002 implementation, manuals, training, suppliers' conformance
- Statistical analysis
- Process optimization
- Conformance with international regulatory requirements – FDA, BGA, UL, AAMVA
- **Accomplishments:** The ISO implementation program was completed on time despite numerous obstacles, and the market development program was also completed on time and within budget with the result that the company's market share has increased 3%.

Extensive experience related to asphalts
- Market and Product Evaluation Project related to asphalt membranes for MOTOROLA in Brazil in 1997
- Soil Stabilization Project in Mexico in 1995
- Soil Stabilization Project in 1997 related to road construction, airports, and railway embankments in San Argentina
- Projects involving Evaluation of Impact Modifiers in asphalts

Considered one of the world's foremost experts in the technologies described above, I am interested in assignments where I can make a leading contribution. I am eager to be held accountable for my results and hope you will contact me soon.

Yours sincerely,

Roy Parker, Jr.

LETTER OF INTRODUCTION

A consultant might use a letter like this to introduce himself and his services to companies which might be able to use his experience and abilities.

Date

Exact Name
Chief Executive Officer
Exact Company Name
Address
City, state zip

LETTER OF INTRODUCTION TO A BUSINESS

This letter of introduction is intended to accompany the business fact sheet on the facing page. Together they introduce and market the services of a business.

Dear

With the enclosed fact sheet, I would like to introduce myself and the services I can offer your company. If you answer "yes" to any of the following questions, you may be in need of my services:

Would you like to give your exteriors a "facelift" and make your business "shine?"

Would you like a free demonstration of how we can save you money through our quality services?

For an overview of who we are and what we do, please look at the enclosed "fact sheet" about our business and services. We can work anytime during the day or night in order to cause the least disruption to your business, customer traffic, and cash flow!

Please call me as soon as you look over the fact sheet enclosed, and I can schedule a time to give you a free estimate and demonstration of our services. Even if you are not sure if you need our services, let me come to see you for 15 minutes to show you what I can do for your business!

Best wishes,

Kyle Hendricks, Owner

PACIFIC PRESSURE WASHING & COATING

Kyle Hendricks, Owner
1605 Morganton Road, Dallas, TX 34099
Phone: 910-430-6611   Pager: 1-800-555-1212   Fax: 910-483-2439

OBJECTIVE *To offer quality services related to pressure washing and coating.*

THINGS YOU CAN COUNT ON:
- Perfect safety record
- Fully insured through BB&T and licensed for all jobs; $1 million of protection.
- Full Worker's Compensation available on all employees
- Competitive rates
- Satisfaction Guaranteed

SERVICES, MATERIALS, AND COATINGS:
In addition to pressure washing your exterior, we are expert in applying a variety of coatings to help you revitalize your old and worn concrete and spare you the expense of replacing it. Coatings come in a variety of patterns, designs, and colors. Pictorial portfolio available for review. Revitalize your concrete and select from the latest patterns which include rock patterns and brick patterns! Monthly and quarterly cleaning services provided!

SOME OF OUR CUSTOMERS:
We serve primarily business and commercial customers, who include:
- Dellwood Schools
- Dellwood Housing Office
- Cargill, Inc.
- Burger King and McDonald's Corporations
- Dellwood Apartment Association

WHAT OUR CUSTOMERS SAY:
Atlantic Pressure Washing and Coating saved me thousands of dollars and inconvenience by coating my concrete. Coated concrete is easier to clean and maintain!"
—G. Byrd, business owner
"I appreciated the way Atlantic was willing to work in the early hours of the morning to clean my concrete parking lot. This allowed me to give my business a clean look without causing my customers any inconvenience, and without interrupting my cash flow!" —N. Bates, restaurant chain CEO

EQUIPMENT USED:
We believe the best result is achieved by utilizing the best equipment in addition to well-trained personnel. We use state-of-the-art equipment including: Two LANDA self-contained units. Hot water units: one mounted on 16' trailer; one self-contained unit in full-size mobile van. 3,000 PSI. Temperature: 300 degrees maximum. Special adapters for special jobs.

ABOUT THE OWNER:
Kyle Hendricks holds a B.S. degree in Business.

FACT SHEET INTRODUCING THE SERVICES OF A BUSINESS

The letter on the facing page and this business fact sheet were designed as companion documents to be used in mass mailings, to hand out to potential customers on site, and to utilize in a variety of ways to introduce the business and its services.

Letters Of Invitation

There are many situations in life in which we find ourselves in need of writing an invitation of some type. In this section you will find suitable letters of invitation for social and business purposes.

Invitations can be in the form of a letter or can be presented in other styles. You will see optional techniques of inviting people to functions and events.

Unless your invitation must be very formally presented, you can even consider expressing your invitation in the form of a post card if you want to economize on mailing costs.

If you want people to respond to your invitation and notify you in advance if they will be accepting your invitation, you may ask them to "R.S.V.P." either in writing or by telephone. Borrowed from the French language, "Respondez s'il vous plait" means "please reply." If is often helpful to know how many guests will be attending your event if, for example, you are serving food and want to know how many people to plan for. See the invitation on page 154 for an example.

PEOPLEFIND, INC.
1110 Hay Street, Peoria, GA 23986
910-483-1166

Date

Ms. Samantha Smith
234 Litener Street
Albuquerque, GA 28301

Dear Ms. Smith:

You are cordially invited to a Job Fair sponsored by PEOPLEFIND. This Jobs Fair program will be held in Albuquerque, GA, on April 26-27. This is an all-expenses-paid program, although there is a $30 security deposit for damages. There will be two persons per room.

Transportation will be made available on a first-come, first-served basis. Hope to see you!

Please call for more information at 1-910-483-6611 and to make your room reservations and arrangements for transportation.

Sincerely,

Wyette Jones
Vice President

LETTER OF INVITATION

Businesses have numerous reasons to invite people to events, and this letter shows how a letter of invitation can be prepared.

INVITATION TO A BOY SCOUT EAGLE CEREMONY

An Eagle ceremony is a big event in a young man's life, and this is one form in which the invitation to this special event can be extended.

Mr. and Mrs. Delaney Jones

cordially invite you to attend

Boy Scouts of America Troop 787

Eagle Scout Court of Honor

for their son

BRANDON ERVIN JONES

On Tuesday, December 22, 1999

at 7:15 P.M.

St. Anthony Episcopal Church

1875 Ellerslie Road

Ft. Worth, TX

Please join us for the reception which follows.

R.S.V.P. 483-6611 by December 18

Date

Exact Name
Chief Executive Officer
Exact Company Name
Address
City, state zip

Dear Sir or Madam:

This letter is to invite you to the inaugural meeting of the Save America Foundation, designed to promote better government. You have been specially selected to receive this invitation because someone has recommended that you receive an invitation based on your reputation as a patriotic American.

The purpose of the Foundation is to promote better government through letter-writing campaigns, political rallies, and other events designed to raise public awareness of and involvement in local, state, and federal government.

Appropriately, our first meeting will be held on Independence Day, July 4, 1999, at 12 noon, in the sanctuary of First Baptist Church, 22 Conroy Street, Atlanta. Possible activities may include public speakers, patriotic songs, and the discussion of future activities for the Foundation. Refreshments will be provided.

Thank you in advance for you support. We look forward to seeing you on July 4th!

Yours sincerely,

Mason Brite III

LETTER OF INVITATION

There are numerous charities and nonprofit organizations in the world, and they all have their first meeting! This letter invites like-minded spirits to an organizational meeting of a political group.

Letters Of Negotiation

Sometimes we find ourselves in situations in which we must negotiate a satisfactory conclusion to a matter about which there have been differences of opinion.

Often letters of negotiation involve monetary settlements but not always.

In this section, you will see an example of a letter of negotiation, and you will see that the language is precise and the tone objective.

There are other letters of negotiation in this book. For example, on page 108 you will see a letter sent to an attorney to settle an account for less than the amount billed. In the Collections Letters section, you will see letters intended to negotiate the resolution of a debt.

In the Letters of Appeal and Letters of Complaint sections, there are letters designed to negotiate matters ranging from a medical board's decision to a supervisor's written performance evaluation. You will also find letters with a negotiating spirit in the Legal Letters section and in the Letters related to Consumer Credit and Finance section.

Date

295 DoLittle Road
Ft. Lauderdale, FL 92387

Commissioner of Insurance
Post Office Box 26387
Miami, FL 29887

Dear Sir or Madam:

In reference to Abundant Insurance Company, file number P-1999-08-00456, we have not received any response from our last letter. As previously stated on the enclosed letter, our offer to settle was $11,048.64 net.

Abundant Insurance's offer was $10,325.00 net. The difference is $723.64. In the spirit of compromise, we are prepared to reduce our offer respectively by $361.82 in an effort to meet Abundant Insurance halfway and resolve the issue. Our new net offer stands at (1) $10,686.82 or (2) the vehicle and $9,086.18.

We question the legality of Abundant Insurance taking control of the vehicle and refusing to pay fair market value. In addition, I enclose a letter from the loan company demanding payment on the vehicle.

Sincerely,

Jason Edwards

Enc.

LETTER OF NEGOTIATION

Although much can be done verbally in negotiating prices and deals, there usually comes a point when things have to be put in writing. Here is an example of a letter intended to negotiate an insurance claim.

About Enclosures

This letter mentions that the writer is sending an enclosure. At the bottom left of the letter, the "Enc." refers the reader to that enclosure. If you do enclose another document with your letter, the general rule is to refer to the enclosure in your letter.

DAVIS CONSULTING
1110 ½ Hay Street, Dallas, TX 28305

Telephone: 483-6611　　　fax: (910) 483-2439　　　preppub@aol.com

Date

Mrs. Judy Gilverson
525 Morganton Road
Dallas, TX 84509

LETTER OF NEGOTIATION

Unfortunately, people sometimes have differences of opinion in business relationships which cause their relationship to sour. A series of events caused this business to lose the services of its freelance graphics designer, and this letter in intended to clarify the remaining financial obligations and technical responsibilities of the parties involved.

Dear Judy:

This letter is intended to clarify our professional relationship and to notify you of the conditions which must exist if that relationship is to continue. As you are aware, in June 1999 you solicited our office by telephone and made us aware of your services as a publicist and freelance graphics designer. We met in my office and in June 1999, you agreed to become our freelance graphics designer for seven projects which you knew had a completion date of Fall 2000—and therefore a printing deadline of May 2000. In selling you and your services to David Consulting, you bragged about how you could take information in any form—even on the back of envelopes, etc.—and turn that information into professionally designed matter.

A joyful event occurred in your life—you became pregnant—during the process of your creating the advertising and publicity materials for those projects, and your lack of availability to do your job as your pregnancy advanced caused problems in our production schedule. To make matters worse, you encouraged us to change typography and layout in the last stage of the design process, and the changes you made caused numerous internal problems, which you were unavailable to help us resolve because you were bedridden and then recovering from pregnancy. In your final stages of pregnancy, you submitted the materials for the final three projects, and those materials were clearly not up to your usual standards. You even apologized when you submitted the materials to me, saying that you felt like a failure and that you thought you should just "start over, from scratch." I told you to give me the materials anyway, that I would look them over.

You have acted quite petulant during the final stages of finishing these publicity and advertising materials. After my office assistant drove some printed pages by your apartment one day (because you were in advanced pregnancy and unable to drive), you called our office to express your hostile indignation and to say that you thought you should pull out of the project and let us create the advertising. You were insinuating that we were as much the graphics designer as you were. The only reason my staff was very involved in the graphics design process was that our deadlines were right on top of us and you were unavailable to do what you should have been doing.

You also pestered me repeatedly in January and February, insisting that you wanted us to change printers because you felt the out-of-town printer was more aesthetically in tune with your design sensibilities. I told you repeatedly that we had worked with our printer for years and had negotiated excellent prices and turnaround times. You seem to have held a grudge because I did not want to change printers halfway through the project, and your attitude deteriorated because you could not exercise complete creative control of the project (from your bedridden state).

I believe it has been almost a month since your son was born, and it is time for you to finish your commitments to Davis Consulting if you intend to. As I told you on the phone tonight, I believe you should start over, as you suggested yourself, on the advertisements and brochures for the final three projects.

And, no, we do not want the hospital picture of your baby to be in the seventh ad which relates to the long-term advantages of term life insurance. (Your son's baby picture is beautiful, but we do not want his newborn picture in the ad.)

I need you to finish your responsibilities, which will involve your coming into my office to discuss the problems on the remaining advertising and publicity materials and to finish them off in a very timely manner. You are aware that there are remaining publicity materials which need to be sent to the printer by May 15. If you are unable to finish this work because of physical or mental problems, I will have no choice other than to make other arrangements to have the work completed which you agreed to do. If that happens, I will not pay the final invoices which you have submitted because I do not accept the creative concept or the work presented on the final three projects.

If I do not hear from you by close of business on Monday, April 12, indicating your interest in continuing in and finishing the projects, I will consider our relationship terminated and I will consider my financial obligations to you to be paid in full.

Yours sincerely,

Bryant Davis

LETTER OF NEGOTIATION

The next step for these two parties will probably be small claims court. This letter can be used later to clarify what the business felt were its rights and responsibilities at the date of the letter. As you can see, this is also a **letter of notice of impending termination** if specific responsibilities are not met in a timely way.

Letters Of Nomination
(see also Reference Letters)

Sometimes we wish to nominate someone for an award or position, and the vehicle for doing so is often a letter.

The language in a letter of nomination is often flowery and poetic, although a letter must give sufficient details to provide credibility.

For example, in the letter of nomination in this section, you will see a letter written by a college professor for a young college student whom the educator wanted to nominate for a prestigious leadership award. Notice that the professor has cited specific examples of the young lady's leadership qualities and accomplishments. Remember that it's usually the details that create credibility, so be prepared to provide specific "testimonials" and examples of situations which illustrate your opinions.

If you can make your reader aware of three main points about the individual you are nominating, your letter will probably have coherence and clarity. For example, you might want to give your reader the impression that the nominee (1) has integrity, (2) is persistent, and (3) is academically gifted. Focusing on no more than three main points in a single letter will make your observations seem detailed and specific, and you will probably be able to describe at least one situation illustrating each of the points you are trying to make.

Other letters of this type may be found in the Reference Letters section on page 200.

Date

Nancy Susan Reynolds Awards
Z. Smith Reynolds Foundation
101 Reynolds Village
Winston-Salem, NC 27106-5199

Dear Awards Committee:

In nomination for A Special Kind of Leadership Award, I would like to place the name of Mamie Gilbert.

I have had the pleasure of observing Ms. Gilbert in leadership situations during the four years she has been a student on the campus of Florida State University. In her freshman year, she became a valuable member of her intramural basketball team, and she was elected team captain. In the fall of her sophomore year, she ran for elected office and was defeated in a close race for a spot on the Student Senate. While many people give up after such a defeat, Ms. Gilbert plucked up her courage and ran for a senate seat six months later. The second time, she won. I have much admiration for the kind of leader who does not give up. She seemed to understand that from defeat we often learn how to win the next time. She seemed to view her earlier defeat as a learning experience and she turned a negative result into a positive outcome later.

I have come to admire Ms. Gilbert for the generous way in which she donates her spare time to worthy volunteer causes. She has utilized her leadership ability in garnering support for Habitat for Humanity activities. A vivacious individual and a charismatic public speaker, Ms. Garner has spoken at church meetings and civic organizations about Habitat activities, and local Habitat officials privately give her much credit for the growing number of college students now involved with Habitat.

Although many recipients of the Leadership Award might view the award as a "badge" and honor that would look good on a resume, I believe Ms. Gilbert would view the A Special Kind of Leadership Award as inspiration for even greater leadership accomplishments in the future.

If the Z. Smith Reynolds Foundation intends to motivate and inspire gifted young leaders and to impel them to even greater actions on behalf of humanity, then I nominate Mamie Gilbert for the A Special Kind of Leadership Award and urge the board to favor this outstanding young leader with the special encouragement and blessing that the Nancy Susan Reynolds Awards Program has come to represent.

Thank you.

Sincerely,

David Diaz

LETTER OF NOMINATION

It is such a pleasure to nominate a special person for a special award which they deserve, but it can be nerve-wracking if you aren't sure of the format and style you should use in order to do justice to the nominee. Here is a letter written from the heart and containing the kind of details which create credibility.

Letters Of Notice

It may not be your favorite thing to do, but sometimes you must provide written notice of your intention to do something. On the page which follows, you will see examples of letters composed to provide official notice of an event or action.

There are other letters of notice in other sections of this book. For example, in the Collections Letters section, you will find letters which give notice of the intent to file action in small claims court if a debt is not paid.

In the letter on page 108, you will see a letter written to notify an attorney that his fee will not be paid in full because of malfeasance.

The letter on page 174 gives notice to a marginal employee that her misconduct will not be tolerated.

On page 158-159 you can read a letter written to a freelance designer defining terms of project completion and giving notice that the business relationship will be terminated if key responsibilities are not taken care of.

SIMONS COMMERCIAL REAL ESTATE
22 Carowinds, Suite 120
Dallas, TX 89345
(910) 483-6611

Date

Texas Real Estate Commission
P.O. Box 17100
Dallas, TX 89319-7100

Dear Sir or Madam:

Effective today—October 30, 1999—the address for Simons Commercial Real Estate is 22 Carowinds, Suite 120, Dallas, TX 89345.

The old address was 620 Bow Court, Dallas, TX 89456.

The applicable license number is TX 7098.

Sincerely,

Perry Simons

LETTER OF NOTICE TO REAL ESTATE COMMISSION

A letter of notice can be brief and to the point, such as this one.

Date

Daughters of the American Revolution (DAR)
Atlanta Chapter
c/o Delores Vanderbuilt
1921 Weymouth Street
Atlanta, GA 87645-4115

LETTER OF NOTICE FROM A TREASURER REGARDING A BANK ACCOUNT

Those who administer finances for volunteer and other organizations often need to prepare letters of notice in their capacity as treasurer.

RE: Account #87667027898

To whom it may concern:

    I, Martha Baer, serve as Treasurer for the Atlanta Chapter of the Daughters of the American Revolution (DAR).

    On the 22nd of September, 1999, I was sworn in as Treasurer for the chapter. On the 24th of September I updated the signature card for the chapter's savings account. The only two (2) authorized signatures for the account were Annie McMillan and Eloise Stephens.

    We will resolve the savings account issue by converting this account to a Certificate of Deposit (CD).

Yours sincerely,

Martha Baer

FORTUNA O'CONNELL
65 Namath Street
Livermore, KY 89776
(910) 483-6611

Date

Department of Defense
Defense Finance and Accounting Service
Cleveland Center
1240 East Ninth Street
Cleveland, OH 44199-2056

To whom it may concern:

On June 17, 1999, I sent a certified letter with return receipt requested to your office. This letter was in reference to my alimony payment which I had not received for the month of May from my ex-husband, Joseph O'Connell (SSN# **000-00-0000**). There was no reply to my inquiry, and the receipt from the certified letter was never returned.

On several different occasions since, I have spoken with different individuals in your office, but I still have not received this payment.

The last person with whom I spoke suggested that this matter would be dealt with more quickly if I could fax you a letter explaining the situation. In the hope that this will provide a quick resolution to this problem, I am doing so now.

I thank you in advance for your prompt attention to this matter.

Yours sincerely,

Fortuna O'Connell
SSN# 000-00-9999

NOTICE REGARDING LAPSED ALIMONY PAYMENT

Often letters of notice concern financial matters. This letter deals with lapsed alimony payments.

Notice of Sealed Bid Land and Timber Sale
Date

NOTICE OF SEALED BID LAND AND TIMBER SALE

This letter makes the public aware of a sealed bid sale and provides the who, what, when, and how details of the bidding process.

As an authorized agent for Milton Frecia III and the James McDowell heirs, I am offering for sale all merchantable timber (all species, predominately Southern Yellow Pine) on 73.83 acres of land in the Landover area north of Montgomery. I am also offering the land at the same time. You may present a bid on the land and timber together, or either the land or the timber separately. Please stipulate which way you are bidding when you prepare your bid. Survey and location maps are enclosed.

Date and Time of Sale

The Sale will take place on December 15, 2000, at 10:30 A.M. at the office of Milton Frecia III (Frecia Lumber Supply Co.), 1605 Morganton Road.

Mail bids to Fulton Real Estate, Post Office Box 52, Montgomery, AL 78348, or bring to bid opening.

No tops or trees left in cleared area. All ditches to be left open. All roads used to market timber must be left in good condition and passable.

We reserve the right to reject any and all bids.

The successful bidder will receive a deed no later than ten (10) days after the sale.

Timber must be harvested within twenty-four months of closing, unless the successful bidder buys both the land and the timber. If you need more information, please call (910) 483-6611 or (910) 483-2439 (mobile).

NOTIFICATION & CERTIFICATE OF DESTRUCTION

BM-SES Environment, Inc., Hereby Certifies

That The Following Tanks Have Been Destroyed

Client_____ Date_____

Number of tanks _____

Tank IDs   Product formerly contained

_____   _____

_____   _____

_____   _____

_____

NOTIFICATION & CERTIFICATE OF DESTRUCTION

Highly technical matters such as issues related to compliance with environmental issues often need to be put in writing in official notices.

Scrap steel was/will be sent for recycling at:

_____

All tanks have been cleaned of all liquids and accumulated sludges and residues and have been destroyed and disposed of in accordance with EPA regulation 40 CFR part 280.71 and API recommended practices 1604.

All liquids sludges and residues have been disposed of in accordance with all federal, state, and local regulations at an EPA-approved disposal facility.

CERTIFICATE # _____

Letters Of Opposition
(see also Letters of Appeal and Letters of Complaint)

Sometimes it's necessary to write a letter of opposition if you oppose something.

Giving the details is important
A main thing to keep in mind when writing a letter of opposition is that you need to give as many details, dates, specific names, and so forth as possible so that the individual reading your letter of opposition will clearly follow your train of thought and be persuaded by your point of view. If the facts are on your side, make sure you give the facts in very detailed and explicit ways. It's OK to show your emotion in such a letter but make sure you don't substitute emotion for factual information.

Remember that you are writing to persuade, not just oppose
A letter of opposition is similar to an appeals letter, but a letter of opposition is often written in an attempt to influence a decision-making process. Often the letter of opposition is directed at a municipality. In this section you will see a letter written to oppose a rezoning change.

Remember that you are writing to persuade, not just oppose
In addition to the letter of opposition shown here, there are other letters of opposition in other sections of the book. For example, in the Letters of Complaint section, you will see a letter written to challenge an insurance company's policies about agency ownership. An important thing to remember about a letter of opposition is that you are writing to persuade, so you must maintain an agreeable tone.

Date

Planning Services Division
33 Bay Street
Normandy, OK 89976
RE: Case #Q98-02F

Dear Members of the Planning Services Division:

The property in question for rezoning joins my property on three sides: South, East, and West, as shown on the plot layout on the reverse side of the notification letter. We oppose the rezoning unless the following stipulations are made and concerns noted:

1. **Existing water line:** In future use of the property, care and concern must be shown related to my copper pipe water line which proceeds from the meter on Dell Lane to our house at 8972 Dell Lane, with the line approximately 700 feet between the present nursing home and Gables Drive, running due South. **At approximately 400 ft., the pipe angles 45 degrees due East to our house, across part of lot #55 and my driveway.**

2. **Driveway:** The driveway is approximately 16 to 20 feet wide, and I have considerable expense in the driveway to include paving it and other improvements to take care of the water run off as well as the maintenance of said property. **If either the driveway or existing water line are moved and/or damaged in any way (for example, during construction of any site addition), then the owner of the nursing home should bear the expense of immediately replacing the asset to a like condition according to its current well-maintained status.**

3. **Safety and Privacy Buffer:** I would like to also stipulate that a buffer in the form of a six-foot red wood fence be installed, as is at present on the East and South side of the existing nursing home, in the event that any special use permit is issued for any activity of the nursing home. If any special use permit should ever be granted to the nursing home, it should furthermore be stipulated that the nursing home would need to erect such a barrier before commencing such construction and maintain that buffer in excellent condition.

In conclusion, I would like to make a matter of public record my letter of August 17, 1988, which I wrote in order to express my concerns related to asset protection as well as security, privacy, and protection against vandalism. My concerns remain essentially the same in 1999 as they were in 1988. If special use rezoning is permitted which allows either further growth of the nursing home or allows any use of the land which increases public traffic, I respectfully ask the Planning Board to respond in a professional manner to my concerns in 1999 as they were kind enough to do in 1988.

Yours sincerely,

Delbert Willard

LETTER OF OPPOSITION TO A REZONING PROPOSAL

Rezoning proposals are often not in your best interest, and this letter is a formal opposition to a rezoning request by a corporation which wishes to erect commercial structures on land adjacent to this person's home.

Letters Of Regret and Condolence

Unfortunately, we all have situations in life which require us to convey news which others will find disappointing. For example, sometimes we have to write a letter to an eager young job hunter who was the unsuccessful candidate in a job search.

You will see a letter written to express personal condolence. Regretably, we all have many situations in life which present us with the need to express our sympathy to another human being. Sometimes we fail to write the letter of condolence because we're not sure of the words to use. The model in this book is intended to provide you with an example of appropriate and tasteful language.

In this section, you will also see a letter written by a human resources manager conveying the "bad news" to a job seeker.

Date

Ms. Janice Smith
525 Country Lake Terracer
Peoria, IL 99887

Dear Janice:

Please accept my heartfelt sympathy for the loss of your beloved spouse.

Although I did not know your husband very well, I was well acquainted with his reputation as an honest and hard-working businessman. You must be very proud of the fact that your family name in Peoria is synonymous with decency, fairness, and the highest ethical standards.

On the few occasions yearly when I had the opportunity to interact with Bill—usually at our office Holiday Party and at the Fourth of July company party—I always noticed his obvious respect for and personal devotion to you. I am hopeful that in this sad time you can find comfort and strength in such memories.

Please be aware that all of us at Franklin Industries share your grief and are keeping you in our thoughts and prayers in this time of bereavement.

Sincerely,

Delores Franklin

LETTER OF CONDOLENCE TO AN EMPLOYEE WHOSE HUSBAND DIED

It is a natural instinct to want to comfort someone who has suffered a great loss, but we often hold back because we don't quite know what to say. Here is a letter expressing sentiments all of us can relate to.

Date

Ms. Wendy James
1110 Hay Street
Fayetteville, NC 28305

Dear Ms. James:

    We thank you for applying for employment with our company. It was a pleasure to meet and talk with you. While we felt that you were an excellent prospect, we were ultimately unable to hire you. We are keeping your name, number, and application on file in the event that we develop another opening in the future.

    While we realize this news will probably disappoint you, we wish you to know that the applicant we selected had extensive experience in the accounting software and spreadsheets used by our company, specifically QuickBooks, Lotus, and Excel.

    We wish you the best of luck in your future job search, Ms. James, and we are sorry that we are unable to offer you employment at this time.

Sincerely,

Rufus Edmonston
Manager,
Human Resources
The Main Line Company

LETTER OF REGRET TO A JOB APPLICANT

So often we hear nothing from the companies with which we interview, but this human resources manager makes a special effort to convey disappointing news in a personal letter such as this.

Letters Of Reprimand

Letters of reprimand must sometimes be written to employees whose work or behavior requires written correction and strong reaction.

Such letters of reprimand are best written after consulting your state labor laws. You will notice that some of the letters in this section borrow language from the state labor laws. Frequently letters of reprimand are an early stage in the termination of an employee.

Letters of reprimand are useful for employers because the letters are a "paper trail" related to an employee's poor performance or misconduct, and such letters can help employers demonstrate later on that an employee was fired "with cause." Terminating an employee "with cause" may allow the employer to avoid a charge against his unemployment fund in case a terminated employee files for unemployment benefits later.

It's best to consult the labor law and labor policies in your state for the exact details related to termination rights of employers, but bear in mind that employers are wise to write letters of reprimand with a full knowledge of state and local labor policies.

You will find a similar letter on page 158-159 written to a freelance graphics designer whose non-completion of work led the employer to give notice of pending termination.

Date

TO: Diana Dingbat

FROM: Sally Employer

LETTER OF REPRIMAND TO AN EMPLOYEE

The employer who wrote this letter did so in an attempt to provide a written reprimand to a marginal employee. This letter puts the employee on notice that her unprofessional behavior will not be tolerated, and the employer is covering himself by putting his concerns in writing. If he has to fire the employee, he will be able to do so with cause.

Dear Diana:

This letter is intended as a warning. With regret, I must inform you that I will have no choice other than to terminate your employment if you continue conducting yourself in an unprofessional fashion. This letter will advise you of several matters which are related to your continued employment at PEOPLEFIND.

1. Your verbal outbursts in the office must stop immediately. The attached letter from a customer explains that your unprofessional conduct was noticed by a customer in our office this morning, and she has written the attached letter to clarify what took place within her earshot and eyesight this morning when you and I were conferring over personnel matters. I cannot continue to employ anyone who engages in conduct which is embarrassing to customers and distressing to the image of the business. We are a small, 20-year-old business which prides itself on a professional reputation.

2. When I reminded you that your gross salary is $430 per week and not $440 per week, you became verbally abusive and said that you would not continue to pick up the company's mail in the mornings, which is part of your job. Your insubordination is inappropriate and will not be tolerated on a long-term basis. You cannot capriciously decide that you will do and will not do certain aspects of your job.

3. Please remove the radio from your office. It is not expected that employees would be playing the radio in the background during our workday.

4. You continuously leave your telephone ringing while you go on frequent cigarette breaks. Although occasional cigarette breaks are allowed, your frequent absences from your desk are excessive. As you know, when you leave your desk that leaves only two other employees and often only one other employee handling customer service and taking care of five phone lines which could ring in our office. You are reminded to be at your desk doing your job.

Yours sincerely,

Sally Employer

Date

MEMO TO THE FILE
Prepared by Mrs. Clinton, Owner of PEOPLEFIND

On Tuesday, December 15, 2000, at 4:00 p.m. a man who identified himself as the probation officer of Kelly Purchase called PEOPLEFIND Personnel to ask for Judith Means. I explained that Judith Means was no longer at PEOPLEFIND and that she had been terminated for professional misconduct on Friday, October 3.

When I appeared shocked at the fact that a probation officer was calling on behalf of someone whom Judith had placed in a job, he said that he had previously informed Mrs. Means that Kelly Purchase had a police record. Mrs. Clinton (the owner of PEOPLEFIND) provided to the probation officer the name of Amy Holderness at the law firm where Kelly Purchase had been placed; Mrs. Holderness is the office manager at that law firm.

Mrs. Means had never informed Mrs. Clinton of the fact that a probation officer had told her about Kelly Purchase's record. This is yet another example of Mrs. Means's professional misconduct.

The probation officer wanted to know if Kelly Purchase had, indeed, been fired from the law firm of Dillons & Harper Attorneys as she had told him she had been. Mrs. Clinton replied that Delia Stephens, who began employment in Mrs. Means's former job on October 9, had learned that Kelly Purchase was fired when she tried to call the law offices on October 9 to tell Kelly Purchase that her payments to PEOPLEFIND were delinquent and that she needed to make her payments immediately.

Mrs. Amy Holderness from the law firm of Dillons & Harper Attorneys called on October 15 to say they had just learned in the morning of October 15 that Kelly Purchase had a record of convictions, and they felt they had to change the locks on their law offices and thought PEOPLEFIND should pay for the cost.

Mrs. Clinton called Amy Holderness at 12:30 P.M. to tell her that Mrs. Clinton suggested that the law firm and PEOPLEFIND Personnel could join forces to take Judith Means to Small Claims Court to sue for cost of doing business. Mrs. Holderness said that she would run that concept by Mr. Dillons but that they were disgusted with the whole thing and ready to be finished with it.

The cause of all this needless expense and disgust is Judith Means's professional misconduct.

REPRIMAND AND MEMO TO THE FILE

On occasion, it is useful to write a memo to the file in order to maintain documentation about a problem situation.

Letters Of Solicitation
(see also Letters of Invitation and Reference Letters)

In this section, you will find letters used to solicit funds for worthy causes as well as for commercial ventures.

One of letters was written by a highly intelligent and sensitive gentleman who wanted to find a way to help disadvantaged children by soliciting money from big-league sports.

The other solicitation medium is not a letter at all. You will see how a resume can be used to solicit funds for a commercial activity.

There are letters of solicitation in other sections of this book. For example, on page 219 you will see a letter requesting financial aid or grant money for a mother with Alzheimer's. On page 51 is a letter used in a chain letter mailing. You will find like-minded letters in the Business Marketing Letters and Press Releases section as well as the Collections Letters section. Again, consult the Table of Contents to find prototype letters that meet your needs.

On the facing page, you will see a letter written by actual person. The cause is real, and you will see what Dr. Allen invites you to do if his letter arouses in you a desire to support his worthy cause. The address on his letter is real, and he encourages you to write directly to him if you seek more information.

"BABE" RUTH MEMORIAL
Humanitarian Sports Sale and Auction
Jeffrey Brooke Allen, Ph.D., Promoter
P.O. Box 53143, Fayetteville, NC 28305

Date

Dear

Recent dramatic events inspire me to seek your support. Deeply inspired by the urgent call for greater volunteerism on behalf of America's horribly disadvantaged children issued recently in Philadelphia by several distinguished Americans, I hereby offer to donate to the Yankees' and Mets' favorite New York City children's charities, no less than $10,000 worth of Mets' and Yankees' memorabilia. Based upon seven years of scholarly research and sometimes sizeable donations to five sports charity events, I know my tiny offer will inspire innumerable bequests from generous New Yorkers who care deeply about baseball and your city's poor children.

Research reveals the following: (1) the proudest recent tradition in sports humanitarianism was the annual series of Yankee/Met Mayor's Trophy children's charity games; (2) a single charity game played in Tokyo by loving Japanese and American ballplayers on 7/24/95 netted over $1 million; and (3) a handful of caring and joyful American ballplayers at a Chicago charity autographing show on 12/5/92 raised nearly $250,000 for the precious children of umpire John Hirschbeck.

"The House" built by sports' all-time greatest children's humanitarian, "Babe" Ruth, seats twice as many people as Tokyo's Fukuoaka Dome and over ten times the attendance at the Hirschbeck Benefit. Obviously, by combining two charity events at Yankee Stadium in only a few hours (adding corporate sponsorships, memorabilia sales, charity HR contests, television rights, etc.), the Mets and Yankees could, at no personal expense whatsoever, greatly ameliorate the pain of thousands of New York City's homeless, hungry, sick, and undereducated poor children.

This is all I ask you and your teammates to prayerfully consider: a massive public demonstration of baseball's deep love for children through a simple resumption of the annual Mayor's Trophy Games, slightly expanded so that more poor children will be helped, and so that all of baseball...indeed all of sports...will be inspired to emulate the Mets' and Yankees' moral example, and thus soon feel the immense joy great athletes always feel when they help otherwise defenseless children.

I pray that you will share this letter with your loving teammates and tell me soon that, like over 5,000 young volunteers in New York, you will volunteer just a few hours to help America's finest citizens...our endangered children.

Sincerely,

Jeffrey B. Allen, Ph.D.

LETTER OF SOLICITATION ON BEHALF OF DISADVANTAGED CHILDREN

Americans are enthusiastic volunteers and energetic do-gooders, and this brilliant Ph.D. is a champion of children's rights and a lover of baseball. Dr. Allen really exists and the cause he champions is a worthy one for which he is enlisting financial support. You may write to him at the address on his letter.

DEVLIN DONALDSON

Business: CarPlus, Inc., President and Owner
FORD Service Center
Work: (910) 483-6611

- We at CarPlus Inc. are currently purchasing $60,000 worth of FORD parts from the store #910 in Greenville, SC.
- We anticipate a large sales increase in 1998.
- We travel approximately 35,000 miles along the east coast and Midwest.
- We would be very proud to display the FORD logo on the side of race car and 26' enclosed trailer.

Accomplishments
- Started racing in 1975 as Stock Elimination 360 Plymouth Duster I/SA.
- Held N.H.R.A. national record for two years.
- Division I Champ and two I.H.R.A. national events wins.
- 16 N.H.R.A. class wins between stock and super stock; then proceeded to SS elimination in a 74 Plymouth Duster 360 SS/KA.
- Won one I.H.R.A. national event.
- Won N.H.R.A. Gold Cup national in Lester, NY; also held national record.
- Then proceeded to the rear engine Super Comp Dragster and rear engine B-econo Dragster with Bill Jenkins of Detroit; we won several bracket races in Division 2.

Most Recent Accomplishments
- We have recently built a new 1996 FORD Daytona IROC car which is in the class as SS/GTCA.
- We came 7th in the I.H.R.A. World Championship Points.
- In 1997 – our very first year with this car – we got into the finals of two division events and also one national event at M.I.R. as well as three semifinal finishes. We also won class 3 out of three races.
- We are planning to run the entire I.H.R.A. schedule for the 1998 season and also six N.H.R.A. races.
- We also receive a lot of publicity for having the only FORD GT/CA car on the I.H.R.A. circuit.
- We are now planning on building a new modified engine using W-7 heads and the new FORD block for the upcoming seasons.

What we are requesting from FORD
- We would appreciate any financial help which can be provided to a vehicle and a racing expert who will bring much publicity to the FORD Corporation.
- We would be proud to repaint our car with the FORD logo if this is desired by FORD.
- Our racing schedule begins in February 2000. We are excited about putting our Daytona in the low 9 seconds to high 8.90 elapsed time in this up-and-coming season!

RESUME USED AS A METHOD OF SOLICITING FUNDS FOR BUSINESS SPONSORSHIP

Some activities, like racing, require sponsors. This resume is an attempt to solicit sponsorship money.

Letters Of Support

Sometimes we find ourselves in a situation in which we must write a letter to support some action which a friend wishes to take.

Although the letter of support sounds similar to a letter of recommendation, there are differences.

The letter in this section is a letter written to "take a side" in a bitter custody battle between divorced parents with three children. Since the purpose of the letter is to vigorously support the desire of one party in this case, the letter contains places for the proper signature and declaration of a notary public.

As with most other letters, providing details is important if you are trying to convince a judge of the correctness of your point of view. In fact, details and facts are of vital importance in this type of letter because such a letter has an obvious bias toward one party and is not perceived of as objective by the reader.

If you're writing a letter to show support for a friend or acquaintance, give plenty of details, facts, and examples to show why you feel the way you do.

You will find other examples of letters in the Legal Letters section. On page 14 in the Letter of Appeals section is a letter of support written on behalf of an employee by the franchisee who hired him.

Date

Letter in Support of the Petition by Andrew Farthing

To Gain Custody of His Children:

My name is Corrine Matthews, proprietor of Quick Fix, a graphics design and advertising business which serves commercial customers. I would like provide a statement concerning the children of Andrew Farthing. The children are Jason, Brian, and Melissa Farthing.

I have known and worked with Suzanne Ismael, the wife of Andrew Farthing, since May 1997. I have known Andrew Farthing since June 1998. I have frequented their home on numerous occasions at 2516 Maples Court, Lake Geneva, FL 39087.

I met Andrew's children in June 1999, when they moved in with their father and his second wife Suzanne, and I was aware of the family dislocation which occurred in December 1999 when their biological mother removed them from their father's home.

Within the time stated above, I observed the household to be a harmonious home busy with the hustle and bustle of a family with children involved in summer and school activities. After the children moved in with their father and during the nearly six months they were living with him, I noticed a great change in the demeanor and attitudes of the children; they seemed to transform from shy and reclusive to outgoing, studious, and active children. They were a churchgoing family, and the boys had joined a Cub Scout pack.

Suzanne and Andrew have had a great effect on these young minds. Not only have they been parents to these children, but they have been leaders and spiritual guides for them as well. The love which Suzanne and Andrew have for the three children is obvious, and the children seemed to be thriving on the loving atmosphere created by Suzanne and Andrew and on Suzanne and Andrew's strong encouragement to excel in academics, sports, and personal pursuits.

I wish the best for this family and pray that they will be reunited soon.

Yours sincerely,

Denise Watson _____ Date _____

Sworn before _____

Lake Geneva, FL

Notary _____

My commission expires _____

LETTER OF SUPPORT ON BEHALF OF A PARTY IN A CHILD CUSTODY DISPUTE

You may be asked to provide a letter stating your opinions about a person's character and expressing your view on child custody matters. If you ever have such a letter to write, this is a model.

Letters Of Understanding And Intent

We sometimes find ourselves in situations in which we must express our intentions or our thoughts in writing in a form that constitutes an agreement or a document of understanding between two or more parties. The letters in this section are simple letters which worked for the parties involved, but you may need to seek legal counsel if you feel your own situation is complex. It is not the intention of the letters and agreements shown to provide legal advice.

- You will find a letter of intent between an individual and an organization in which she wishes to invest money.

- You will find a letter of understanding and a service agreement which clarifies the expectations and obligations of the parties involved in an agreement related to the provision of janitorial services.

- You will find a letter of understanding and an agreement between a speech therapy organization and the independent subcontractors who provide the one-on-one services to clients in the field.

Date

LETTER OF INTENT & INVESTMENT AGREEMENT
XYZ Check Cashing Facility, Inc.
82 Monton Street
Decatur, GA 34509

LETTER OF INTENT AND INVESTMENT AGREEMENT

A business arrangement may require a letter of intent and investment agreement, such as the one on this page.

The following agreement is made on the date which appears on this letter of understanding between McKenzie Phillips (SSN: 000-00-0000) of 42 Enterprise Circle, Decatur, GA, and XYZ Check Cashing Facility, Inc. of 82 Monton Street, Decatur, GA.

It is acknowledged that on December 30, 1999, XYZ Check Cashing Facility, Inc., will accept from McKenzie Phillips a cash investment in the amount of $4,500.00. This will serve as an investment to be placed in the account towards operation of XYZ Check Cashing Facility, Inc., 82 Monton Street, Decatur, GA, beginning on February 28, 2000.

It is acknowledged and understood that this investment equates to 5% of profit and for losses in above business beginning February 28, 2000. Under no circumstances may this be inferred or interpreted as a "guarantee" on a definitive return for the above investor (McKenzie Phillips) or company (XYZ Check Cashing Facility, Inc.).

This agreement is made in good faith demonstrated by all parties. It is understood that all efforts possible will be made to turn the business and above investment into a profitable venture. All Alcohol Law Enforcement rules are to be adhered to by all parties. Any deliberate violation of these policies will be considered a breach of contract.

A monthly financial statement will be made available upon request.

The above is agreed upon by the following parties and officers:

_____   _____
McKenzie Phillips   Clyde Taunton, President
Investor   XYZ Check Cashing Facility, Inc.

_____
Marybelle Taunton
Vice President, XYZ Check Cashing Facility, Inc.

JANITORIAL SERVICES OF BUENA VISTA
LETTER OF UNDERSTANDING & SERVICES AGREEMENT

This Agreement is effective as of _____ (date to be filled in by Janitorial Services of Buena Vista (herein referred to as "Contractor") and _____ (herein referred to as "Client").

Contractor agrees to furnish the following services (check services which are applicable):

Install Flooring _____	Refurbish Bathrooms _____
Replace Roofing _____	Refurbish Kitchen _____
Replace Shingles _____	Refurbish Plumbing _____
Room Additions _____	Build/Remove Walls _____
Other (Specify) _____	

Contractor agrees to remove all work-related material from the site at the completion of the job.

Contractor guarantees the aforementioned work for a period of _____ from the date of its completion. All work will be performed in accordance with drawings and specifications submitted by Client.

Client agrees to pay the full contract price of $_____ in the following manner:

(a) 50% down payment
(b) Remaining balance at the completion of the job

IN WITNESS WHEREOF, the parties have executed this Agreement to be effective on the day and year first above written:

Janitorial Services of Buena Vista:

Name _____ Signature _____ Date _____

Client:

Name _____ Signature _____ Date _____

LETTER OF UNDERSTANDING AND SERVICES AGREEMENT

Agreeing on the details when an agreement is entered into can do much to deter problems later on about what was promised and what was expected.

LETTER OF UNDERSTANDING & AGREEMENT WITH INDEPENDENT SUBCONTRACTOR

This Agreement made this _____ day of _____ in the year 2000 by and between Therapy Plus Speech doing business at this address: 3567 Avery Street, Suite 150, Morganton, SC (hereinafter referred to as the "contractor") and _____, an Independent Subcontractor of Therapy Plus Speech whose address is _____ (hereinafter referred to as Subcontractor).

AGREEMENT

1. TERM
The term of this Agreement shall be nine (9) months from the date of its execution. Either party hereto may at any time during the term hereof terminate this Agreement upon thirty (30) days written notice to the other party of such termination. At the end of said thirty (30) day notice period, this Agreement shall forthwith terminate for all purposes, as if said date were the date set forth herein as the termination date of this Agreement, provided that any obligations arising prior to the termination of this Agreement shall be governed by the terms hereinafter set forth until satisfied.

2. SERVICES
The parties agree that the Subcontractor is to provide speech pathology services under the terms and conditions of this Agreement and in accordance with The South Carolina Guidelines for Speech and Language Programs and with any applicable requirements of federal, state or local laws, rules and/or regulations.

3. COMPENSATION
The Subcontractor will be compensated by Therapy Plus Speech for speech and language services rendered from the first to last day of each month (hereinafter referred to as the "billing period") according to invoices submitted to Therapy Plus Speech no later than three (3) working days following the end of the billing period in which said services were rendered. Therapy Plus Speech agrees to pay for the foregoing services at the consultation rate of $35.00 per hour for five (5) days per week _____ not to exceed 6 hours _____ per day. Therapy Plus Speech Services shall pay the Subcontractor upon the conditions hereinafter set forth, for all services rendered by the Subcontractor within fifteen (15) days following the date in which the Subcontractor's invoices have been received by Therapy Plus Speech Services for the applicable billing period.

Any amendments or changes to the schedule of fees herein above stated shall be effective thirty (30) days following the date upon which the parties agree to such amendment or change in writing. Upon the parties' mutual acceptance in writing, the amended schedule of fees shall become part of this agreement.

4. INDEPENDENT SUBCONTRACTOR
It is the parties' intention that so far as shall be in conformity with the law the Subcontractor shall be an independent Subcontractor. In conformity therewith Subcontractor shall retain sole and absolute discretion and judgment in the manner and means of providing speech services to the Meridian County Schools. This agreement shall not be construed as a partnership and Therapy Plus Speech Services shall not be liable for any obligation incurred by the Subcontractor. However, Subcontractor shall comply with

---

LETTER OF UNDERSTANDING AND AGREEMENT WITH INDEPENDENT SUBCONTRACTOR

A business providing services may utilize subcontractors, and an agreement may need to be drawn up to clarify responsibilities and obligations of the respective parties.

all policies, rules and regulations of Therapy Plus Speech Services in connection with provision of Speech Pathology services. All services rendered by the Subcontractor shall be rendered in a competent, efficient and satisfactory manner and in strict accordance with currently approved methods and practices of Subcontractor's profession.

5. SUBCONTRACTOR QUALIFICATIONS
All services to students in Meridian County Schools shall be performed by the speech pathologists who are holders of current licenses of the state in which they are practicing and of the Certificate of Clinical Competence (CCC) in their area of specialization, as issued by the American Speech-Language-Hearing Association. The only exception to the above shall be employees of Provider who are in the process of completing their Clinical Fellowship Year as specified by the American Speech-Language-Hearing Association and who are working under the supervision of a certified and licensed speech pathologist.

6. INSURANCE
Therapy Plus represents that it has in effect appropriate liability coverage, including coverage for any acts of professional malpractice.

7. RESTRICTIVE COVENANTS
The employee agrees for a period of one (1) year following the termination of this Agreement, whether such Agreement is terminated by the Employee or Employer, that the Employee will not, directly or indirectly, engage in either as an Employee or Employer, or in any manner whatsoever, the private practice of speech and language pathology which in any manner whatsoever would be competitive with the Employer within a 25-mile radius of the Morganton office of Therapy Plus Speech.

8. MISCELLANEOUS
Each party to this Agreement acknowledges that no representations, inducements, promises or agreements, orally or otherwise, have been made by any party, or anyone acting on behalf of any party, which are not embodied herein, and that no other Agreement, statement or promise not contained in this Agreement shall be valid or binding.

Any modification of this Agreement will be effective only if it is in writing and signed by all parties to this Agreement.

In WITNESS WHEREOF, we the undersigned, duly authorized representatives of the parties to this Agreement herein above expressed, have entered into this Agreement without reservation and have read the terms herein.

By_____

Director, Therapy Plus   Date_____

By_____

Independent Subcontractor   Date_____

LETTER OF UNDERSTANDING AND AGREEMENT WITH INDEPENDENT SUBCONTRACTOR

If you are ever in the position of signing such an agreement like this, read it carefully.

Letters Of Welcome
(see also Business Marketing Letters and Press Releases)

A letter of welcome can make a new customer or new member of an organization feel appreciated and included.

In this section, you will see an enthusiastic example of a letter used by a church to welcome new members. You will see that it is a "form" letter which can be personalized to each person who joins the church.

So often in life, we only write letters because we have to do so and because we are forced to react or respond in writing to an event.

On the other hand, letters of welcome are discretionary, and for that reason they are often not written. When you read the letter of welcome in this section, we think you will become aware of the tremendous opportunity to create good will which these letters provide. The next time you have an opportunity to write a letter welcoming someone, go ahead. You will reap many benefits in terms of developing an excellent relationship with your reader.

In the Business Marketing letters section, you will also find a letter written by a business to welcome a new customer.

BETHLEHEM PENTECOSTAL HOLINESS CHURCH
9530 Davidson Street
Amazon, AL 76311
(910) 483-6611

Pastor Eldress Eloise Henretty
Assistant Pastor Evangelist Meriah Boratty

Date

LETTER OF WELCOME

Organizations often send letters welcoming new members, and they are similar to this letter mailed to new members by a church. This letter allows for two signatures.

Dear New Member:

Welcome to the Bethlehem Pentecostal Holiness Church of Great Expectations. Pastor Eldress Eloise Henretty and the members of Bethlehem Pentecostal Holiness Church welcome you to our church family with open arms for you are loved here at Bethlehem. John 4:7 says, *Beloved; let us love one another; for love is of God, and anyone that loveth is born of God, and knoweth God."* Proverbs 3:6 says, *"In all thy ways acknowledge him and he shall direct thy path."*

We thank God for directing your path to the Bethlehem, the growing Church of Great Expectations, with open arms.

May God continue to bless you under his ministry. May you grow spiritually through guidance by the Holy Spirit. Once more, welcome to Bethlehem Pentecostal Holiness Church.

Yours In Christ,

Pastor:
Eldress Eloise Henretty

Assistant Pastor:
Evangelist M. Boratty

Letters To Public Officials

At some time in your life, you may feel the need to write to an elected official or to a public official.

In the first section of this book, you will find helpful information on how to prepare the salutation and address when writing to public officials. See page 6.

In this section, we will show you two examples of letters to public officials. One letter is asking an elected official to send a written letter of congratulations to a boy upon attaining the rank of Eagle Scout.

Another letter is a letter written to a Congressman requesting an appointment to the U.S. Military Academy at West Point.

Elected officials can be very helpful when you are having trouble and wish to involve your elected official—Congressmen or Senators—in helping you to resolve the matter.

You will find letters to public officials in other sections of this book. For example, on page 112 you will see a letter to a senator asking his help in securing a father's legitimate medical benefits for the wife who has survived him.

Date

The Honorable Jesse Helms
United States Senate
Washington, DC 20510

Dear Senator Helms:

As a Scoutmaster in Troop 748, I am respectfully requesting that you participate once again—as I have requested many times in years past—in an Eagle Scout ceremony at our church.

As you are well aware, it is a tradition that your office sends a letter of congratulations to a Boy Scout once he has attained the rank of Eagle Scout.

I am requesting that you send your usual kind and encouraging letter of congratulations to Kyle Stephens in care of my address:

> Kyle Stephens
> c/o Scoutmaster Vincent Masters
> 1110 Hay Street
> Payton, SC 83567

Thank you in advance for the courteous and prompt way in which your office always responds to my requests for a letter of congratulations, and let me assure you once again that it is a most meaningful letter for each and every boy receiving such a letter.

Sincerely,

Vincent Master
Scoutmaster

LETTER TO A SENATOR

Your senators or congressmen can be very helpful to you in numerous ways if you write to them. Here you see a letter written to North Carolina Senator Jesse Helms asking him to send a letter of congratulations to a young man who has earned the highest rank in Boy Scouts. For information on how to address public officials, see the section at the beginning of the book entitled "Addressing Your Letters."

Date

The Honorable Jesse Helms
United States Senate
Washington, DC 20510

LETTER REQUESTING AN APPOINTMENT TO A MILITARY ACADEMY

If a young man or woman desires to be admitted to a U.S. military academy, that requires the candidate to be successful in obtaining an appointment. The process of obtaining an appointment involves getting a letter of nomination from an elected public official, most often a senator or congressman. This is the kind of letter that should be written to the senator or congressman from your state if you are seeking such an appointment.

Dear Senator Helms:

As a high school junior, I would like to make you aware of my deep desire to serve my country as a military officer, and I am respectfully requesting that you nominate me for an appointment to the U.S. Military Academy at West Point.

I am sending several documents which, I believe, indicate that I am worthy of such a high honor as that of serving my country. In a senior class of nearly 400 students, I am ranked number 8 in my class and am a member of the National Honor Society. Just recently I made 1420 on my Scholastic Aptitude Test (SAT). I have studied hard throughout my life, and I believe I am well prepared for the extensive academic challenges which will face me at West Point.

I am also an Eagle Scout. I began in Cub Scouts when I was in the second grade as a Wolf, and I have continued until my 17th birthday, when I achieved the rank of Eagle Scout. I am a strong believer in the moral and ethical values stressed by the Boy Scouts, and I am a deeply religious person.

I realize that West Point will also hold many physical challenges, and I believe I am ready. I am proficient in both judo and karate, and I am a keen biker.

If you would consider me for this great patriotic honor of serving my country, Senator Helms, I would be grateful, and it would indeed be a great honor to receive the nomination from such a great statesman and patriot as yourself, sir.

Thank you for all you do to help and serve our country.

Yours sincerely,

Kyle Wesley Stephens

Minutes And Agendas

Although they are not strictly letters in the traditional sense, the editor of this book was strongly encouraged to include this section which shows sample minutes and agendas.

The minutes of a meeting are a record of the discussions and decisions made at the meeting. Written minutes provide a means of doublechecking facts and figures later when memory fades.

An agenda is the tentative "roadmap" for a meeting. Agendas focus attendees on the main items of business and help to ensure that the main purposes of the meeting are achieved.

DELTA CHAPTER
CFC FRATERNITY, INC.
PO Box 928, Klamath Falls, AZ 78302

AGENDA FOR A FRATERNAL ORGANIZATION MEETING

Although not strictly a letter, an agenda for an organizational meeting is a "cousin" of a letter, and it is a piece of written communication that many people have to prepare from time to time. Therefore, we wanted to show you a sample format.

Brothers, our June meeting will be Friday, 7 p.m., December 20, 1999, at the Anne Street School. We will use this meeting to attend to all final matters pertaining to the scholarship dinner/dance program. Also, you will be asked to assist with various tasks for the dance, which is scheduled for **Friday, December 27.** Cocktails and reception will begin at 7 p.m., and dinner will be served at 8 p.m.

In preparation for the next fraternal year, please jot down and bring with you one good program idea for the chapter to pursue.

MEETING AGENDA

Call to order and prayer
Meeting new brothers
Minutes
Treasurer's report

Old business:
Scholarship Dinner/Dance Committee Report   Fred Phillips
Award Presentations   Brother Dick Smith

New business:
Summer outing   Needs chairman
Golf tournament   Brother Jorge Gonzales
Scholarship Committee Report   Brother Dimitri Zorabel

Announcements

Adjourn

Hymn

Social Hour

Brothers, the Blue and Gold Committee needs your guest list, money, and a firm commitment that this scholarship dinner/dance will be the best ever.

DELTA CHAPTER
CFC FRATERNITY, INC.
PO Box 928, Klamath Falls, AZ 78302

Minutes of the Meeting of December 30, 1999

On December 30, 1999, at 7:30 the meeting of the Delta Chapter of **CFC** Fraternity was called to order by Brother Gilforth, President. The meeting was called to order and Pastor Namath was asked to give the invocation.

As the first order of business, the slate of new officers for 2000 was presented to the membership. A motion was made by Brother David Jones to accept the slate of officers as presented, and Brother Mason Hicks seconded the motion. The vote to accept the slate of officers was unanimously carried by the 53 members in attendance.

As the second order of business, the new members recruited during the month of November were presented to the membership. Members welcomed into the brotherhood Patrick Phillips and Roger Dillmuth.

The Treasurer's Report was brief. Treasurer Tom Lemmons reported that the balance in the checking account is $2,390 of which $1,998 were funds made from the fall fund raiser. The treasurer asked for a vote on the charitable beneficiaries of the $1,500 which had been designated to be donated to worthy causes. After some discussion by the membership, the decision was made to present a check for the entire $1,500 to the Children's Home Society. Members felt strongly that they wanted to assist in repairing the orphanage after the October fire which damaged the facility.

New business items discussed briefly were the summer 2000 outing, the golf tournament, and the scholarship awards program. Because the December meeting is mostly social in nature and because members were eager to enjoy the dancing and dinner, the board of directors was instructed to discuss the new business matters in great detail at its January 2000 meeting and report to the membership with recommendations at the meeting in January 2000.

Brothers, our January meeting will be Friday, 7 p.m., January 20, 2000.

Respectfully submitted,

David Jones
Secretary

MINUTES OF A MEETING OF A FRATERNAL ORGANIZATION

There isn't one format for preparing minutes, but this format is certainly an appropriate one. Remember that the minutes of an organization's meeting are prepared in writing so that there can be a record of the discussion and decisions.

Networking Letters
(see also Business Marketing Letters and Press Releases)

There are situations in life in which you can benefit from a letter of networking. Networking is particularly used to advance careers, and it has to do with simply making others aware of one's capabilities and interests.

The networking letter you will see in this section was used by an executive to communicate with acquaintances in his field. Although this executive was satisfied in large measure with his current position and responsibilities, he felt a growing urge to take on a new challenge.

What better way to find a new career challenge than by letting the "movers and shakers" in one's industry know of one's desires and abilities? In a way, the networking letter is simply a personal marketing letter used to promote one's ambitions in a certain area and to advance one's interests through enlisting the support of others.

Date

Exact Name of Person
Title or Position
Name of Company
Address (number and street)
Address (city, state, and zip)

Dear Exact Name of Person: (or Sir or Madam if answering a blind ad.)

It was great talking with you recently at the annual Toy Manufacturers Convention in Los Angeles, and I wanted to get back in touch with you confidentially about some matters of a professional nature.

Since 1995 I have been handling responsibilities equivalent to those of a General Manager for the International Toy Emporium. Although I am excelling in my job, am highly regarded, and could probably stay with the Toy Emporium organization until I retire, I am interested in very selectively exploring management positions in other organizations.

I am writing to you because I respect you and would appreciate your mentioning my name or giving me a call if you hear of a situation in which you think my executive talents and retailing know-how could be of value. (I am sending you two business cards, one to keep and one to give away if you find yourself in a situation where that seems appropriate).

I have a great job and the Toy Emporium is a fine organization, so the kinds of things which would attract me to another organization would be outstanding coworkers, an organization with a distinctive competence and aggressive future growth plans, and a structure which rewards initiative and exceptional performance. I am open to any new adventure and new challenge worldwide.

If you learn from a headhunter of an opportunity which does not interest you, I hope you will refer that individual to me. If I can help you in some similar or other way, I hope you will give me a call. It's always a pleasure talking with you and I hope our paths cross again soon.

Yours sincerely,

Eric McDonnell

NETWORKING LETTER SENT TO AN INDUSTRY COLLEAGUE

Statistics about job hunting reveal that "who you know" counts for a lot when it comes to getting in the door for interviews. The savvy retailer who signed this letter used this letter as a model or template, and he sent the letter with slight modifications to acquaintances and colleagues in the spirit of networking and to let them know that, for the right opportunity, he was available and would be glad to hear from them if they heard of a situation that might be right for him.

Postponement Requests
(see also Letters of Appeal)

Sometimes we find ourselves in a situation in which we must ask for a postponement or rescheduling of an event which we want to happen.

In this section, you will see the letter used by an individual to postpone an interview with a company for which she really wanted to work.

Sometimes you must ask a prospective employer if you can postpone your starting date on a new job, or perhaps even reschedule an interview. On page 130 in the Follow-Up Letters section, you will see a follow-up letter used to express interest in a job while simultaneously proposing a delayed start date.

You may also wish to request extra time for completing a job, as is the case with the letter on page 20, written by a contractor who cites numerous factors outside his control as the causes for his non-completion of work according to set deadlines.

Date

Ms. Eloise Smith
Merck Pharmaceutical Products
32 Wagon Hitch Lane
Coral Springs, FL 89023

Dear Ms. Smith:

I would very much like to accept your invitation to meet with you to discuss the possibility of joining Merck Pharmaceutical Products as a pharmaceutical sales representative or in some other similar capacity in which you could utilize my strong sales and management background. You will recall that we were scheduled to meet on Thursday, December 19.

As you are also aware, in terms of the timetable of our meeting, I would like to respectfully ask if we could schedule our meeting for a later time in December. I am in the process of getting married with the wedding scheduled for December 26, and my inlaws, who are from Europe, will be arriving in the U.S. on December 18. Because of plane arrivals with the added complication that European relatives will be arriving in three separate U.S. cities (Atlanta, New York, and Chicago), I fear I may have to be "on call" on December 19 in case something goes awry.

Please be assured that I am very interested in discussing employment opportunities within Merck Pharmaceutical Products, and I hope that this delay will not diminish your interest in me. I feel I could rapidly become an asset to your organization, and I wonder if you would be kind enough to check your calendar and let me know if you see a suitable time when you could fit me into your busy calendar.

It will be a pleasure meeting with you in person, and I appreciate very much your interest in my background and your professional courtesies to me. I hope to make myself available at your convenience at some point in the next few weeks. I certainly wish you to know that I would be appreciative of your understanding in this matter, and I hope you will contact me to suggest another meeting date.

Sincerely,

Eileen Johnson

LETTER REQUESTING POSTPONEMENT

Getting a job as a pharmaceutical representative was what the writer of this letter considered her ideal job, so she wanted to be careful about requesting postponement of an interview time which she had worked very hard to get.

Promissory Notes
(see also Letters of Understanding and Intent)

A promissory note is a promise to pay later, and if you ever loan or borrow money, services, or products, you will probably need to construct your basic understanding with the other party in a quasi-letter document called a promissory note.

In this section, you will find a simple example of a promissory note written to communicate the basic understanding between two people who were entering into a promise to loan and a promise to repay the sum of $5,000.

There are other letters in this book outlining financial agreements between parties. On page 142 in the Legal Letters and Notices section, you will see an agreement outlining financial responsibilities between divorcing parties. On page 182 in the Letters of Understanding and Intent, you will find a leter of intent and investment agreement.

EDWARDS TREE SERVICE
4267 Angel Street
Del Rio, TX 87023
(910) 483-6611

PROMISSORY NOTE

To: Tex Panter, Inc.
Sampson County
P.O. Box 18
Del Rio, TX 87023

Lender, Tex Panter, Sampson County, agrees to lend the amount of $5,000 (five thousand dollars) to Edwards Tree Service, 4267 Angel Street, Del Rio, TX 87023.

In return, the undersigned will pay back $6,500 (six thousand and five hundred dollars) plus $2,250 (two thousand, two hundred and fifty dollars) on existing loan for a period of 43 (forty-three) weeks, beginning on January 12, 2000, with last payment being $350.00 (three hundred and fifty dollars). TOTAL LOAN OF $8,750 (eight thousand, seven hundred and fifty dollars).

Collateral for loan as follows:

One (1) each Mobark Chipper – 88 model #290.

SN: 5072

Date: _____

Signature: _____

Joseph R. Edwards
Owner

PROMISSORY NOTE

A letter can be used to capture in writing someone's promise to pay. A promissory note is a written piece of communication which expresses the timing and amount of future payments so that both parties will be in agreement as to the details.

Reference Letters and Letters of Recommendation (see also Letters of Support)

You may have numerous occasions in your life to write letters of reference and letters of recommendation. The most common use of such a letter is for a former employee who is seeking a job in another company, or an internal promotion, or a special honor based on exceptional performance.

You will see that you have wide latitude in writing letters of reference. You are simply trying to give someone (usually a prospective employer) enough information so that an informed decision can be made. If you did not supervise that individual, of course you cannot comment from a supervisor's point of view, but you can identify personality traits and describe encounters you had with the individual which would help you illustrate the person's character and personal qualities.

PEOPLEFIND, Inc.
1110 Hay Street, Dallas, TX 28305
Telephone: (910) 483-6611
Fax: (910) 483-2439
http://www.prep-pub.com
e-mail: preppub@aol.com

Date

To whom it may concern:

It with great pleasure, mixed with some sadness, that I write an enthusiastic letter of recommendation for Mrs. Eloise Johnson, who has served with distinction as office manager of PEOPLEFIND Personnel Service for the past five years.

When Mrs. Johnson joined PEOPLEFIND in 1996, she was already a hard worker and congenial individual with a strong work ethic and excellent communication skills. During her tenure at PEOPLEFIND she blossomed out professionally as she took charge of our 16-year-old advertising agency, our 10-year-old outplacement business, and increasingly became a part of an executive recruiting business which is now in its fourth year of operation.

Mrs. Johnson displayed a willingness to adapt to change, and that was, indeed, an implicit condition of her employment at PEOPLEFIND, since she worked for a hard-charging entrepreneur who was continuously creating and implementing new profit-making ventures at PEOPLEFIND while refining ways in which PEOPLEFIND serves its customers.

The owners of PEOPLEFIND are deeply appreciative to Mrs. Johnson for the professionalism she displayed at all times at PEOPLEFIND, and we heartily recommend her to any prospective employer seeking a resourceful and congenial young professional who will become a valuable asset to any organization she joins.

Please feel free to call me for any additional questions you might have about the aptitude and attitude of this highly talented young person.

Yours sincerely,

Grace Jones
Owner

LETTER OF REFERENCE FOR A RESPECTED OFFICE MANAGER

The employer who wrote this letter was sad that such a valuable employee was leaving for a job in another city.

Date

TO: Human Solutions

FROM: Joyce Thomas

LETTER OF REFERENCE FROM A BUSINESS PROFESSIONAL

You will probably be asked to write a letter of reference for various people through the years. Here you see a letter written by a family friend who has not supervised the young lady in an employment situation but who has nevertheless known her long enough to comment on her character and personal qualities. If you have not supervised the person for whom you are writing a letter of reference, you are actually providing a character reference for the potential employer.

Dear Sir or Madam:

I would like to strongly recommend Ms. Laura Kier for a position within your organization which involves working with others. I have known Laura since her childhood (more than 12 years) and I have watched her grow up into a stable, well adjusted, and hard-working individual.

One of the things I have always known about Laura is that she is oriented toward helping others and has always possessed a desire to be involved in helping others with special needs. I believe she is especially gifted with the patience, outgoing personality, and resourcefulness which could be vital to success in such a helping role. She is a warm and gracious person who is known for her kindness and compassion.

Although she is excelling in her position with Food Lion and is being groomed for promotion into management, I know that her true desire is to be in a human services organization in which she can be helping children or adults with special needs.

Laura was brought up by parents whom I know personally and respect tremendously. Her mother is a free-lance writer and her father is a retired senior warrant officer who now is employed in a management position in the postal service. Laura was brought up in a loving home by stable and caring parents, and I am certain she could become a loving and stabilizing presence for anyone with whom she comes into contact.

I would be delighted to answer additional questions if you would like to call me at the number below. Please give her every consideration for whatever job she is applying for as I can assure you that she would be a valuable and reliable employee.

Thank you,

Joyce Thomas
910-483-6611

Date

To whom it may concern:

It is my pleasure to provide a letter of reference on behalf of Nadine Wasserman.

I have been acquainted with Mrs. Wasserman for more than half a century, and I can assure you that she is a reliable and trustworthy individual of the highest character and integrity. Currently she is operating a group home, and she has also excelled in previous positions as a seamstress and nurse's aide.

Mrs. Wasserman has a gift for working with others. Especially with those who are discouraged, Mrs. Wasserman's cheerful and positive personality is uplifting and encouraging, and she has devoted much of her time to helping the less fortunate and the disadvantaged.

Without any question, Mrs. Wasserman would be an asset to any organization, and I am certain that any group she becomes a part of will benefit greatly from her versatile professional abilities as well as from her sunny disposition and unselfish nature.

Yours sincerely,

Vince Hintz
Retired Military Officer

LETTER OF REFERENCE FROM A FRIEND

Sometimes you are asked to simply provide a letter of reference as a friend. You can comment on the individual's personal qualities in such a letter. The things you say may help the new employer to manage the individual in order to help the employee achieve the maximum job satisfaction and productivity.

LETTER OF REFERENCE FROM A SUPERVISOR

Compare this letter of reference to the letter on page 201. Both letters were written for very valuable employees by employers who were sorry to see them leave. If you are ever leaving a job, be sure to ask your employer for a written letter of reference. That may save your new potential employers the time and expense of playing "telephone tag" to contact your previous employers for a verbal reference.

Date

To: Whom it may concern
From: Wylma Hinkley

Dear Sir or Madam:

It is with much sadness that I sit down to write this letter of reference for Mrs. Annie Lou Herron. She has voluntarily resigned from her position with our organization in order to relocate with her husband, and we are indeed sorry that she is leaving. I still am not quite sure how I will replace her.

When Mrs. Herron joined our staff nearly three years ago, she was seeking her first job in the public relations field, and she had just finished a degree in journalism. Although she had no experience in that field, we were attracted to her warm and vivacious personality and felt she would have the natural abilities to "catch on."

During the first six months of her job, she went up a steep learning curve. She proved her ability to master a variety of sophisticated software programs for which she had received no formal training. She always maintained a "can-do" attitude and persevered until she figured out the solution to a software problem.

Her work habits are excellent. To my knowledge, she was out sick only two days during her employment with us, and she demonstrated a capacity for hard work and long hours throughout her employment with Better Image Public Relations, Inc.

Although Mrs. Herron had never had a sales job, she exhibited a knack for establishing warm relationships with others, and she became one of our most aggressive account representatives. She welcomed every opportunity to have her results measured, and she cheerfully and aggressively tackled ambitious sales and marketing goals.

It is my pleasure to recommend Mrs. Herron enthusiastically for any job for which she applies, and I would be delighted to elaborate on her outstanding performance as well as the personal qualities of this highly talented individual if you wish to telephone me.

Yours sincerely,

Wylma Hinkley
President, BIPR, Inc.
63 Dixon Boulevard
Houston, TX 98087
1-910-483-6611

Date

To Whom It May Concern:

This letter is a recommendation that JoAnn Panter be accepted for admission in the School of Veterinary Medicine. I have had an opportunity to observe Ms. Panter in a classroom environment, as I taught her Principles of Wildlife Management in her junior year (she made an A), as well as in a professional setting outside the school when she was volunteering her time to help animals in distress.

As a mature woman, JoAnn is able to define, plan, and apply herself towards achieving goals. She is an exceptionally hard worker with the stamina required to maintain a heavy schedule when necessary. She is also realistic and aware of time and personal limitations.

JoAnn is intelligent, gregarious, and articulate. Her training and work as a counselor will give her the ability to relate to and effectively communicate with clients facing difficult decisions concerning their animals.

In my association with her in the field of wildlife rehabilitation, I am continually impressed with her pursuit of additional knowledge through attendance at various classes offered, attendance at national wildlife rehabilitation symposiums, and personal communication with other experienced professionals in the field.

She has a high moral and ethical commitment to animals in her care and makes every effort to ensure that diets, housing, and supportive care are not just adequate but optimum.

It is my belief that JoAnn Panter would be an excellent student and would graduate to become an excellent member of the veterinary profession. Please feel free to contact me if you require additional information.

Very Truly Yours,

Zimbalist Ziguawe
Faculty Member,
School of Science
NC State University
P.O. Box 66
Raleigh, NC 28302
1-910-483-6611

LETTER OF REFERENCE FROM A TEACHER

A letter of reference from a teacher or faculty member is usually designed to assure an admissions committee of scholastic ability and/or potential to excel in a field.

Relocation Cover Letters

If you are not only changing jobs but moving out of one town and to another, you will almost certainly need to send prospective employers your resume accompanied by a cover letter.

The letters in this section are really cover letters for resumes, but they are cover letters especially designed for individuals who are moving to a new town or state and who need to help prospective employers "make sense" of their approach.

Understand this about potential employers to whom you are writing: They are "nosy" people who simply wonder why you are writing to them if you have been working in another city. That's why the goal of the relocation cover letter is to give a few more details explaining your move so that you will look just as reliable as the "local yokel."

Date

Current address:
523 Delaware Drive
La Mesa, CA 91941

Permanent address:
525 Country Club Drive
Sheboygan, WI 53081

Director, Windsor Point
P.O. Box 1330
Sheboygan, WI 53081

Dear Director:

Providing quality health care to the older population is a very important job. I read of your recent certification as a Continuing Care Retirement Community. What an exciting time for Windsor Point!

As a certified Gerontological Nurse Practitioner, I am aware of the complexity involved in working with the older population and their families. I presently provide health maintenance, prevention, and promotion for 39 Nursing Home/Rehab patients at the La Mesa Veterans Affairs Medical Center. I also work in the Geriatric Outpatient Clinic and serve as the Pressure Ulcer Consultant throughout the hospital.

I am in the process of relocating back to the Sheboygan area where I grew up and where my extended family resides. As you will see from my resume, I have a Sheboygan address already, and I am frequently in your area finalizing details of my upcoming relocation.

If you can use a hard-working practitioner for your fine retirement community, I hope you will contact me to suggest a time when we might meet to discuss your needs and how I might serve them.

I would love to discuss with you any opportunities you might have available for a GNP at your facility, and I would certainly love to see the facility firsthand!

Sincerely,

Benita Gaillard, RN
MSN, GNP-C
910-483-6611

COVER LETTER FOR A NURSE RELOCATING TO A NEW TOWN

Employers in another state might not take you seriously unless you make them understand that you are serious about relocating. In the case of this nurse, she communicates her current address as well as her address in the town to which she is moving.

Date

Exact Name of Person
Title or Position
Name of Company
Address (number and street)
Address (city, state, and zip)

COVER LETTER FOR A VERSATILE YOUNG MANAGER

Employers are nosy people! If they receive a resume from someone whose last (or current) job was in another town or state, they wonder why you've relocated. Go ahead and satisfy their curiosity in the cover letter you send in advance of your arrival in town and tell them why you are moving. In this person's case, it's "family ties."

Dear Exact Name of Person: (or Sir or Madam if answering a blind ad.)

With the enclosed resume, I would like to initiate the process of being considered for employment within your organization. Because of family ties, I am in the process of relocating to the Houston area by a target date of December 5. Although I already have a Houston address which is shown on my resume, it is my brother's home and I would prefer your contacting me at the e-mail address shown on my resume or at my current telephone number if you wish to talk with me prior to February 28.

Since graduating from the University of North Carolina at Chapel Hill, I have enjoyed a track record of rapid promotion with a corporation headquartered in Miami Beach. I began as an Assistant Branch Manager and Head Buyer, was cross-trained as a Sales Representative, and have been promoted to my current position in which I manage the selling process related to 3,500 different products. In that capacity, I am entrusted with the responsibility for nearly $15 million in annual expenditures, and I maintain excellent working relationships with more than 150 vendors of name-brand consumer products sold through chain and convenience stores.

In my job, rapid change is a daily reality, and I have become accustomed to working in an environment in which I must make rapid decisions while weighing factors including forecasted consumer demand, distribution patterns, inventory turnover patterns, and vendor capacity and character. I have earned a reputation as a persuasive communicator and savvy negotiator with an aggressive bottom-line orientation.

If you can use my versatile experience in sales, purchasing, distribution, and operations management, I hope you will contact me to suggest a time when we might meet to discuss your needs and how I might serve them. I can provide excellent personal and professional references, and I assure you in advance that I am a hard worker who is accustomed to being measured according to ambitious goals for profitability in a highly competitive marketplace.

Yours sincerely,

Dale P. Jensen

Date

Exact Name of Person
Title or Position
Name of Company
Address (number and street)
Address (city, state, and zip)

Dear Exact Name of Person: (or Sir or Madam if answering a blind ad.)

With the enclosed resume, I would like to make you aware of the considerable sales and purchasing experience which I could put to work for your company. I am in the process of relocating to New Hampshire, and I believe my background is well suited to your company's needs.

As you will see from my resume, I have been excelling as the purchasing agent for a large wholesale food distributor with a customer base of schools, restaurants, and nursing homes throughout the southeastern United States. While negotiating contracts with vendors and handling the school lunch bid process, I have resourcefully managed inventory turnover in order to optimize inventory levels while maximizing return on investment. I have earned a reputation as a prudent strategic planner and skillful negotiator.

In a prior position as a Sales Trainer and Sales Representative with Kraft Foods in Tampa, I increased sales from $250,000 to $1.3 million and won the Captain Max award given to the company's highest-producing sales representative.

With a B.S. degree, I have excelled in continuous and extensive executive training in the areas of financial management, purchasing, contract negotiation, and quality assurance.

I can provide outstanding personal and professional references at the appropriate time, and I hope you will contact me if you can use a resourceful hard worker with a strong bottom-line orientation. I am in the Concord area frequently and could make myself available to meet with you at your convenience. Thank you in advance for your time.

Sincerely,

Barry P. Sonderfan

COVER LETTER FOR A FOOD SERVICE PROFESSIONAL RELOCATING TO NEW HAMPSHIRE

This purchasing agent is relocating to New Hampshire, and he is using this letter to attempt to set up some interviews with prospective employers prior to his final move.

Date

Exact Name of Person
Title or Position
Name of Company
Address (number and street)
Address (city, state, and zip)

COVER LETTER FOR A VERSATILE YOUNG PROFESSIONAL

Sometimes you relocate back to a place where you lived and worked previously. Go ahead and say so in the letter. That tends to make the employer feel that you are more of "a local."

Dear Exact Name of Person: (or Dear Sir or Madam if answering a blind ad.)

With the enclosed resume, I would like to make you aware of my interest in employment with your organization in some capacity in which you could use my strong administrative and office management skills in addition to my strong personal qualities of unlimited initiative, honesty, and reliability.

As you will see from my resume, I have recently returned to the Des Moines area with my husband, and we are glad to be back in Des Moines. We lived in Des Moines from 1995-98 and, during that time, I excelled in jobs in property management, hospital purchasing, medical scheduling and insurance verification, and small business management. From 1996-97, I worked as the Office Manager for Budget Auto Sound. I began with the company during its start-up and was instrumental in helping it grow into a business which produced more than $150,000 a year in revenues. In addition to handling all accounting and bookkeeping activities, I performed liaison with the company's corporate accounts for which we performed volume contract work. I have recently been recruited by Budget Auto Sound and am currently working as Office Manager.

Known for my friendly, outgoing personality and professional manner, I enjoy working with others and am skilled in handling multiple responsibilities. In one job as a Property Manager, I managed a staff of eight maintenance personnel while overseeing more than 100 single-family rental units.

If you can use a highly motivated self-starter who could become a valuable member of your organization, I hope you will contact me to suggest a time when we could meet to discuss your needs. I can provide outstanding personal and professional references at the appropriate time.

Yours sincerely,

Ruth Basore

Date

Exact Name of Person
Title or Position
Name of Company
Address (number and street)
Address (city, state, and zip)

Dear Exact Name of Person: (or Sir or Madam if answering a blind ad.)

With the enclosed resume, I would like to make you aware of my background in accounts management, personnel supervision, and customer service as well as my strong organizational, interpersonal, and communication skills. My husband and I have relocated back to Rochester, where our respective families are from.

While recently completing my Bachelor of Science degree, I excelled academically and was named to the Dean's List seven times. Prior to earning my degree, I excelled in both military and civilian environments.

In one job in North Carolina, I began as a Receptionist answering a 30-line phone system for a 1,100-employee company which provided on-line computer services. I rapidly advanced to Accounts Manager and Shift Supervisor, which placed me in charge of eight people. In that job I made hundreds of decisions daily which involved committing the company's technical resources. In addition to dispatching technicians and managing liaison with companies such as The Bank of Chicago, United Carolina Bank, and Stein Mart, I was authorized to commit company resources valued at up to $500,000.

With my husband's retirement, we are eager to replant our roots in New York, and I am seeking employment with a company that can use a highly motivated hard worker who is known for excellent decision-making, problem-solving, and organizational skills. If you can use a resourceful and versatile individual with administrative and computer experience, I hope you will contact me to suggest a time when we can discuss your present and future needs and how I might meet them. I can provide outstanding personal and professional references, and I thank you in advance for your time and consideration.

Sincerely,

Antoinette Pardue

COVER LETTER FOR AN OFFICE PROFESSIONAL

Employers like the sound of the fact that you have relocated permanently back to the place where you're from. That fact tends to communicate that you might be a permanent and stable employee in the work force of a local employer.

Requests For A Raise

Sometimes you find yourself in a work situation in which you feel you must write a letter requesting a raise.

In this letter, you are often writing to someone whom you know very well. That is the case in one of the letters you will see in this section. You will see a letter from a comptroller to the president of the company with whom the comptroller worked on a daily basis.

There are other situations in which an individual must write a letter requesting a raise as a kind of petition to an individual many levels up the organizational chain of command. That is the situation in the second letter in this section. In that letter, an individual is writing to a plant manager about a promise which had been made to him by a mid-level manager which had never been implemented.

Date

Mr. Gerald D. Wolfe
President
Wildlife Services Federation
62 Boston Street
New York, NY 10229

Dear Gerry:

I would like to draw your attention to the contributions I have made to Wildlife Services Federation, Incorporated, during the past two years since I have served the organization as Comptroller, in transition most recently to Chief Financial Officer.

Although I am quite happy in my current position and enjoy my colleagues, I must make you aware of the fact that I have been approached by my previous employer, Booz Allen Company, because it is their desire that I rejoin their organization as Vice President of Finance. The position they are offering me would give me a 30% increase in salary compared to my current salary at Wildlife Services Federation. Since my wife is currently in the process of considering a move to a part-time position from her full-time job, the increase in compensation is obviously most attractive.

I would like to formally ask you to review my salary in light of the following demonstrated track record of accomplishments for Wildlife Services Federation, Inc.:
- I have improved the overall reporting of operations, specifically monthly cash flow statements, profit and loss statement with variance analysis, and the quarterly staff allocation spreadsheet.
- I have reduced insurance costs through bidding and through changing the system of co-payments while also hiring a consultant at no additional cost to the organization.
- I have reduced telephone costs by hiring a consultant at no cost to the organization; in this area alone, I have produced a savings of around 6-10%.
- I have improved the budget process in significant and dramatic ways.
- I have coordinated the effort to hire a new accounting firm.
- I have also improved the standards and accountability in the accounting department so that even more valuable and timely information is provided to management for decision making.

I am certain you understand that, in such a situation as I now find myself in, I am torn between my loyalty to my family as a breadwinner and my loyalty to Wildlife Services Federation, Incorporated. My wife and I are discussing what is best for our family, and I would like to involve you in this decision-making process before a final action is taken. Thank you for your understanding.

With sincere best wishes,

Ron Rudd, CFO

LETTER FROM A COMPTROLLER REQUESTING A RAISE

If you like your job but have been offered more money somewhere else, a letter such as this can initiate the process of exploring whether it might be possible to make more money at your current job instead of moving on.

Date

Mr. Jeff Cornwell
President and Owner
House of Oostburg
23 Central Street
Oostburg, WI 53070

Dear Mr. Cornwell:

I, William Nelson, am writing to you because I believe that I have an honest and legitimate concern regarding the financial compensation which I receive for performing my current duties.

More than a year ago, I was approached by and had a meeting with Mr. Fairfield (Cut-up and Operations Manager) and Mr. Dixon (Plant Manager). Their purpose in holding this meeting was to request that I take on added duties and responsibilities within the plant. In addition to transporting meat to the new plant, I was asked to load and reload the tanks. I was assured by Mr. Fairfield that shouldering these extra burdens would bring about an increase in income commensurate with the additional tasks involved. I was informed by Mr. Fairfield that the employee who had previously been handling this task had been earning $20,000 per year. Although a specific amount was never given, Mr. Fairfield stated that my salary would increase by "several thousand" for accepting these additional duties.

Three weeks after I accepted these extra responsibilities, my duties were again increased. At this point I was responsible for loading between 66,000 and 88,000 lbs. worth of material using a hand-powered pallet jack, safely transporting these items to the new plant, returning all empty tanks, listing all products, and verifying that the temperature remained below 40 degrees Fahrenheit. I was also asked to make copies of the accompanying documentation for Mr. Fairfield as well as for the Quality Control Department. All of these additional duties are covered under the Hassle Program. The increase in my compensation for taking on these extra responsibilities was only $10 per day.

My attempts to meet with Mr. Fairfield and/or the Plant Manager in order to discuss my compensation, which is disproportionately low when weighed against the additional responsibilities I have assumed, have been futile.

My job performance consistently meets or exceeds company standards, and I work hard to ensure that this is so. I have attached copies of the product sheets and pre-shipment reviews, which provide ample support for the validity of my grievance. I would also like to point out that company policy clearly states that if fresh meat is being sold to a customer, then it is to be checked by an employee from the Quality Control Department to ensure that the customer is receiving a product of the highest possible quality. This inspection is to be performed every single time that fresh meat is sold to a customer, without fail. I have consistently conducted these pre-sale inspections, in rigorous compliance with company standards.

LETTER FROM A PRODUCTION WORKER REQUESTING A RAISE

This particular letter makes the point that some verbal promises were made which were not delivered. After waiting and waiting, it seemed that the only thing to do was to take the matter to the next level by putting the facts down in writing.

I strongly believe, and I feel that Mr. Dixon would concur, that each employee is an integral part of the company, and each part is necessary in order to ensure that the highest possible levels of product quality and customer service are consistently achieved. All employees deserve fair and appropriate compensation for their efforts. I graciously accept all of my job duties—indeed, I take on additional responsibilities in order to assure that I continue to achieve personal excellence in the performance of my job. In fairness and in recognition of this willingness to take on additional responsibility, I feel that I am entitled to be fairly compensated for my additional labors as indicated below:

Expected back pay:
Quality Control employees would make approximately $280 per week, allowing for a 40-hour work week at $7 per hour. Multiplied by eighteen months, this would come to $21,840.
- My present rate of pay is $110 per day.
- In compensation for the additional responsibilities I have taken on and my excellent performance, I feel that $150 per day is a fair and equitable compensation.

I am a dedicated and hard-working employee who is totally committed to helping House of Oostburg achieve its goals for profitability and efficiency. I respectfully ask that you consider my request for fair compensation based on my outstanding work performance as well as the company's representations and promises of increased compensation. I thank you in advance for your time and consideration.

Yours sincerely,

William Nelson

LETTER REQUESTING A RAISE

Providing details and specifics is important in this type of letter.

Requests For A Transfer
(see also Letters of Appeal)

Sometimes you find yourself in a work situation in which you feel you must write a letter requesting a transfer.

In the one example of such a letter which we give in this section, you will see that a professional woman felt she was the victim of sexual harassment and wrote a letter seeking a transfer.

There are many reasons to put such a request for a transfer in writing. Hopefully, the matter would get quickly resolved by the granting of the transfer request. However, if that doesn't happen, such a letter allows you to make management aware of your circumstances and you have in effect thrown the ball into management's court for action.

Date

Dear Sir or Madam:

Due to unfavorable work conditions, I would like to request a transfer to another duty station.

Unfortunately, during recent months I have been a victim of sexual harassment, discrimination, and unfair working conditions. I am willing to believe that personality conflicts are at the heart of the problems I am encountering, and that is why I am respectfully requesting a transfer to another duty location so that my current supervisor and I will not have to work together.

Because of the difficulties I have encountered with my current supervisor, after 15 years of dedicated and unwavering service, I have been denied cash bonuses and overtime requests for the first time since I have worked for the organization. If you will examine my past performance evaluations, you will see that I have always been evaluated in the top 5% of employees in every rated category.

Since my current supervisor took over his position nearly 18 months ago, my performance has been evaluated as marginal, although I am actually continuing to perform in a dedicated and outstanding manner. This unfairness on the part of my supervisor has resulted in my suffering from severe ailments including depression, stress-related disorders, frustration, and low self-esteem. For the first time in my life, I have sought counseling from a trained therapist.

I would appreciate your compassion and understanding in this matter and hope you will honor my request. There are many issues related to the situations described above which I do not feel comfortable revealing in a letter, but I would be delighted to discuss the private details of my distress and unhappiness with you in person. I would be more than happy to be subjected to a lie detector test or any other method you may wish to use to verify the accuracy of my statements.

It is not my desire to cause trouble for any individual, but it is my desire to continue my long and faithful service to the company. I respectfully request a transfer to another duty location in the same town, and I would greatly appreciate your rapid response to my request.

Sincerely,

Judy Melvin

REQUEST FOR A TRANSFER BECAUSE OF A SUPERVISOR

A letter like this is not easy to write, but sometimes it must be done. You should try to compose such a letter without writing anything mean-spirited.

Requests for Financial Aid
(see also Letters of Solicitation)

There may be situations in life in which you must write a letter requesting financial aid.

In this section, you will see a letter used by the daughter of an elderly woman to obtain some financial assistance from organizations.

Consult the Table of Contents and you will find letters requesting financial aid in other sections. For example, in the Letters of Solicitation section, you will see a letter written by a devoted volunteer to raise money to help disadvantaged children.

Date

Dear Sir or Madam:

In utter desperation and yet with hope that I pray will not be answered with disappointment, I am writing to **request your immediate intervention and assistance with regard to the plight of an elderly needy woman in an advanced stage of Alzheimer's disease.**

At 65 years of age and in failing health, Pauline Louise Wilson is an indigent senior citizen who is unable to care for herself. In her youth and young adulthood, Mrs. Wilson, the loving mother of four children, was a hard-working employee of a chicken factory as well as a law-abiding citizen who was active in church and community affairs. Her husband, Robert E. Wilson, Jr., also a factory worker for most of his life, died in June 1996 of prostate cancer at the age of 68, leaving the family with medical debts of more than $20,000 while also leaving his beloved Pauline Louise Wilson a widow without her devoted primary caregiver. After Mr. Wilson's death, Mrs. Wilson's only living daughter (her other daughter died several years ago of kidney failure), Angela Wilson, moved in with her mother to attempt to step into the role of caregiver. A factory worker, Mr. Wilson had provided part of the financial assistance which allowed Angela Wilson to complete her college education, and Ms. Angela Wilson is now a Counselor Technician at LaRue Training College.

Although Ms. Wilson, who is single, had the best of intentions when she moved in with her mother in an attempt to become her caregiver, Ms. Wilson is simply financially and physically unable to meet the overwhelming needs of her mother. Financially, Ms. Wilson is barely able to meet her own financial needs since she herself has financial obligations of a car payment, student loans for college expenses, and normal credit card expenses. Ms. Wilson now drives nearly one hour each way to and from her job every day, so she is literally not able to provide the daily companionship and caregiving which the elderly Mrs. Wilson desperately needs. At the present time, Ms. Wilson's brothers are providing round-the-clock care for their mother at the expense of their families. One of the brothers is separated from his wife and both brothers have teenagers who are experiencing emotional suffering and exhibiting behavioral problems due to the loss of their father's companionship while they spend their few "free" hours outside work providing care for Mrs. Wilson. Drained physically, emotionally, and financially, the brothers and Ms. Wilson simply cannot meet these extensive needs of their mother and grandmother.

- **Need for a Senior Companion.** Mrs. Wilson is in great need of a Senior Companion who has some knowledge of Alzheimer's disease. Mrs. Wilson suffers from an overactive thyroid which makes her hyperactive and she rarely sleeps. Furthermore, while she is awake, which is most of the day and night, she is in need of being watched like a child nearly all the time. For example, one month Mrs. Wilson ran up a $66 water bill simply because she kept the water running nearly all day and night and insisted on washing her clothes one piece at a time. She is very much like a baby who has no concept of day and night. Mrs. Wilson is a gentle, kind soul who would respond warmly to a patient senior companion.

REQUEST FOR FINANCIAL AID FOR A MOTHER WITH ALZHEIMER'S

The extended physical disability of a family member can be a financially and mentally draining experience, as it was for the offspring of the woman about whom this letter was written. The letter is an attempt to obtain financial assistance.

LETTER REQUESTING FINANCIAL AID

By doing some research at the library, you could find the names of organizations to which you could write in order to obtain financial aid for family situations such as this writer has experienced.

- **Need for Home Repairs Before a Senior Companion can be secured.** Because of the medical problems experienced by Mr. and Mrs. Wilson, the home in which Mrs. Wilson now lives with her daughter is in such a dilapidated state that Mrs. Wilson cannot qualify for an attendant to reside in the home with her at the present time. Several knowledgeable individuals have suggested that it would be more cost effective to demolish the house and build a new one rather than make the significant repairs needed which would include the replacement of all major heating, plumbing, and other systems in the home. The house in which Mrs. Wilson is living is considered unfit for habitation according to minimum standards required before a senior companion can be provided. Reliable estimates suggest that repairing the home would be $40,000 while tearing it down and rebuilding would be around $60,000.

- **Mrs. Wilson is afraid of going to a nursing facility.** Although it is in theory possible that Mrs. Wilson could go to a nursing facility for the extended and round-the-clock caregiving which she requires, the family is apprehensive about this option since Mrs. Wilson's 85-year-old mother was sexually and physically abused at two different nursing facilities in two different states. Furthermore, Mrs. Wilson has no money with which to pay for full-time nursing home care.

- **Mrs. Wilson is in need of medical aid.** Reliable sources have suggested that Mrs. Wilson's current stage of Alzheimer's makes her a viable candidate for some type of medication or treatment which could boost her memory.

- **All attempts to secure assistance for Mrs. Wilson have thus far been fruitless.** As Mrs. Wilson's primary caregiver, Angela Wilson has aggressively pursued several avenues of securing help for this indigent elderly woman. Applications for Emergency Food Stamps, Government Home Repairs, and additional home health care services all have been denied. When the Department of Aging and other such offices were contacted, they simply directed the family toward county agencies. However, Mrs. Wilson resides in LaRue County, which is 98th poorest of South Carolina's 100 counties. The wealthier surrounding counties have made it clear that they provide assistance only to their residents.

Please hear the desperate cries for help of a family which is at the breaking point in terms of emotional reserve, financial ability, spiritual vitality, and mental capacity. The only thing still in unlimited supply is the love which the grown children feel for their mother and their desire to see her spend her final years in a state of dignity, safety, and emotional well being. If you can take up this worthy cause, or point the family in the direction of some agency or foundation that can assist this elderly needy woman, please contact Angela Wilson at the address and phone number below. There are so many alleged "cash grant" scams which have tried to take advantage of the family's desperate situation, and this letter is sent in hope that you will be able to light the family's way out of its darkness.

Sincerely,

Angela Wilson
54 Cable Falls Drive
Larue, SC 99086

Requests for Promotion

In this section you will see letters which will show you how a few people communicated in writing their desire to seek upward mobility within the organizations in which they currently work.

Although you are a "known quantity" within your current employing organization, you must not assume that the person to whom you are writing knows of your accomplishments and fine qualities. You must still market and sell yourself as you must do in any cover letter.

You will find other letters requesting financial consideration for internal promotion in the Career-Changing Letters section.

FROM: CWO2 Kent Quackenbush 000 00 0000
TO: Commander, Coast Guard Personnel Command (CGPC-opm-1)
DATE: December 30, 1999
Via: Commanding Officer, USCGC Red Birch (WLM 687)
SUBJ: APPOINTMENT FOR APPOINTMENT TO TEMPORARY LIEUTENANT
REF: (a) Personnel Manual, COMDTINST M1000.6A, Article 5-B
 (b) COMCOGARD MPC Washington DC 291821Z AUG 97/alperscom 062/97

FORMAL LETTER IN MILITARY STYLE SEEKING PROMOTION TO LIEUTENANT

In the military, requests for certain kinds of promotion need to be made in writing. Here you see an example of a Navy professional who wishes to move into the management ranks.

1. This letter is intended to express my strong desire for consideration for appointment to Lieutenant in the Naval Engineering Occupational field per references (a) and (b) and to demonstrate my suitability for such a leadership position.

2. As a CWO-2, I expect promotion to CWO-3 (ENG) on 1 April 2000. I have advanced rapidly in my career field due to my demonstrated commitment to the Coast Guard's core values of honor, respect, and devotion to duty while leading my subordinates by strong example. The recipient of numerous medals and awards, I have excelled in every test of my leadership and technical proficiency, and my outstanding career achievements clearly indicate that I will also excel in an appointment as a Lieutenant.

3. Known for my tireless enthusiasm for the goals and ideals of the Coast Guard, I am also known for my commitment to the Coast Guard personnel whom I manage. For example, as W2 Engineer Officer on board the USCGC AMERICA, on my own initiative I convened and chaired a monthly safety meeting and took aggressive and resourceful actions to resolve outstanding potential safety issues. The safety and well-being of the men and women I train, lead, and manage are vital considerations of mine at all times.

4. I am respected for my strong administrative and writing skills. In my most recent job I have resourcefully managed a budget of more than $100,000. While attached to the USCGC AMERICA, I applied my creativity in highly practical ways by formulating and implementing major upgrades to reduce maintenance costs and increase operational reliability of the cutter. For example, I made use of DRMO in order to procure high-dollar items such as steam kettles, blowers, and generator heads and thereby saved money which could be re-obligated on other items and projects. With a reputation as an exceptional writer, I offer extensive dockside leadership experience. For example, I have processed hundreds of documents for major contract changes during dockside availabilities. I have earned a reputation for clarity and precision in written communication while drafting letters for signature by the commanding officer, modifying many Coast Guard regulations, and developing numerous damage control outlines. I am proud of the fact, too, that I have used my oral communication skills in training and developing many outstanding young professionals who are serving the Coast Guard with distinction today.

5. Throughout my career, my leadership ability, strong interpersonal skills, and ability to communicate effectively, both orally and in writing, have been noted. For example, recent OERs have praised me as "a highly effective and persuasive speaker" and cited my ability to develop outstanding working relationships with others. On

numerous occasions, I have proven my ability to focus diverse units and personnel on a common goal and to achieve exceptional results under the pressure of tight deadlines, frequently in spite of major obstacles.

6. My technical engineering expertise is unsurpassed by anyone in my field and makes me an outstanding candidate for appointment to Lieutenant. My technical knowledge has been tested in numerous assignments. For example, I have served with distinction as engineering petty officer at a large shore station. I provided leadership in the planning and implementation of two major drydockings and three dockside availabilities. I offer proven expertise in overseeing the safe operation, care, and maintenance of all propulsion and auxiliary machinery.

7. In summary, I believe I would be a credit to the Coast Guard as a Lieutenant, and it is my desire to apply my leadership, problem-solving skills, and decision-making ability for the benefit of the Coast Guard in this capacity.

Yours sincerely,

Kent Quackenbush,
CWO-2

LETTER REQUESTING PROMOTION

You will notice in this letter that he does not take anything for granted. He is meticulous about reciting some of his achievements and accomplishments so that the reviewing personnel can see clearly that he is "lieutenant material."

Date

Morinville County School System
PO Box 2357
Morinville, NC 37091

Dear Sir or Madam:

With the enclosed resume, I would like to make you aware of my interest in the position you recently advertised as Executive Director for Child Nutrition for the Morinville County School System.

As my resume reveals, I offer the extensive knowledge you are seeking in child nutrition along with proven management skills, analytical abilities, and the ability to develop and maintain harmonious working relationships. In my current job as Child Nutrition Supervisor for Morinville County Schools which I have held since 1993, I oversee child nutrition programs in 20 school cafeterias while also planning and implementing all staff development for more than 600 employees. I also plan the yearly orientation program and conduct safety training for all child nutrition employees.

I offer an outstanding personal and professional reputation and am known for my ability to work well with others at all organizational levels.

In previous jobs I excelled as a Home Economics Teacher and Home Economics Extension Agent, and I also served as a Food Service Director in a 120-person nursing care facility and in a 90-patient retirement home.

My Certifications include Certified Child Nutrition Supervisor and Certified Home Economist. I am a member of numerous associations and federations related to home economics and food service, and I have received many honors in recognition of my leadership, character, and technical knowledge of the nutrition field.

I hope you will give me an opportunity to demonstrate to you in person that I am the hard-working professional you are seeking, and it would be a great honor for me to continue my service to the children of Morinville County in the role of Executive Director for Child Nutrition. Thank you in advance for your time.

Yours sincerely,

Martha McNairy

LETTER REQUESTING AN INTERNAL PROMOTION IN AN EDUCATIONAL SYSTEM

Sometimes the best promotional opportunities are within your current employer or system, so don't overlook the stepping stones which are lying all around you.

Date

Mr. Charlie Spencer
Vice President, Human Resources
United Way
223 Geneva Park Road
Chicago, IL 90769

Dear Mr. Spencer:

With the enclosed resume, I would like to make you aware of my interest in the position of **Regional Director for the Eastern District,** United Way.

I am currently excelling as Area Director for area 18, which includes Forsythe, Maroon, and Buffalo counties. When I took over this area, community organization had deteriorated to the point that there was no working relationship at all between the United Way and United Telecom, by far the largest employer in the area. Through revitalization of existing programs, development of new programs, as well as recruiting, training, and careful management of volunteers, I was able to restore United Telecom's confidence in the United Way and we now have a successful partnership with that major sponsor.

To increase community awareness of the United Way, I have initiated a number of new programs, including a highly successful program in which 30 program facilitators served the needs of 400 participants in the last year. I also developed an industrial wellness and education program for employees. Through my efforts, revenues from our major fundraising campaign increased from $56,000 in 1998 to $194,000 in 1999, to $350,000 in 2000.

In addition to my expert knowledge of United Way programs, I offer the strong management and supervisory skills which this position requires. In a previous management position with a profit-making company which was subcontracted by companies to handle quality control functions, I handled key management responsibilities and played a significant role in creating, implementing, and executing the company's business plan. A major responsibility of mine involved traveling throughout the state and adjacent states to establish "from scratch" and then manage offices which were responsible for performing inspections. I hired and trained all satellite office employees and provided continuous training and oversight of their performance as I simultaneously handled liaison with key customers.

It is my sincere desire to be of service to the United Way on an even higher level, and I believe I could make significant contributions to United Way as Regional Director. Please give me the opportunity to talk with you in person about this position.

Sincerely,

Darlene Peddler

REQUEST FOR PROMOTION WITHIN THE UNITED WAY

Most of the time, we get paid the most money to do what we already know how to do and to use the knowledge we have acquired through experience. This job hunter wants to apply her knowledge of the United Way at a higher level of responsibility.

Date

Exact Name of Person
Title or Position
Name of Company
Address (number and street)
Address (city, state, and zip)

Dear Exact Name of Person: (or Dear Sir or Madam if answering a blind ad.)

With the enclosed resume, I would like to make you aware of my interest in the position of **Financial Management Analyst II with the Vermont Department of Revenue.** As you will see from my enclosed resume, I offer a background as a seasoned accounting professional with exceptional analytical, communication, and organization skills. I have handled many responsibilities routinely handled by a Financial Management Analyst in roles as a Field Auditor and Revenue Officer.

With the Department of Revenue, I have advanced in a track record of increasing responsibilities. In my current position as a Field Auditor, I analyze financial reports of businesses and individuals, reconciling various general ledgers, investment and checking accounts in order to accurately determine tax liability. Earlier as a Revenue Officer, I consulted with taxpayers to assist them in determining the validity of deductions and calculating the amount of individual income tax owed. In both of these positions, I trained my coworkers, sharing my extensive knowledge of Internal Revenue Service and Vermont Department of Revenue codes and laws while educating department personnel on correct procedures related to professional auditing and collections.

I hold an Associate of Applied Science degree in Accounting from Central Berkshire Community College and a Bachelor of Science in Business Administration from the University of Oregon at Portland.

Please favorably consider my application for this internal opening, and please also consider my history of dedicated service to the Vermont Department of Revenue. I feel certain that I could excel in this job and could be a valuable asset to the department in this role.

Sincerely,

Kevin Strafford

REQUEST FOR PROMOTION WITHIN STATE GOVERNMENT

We recommend sacrificing no formality when applying for internal promotions. As you see from this cover letter, you still need to "sell" your interest and qualifications, even when the insiders know you.

Date

Exact Name of Person
Title or Position
Name of Company
Address (number and street)
Address (city, state, and zip)

Dear Exact Name of Person: (or Sir or Madam if answering a blind ad.)

With the enclosed resume, I would like to make you aware of the considerable skills I could put to work for the Baltimore Family Health System.

Although I would like you to consider me for any situation where my versatile skills could be of value to you, I am particularly interested in the following positions:
    Access Coordinator
    Assistant Practice Manager
    Network Analyst II (Information Systems)
    Account Analyst

You will see that I offer skills compatible with those and other business office positions. I hold a B.A. in Finance and have acquired experience in internal business auditing activities, payroll calculation and administration, computer operations, and office management. I have worked for only two companies and have been promoted to increasing responsibilities in both organizations because of my initiative, productivity, and office skills. Even in high school, I began working for Camelot Music and was promoted to Assistant Manager for a store with $1.5 million in annual sales and 15 employees. In my current job, I handle a variety of internal auditing procedures, troubleshoot accounting problems, and handle liaison with the home office. I am proficient in utilizing numerous software programs including Excel, Lotus, and many others.

If you can use an energetic and highly motivated hard worker who offers versatile skills and abilities, I hope you will contact me to suggest a time when we might meet to discuss your needs and how I might serve them. Thank you for your time.

Yours sincerely,

Holly M. Vargo

REQUEST FOR PROMOTION & CONSIDERATION FOR MULTIPLE JOBS

There may be several different job openings you wish to apply for within your organization. You could handle your request for consideration for multiple job consideration in this way.

Requests for Reconsideration

If you are changing careers or just thinking about doing so, sometimes your best opportunity is one you considered previously but decided not to act on.

In this section, you will see letters written by individuals who were trying to restore a relationship with employing organizations which had previously considered them for employment.

If you feel you "closed a door" on a relationship some time ago and would like to reconnect with that organization, try writing a letter like the ones you will see in this section.

Date

Exact Name of Person
Title or Position
Name of Company
Address (number and street)
Address (city, state, and zip)

Dear Exact Name of Person: (or Sir or Madam if answering a blind ad.)

As I hope you will recall, several months ago I interviewed with you for a position involving responsibility for advertising sales with the *Hartford News and Observer*. I very much appreciated your many kindnesses to me during the interviewing process.

During the time when I was interviewing with you for a position, my current employer approached me and asked if I would take on a special project which involved performing outside sales for the business. Since I had worked at Cross Roads Chrysler-Buick for five years and was very familiar with the customer base and with the company's style of doing business, he wanted me in particular to take on the project and I felt, because of his business circumstances at the time, that I had a personal and moral obligation to serve the company in that role.

For that reason I was unable to follow through with the final stage of becoming an employee of the *Hartford News and Observer*.

That project has now been completed and I feel I have loyally completed my obligation to the company in that regard. I would like to ask that you reconsider me for an advertising sales position with the *Hartford News and Observer*. I can provide outstanding personal and professional references, including from my current employer, and I can assure you that I would offer the *Hartford News and Observer* the same loyalty as I have consistently shown to my current employer.

My resume is enclosed to refresh your memory about my skills and professional qualifications. You may also recall that we first became acquainted years ago when I was attending St. Joseph's Episcopal Church.

I have a high opinion of you and of the *Hartford News and Observer* and I hope you will consider me for any position within your company which requires a positive, highly motivated individual with a proven track record of excellent performance in sales and customer service.

Thank you again for your past courtesies, and I hope you will welcome my call soon when I try to contact you to see if you have needs I could fill.

Yours sincerely,

Delilah Masonright

REOPENING A DOOR & REQUESTING RECONSIDERATION FOR A SALES JOB

Employers can get their feelings hurt if you turn down a job they offer you. This lady had pulled out of the last round of interviews for a job with a newspaper, and months later she realized she'd made a mistake. This letter accompanying her resume reopened the door for her and led to the offer (and acceptance) of a job.

Date

Exact Name of Person
Title or Position
Name of Company
Address (number and street)
Address (city, state, and zip)

REOPENING A DOOR: REQUEST FOR RECONSIDERATION BY THE CIA

You can reopen a door in life sometimes. This individual was quite far along in the interviewing process for a CIA job when a terminal illness forced him to abort his plans for an employment change. He is reopening the door with this cover letter.

Dear Exact Name of Person: (or Sir or Madam if answering a blind ad.)

Over the course of the last ten years, I have tried to balance my preparations for becoming a CIA Special Agent and my personal responsibilities regarding my wife's terminal illness. Though my wife and I had long discussions about my desire to become a CIA Special Agent, when she was diagnosed with third-stage ovarian cancer I was unable to dedicate my time towards this end.

My wife's death left my goals of achieving a second undergraduate degree in Criminal Justice, a graduate degree and commission from the University of Maryland, and a law degree from Princeton University unrealized. As her cancer slipped into remission I was, however, able to obtain a graduate degree and commission from a local university.

Recently with my wife's passing after a very lengthy illness, I feel that it is time for me to apply for the job that she and I had discussed so many times. I appreciate your attention to my application, and I look forward to the next step in the application process of becoming a Special Agent for the Central Intelligence Agency.

To the future,

Kip Sullivan

Resignation Letters

Almost everyone comes to the point at least once in life, and usually more than once, when he or she decides to change jobs. Often this is a positive change and you may be excited about your new job, but you face the problem of how to resign.

A skillfully written letter of resignation may be one of best ways to make a final positive impression on your current employer. In this section you will see examples of letters of resignation used by real people to resign their positions and attempt to maintain a cordial relationship with the companies they are leaving.

Date

Mr. Ben Diamond
Henry Enterprises, Ltd.
Charlotte, NC 28307
RE: Retirement (e.g.) Medical

Dear Mr. Diamond:

It is with deepest regret that I submit my application for retirement after twenty years and one month of employment with this company.

Multiple medical problems have forced me to this point. They are as follows: diabetes, hypertension, coronary disorders, osteoarthritis of the knees, and tendonitis of the right foot. These medical problems have rendered me unable to perform my duties the way I feel they should be done.

My medical history can be acquired from my primary care physician, Dr. Angela Fields, Greenlawn Family Practice. She can be reached at 1110 ½ Hay Street, Charlotte, NC, and her phone number is 483-6611.

If it is at all possible, I desire that the date of my retirement be December 30, 1999.

Respectfully yours,

Wicklin Smith

Enc: Enclosed please find an In-Service Withdrawal Request Form

---

RESIGNATION LETTER FOR MEDICAL REASONS

Sometimes one is forced to resign for medical reasons. A letter such as this can make your employer aware of the condition which necessitated this change.

Date

Mrs. Patricia Avery
Avery & Johnson, CPAs
1102 12th Street
Tulsa, OK 74128

Dear Patricia:

It is with genuine sadness and many mixed feelings that I must inform you that I will be resigning from my position at Avery & Johnson, CPAs, effective December 30.

The firm of Brice & Smith, CPAs, in Topeka, KS, also a public accounting firm, has offered me a position as a CPA at a salary of nearly $50,000 annually, and I feel it is a time in my life when I must move on.

Leaving the firm of Avery & Johnson, CPAs, is very difficult for me professionally and emotionally. After I passed the CPA Exam in November 1998, you gave me my first job in the public accounting field, and I have thoroughly enjoyed the family atmosphere coupled with the professional style of both you and Mr. Johnson. You have taught me so much about how to solve problems, how to work more efficiently, and how to handle difficult clients. I am deeply grateful for your encouragement, professional mentoring, and strong personal example.

Although the decision to leave Avery & Johnson, CPAs, is difficult, I really feel that I have no choice. As a single parent who provides full financial support of my daughter, I am driven by the desire to provide a decent standard of living for my small family. I will be placing her in a Christian school in Topeka so that she can continue learning in the same Christian environment as she has had in Tulsa.

I hope you know that I have always given 110% to your firm in terms of my financial knowledge, intelligence, and problem-solving ability, and I hope you feel that I have made contributions to its reputation. I feel I am separating more from a family than from an employer, and I felt I wanted to put this information in writing to you as a first step because getting the words out verbally would be a difficult emotional experience for me.

Thank you from the bottom of my heart for all you have done for me professionally and personally.

Yours sincerely,

Tonya Brewer

CC: Mr. Muldoon Johnson

RESIGNATION LETTER FROM A CPA FIRM

You can feel the emotion in this letter. The individual resigning felt like she was leaving home, and the people employing her had become her friends over the years. A letter of resignation such as this one can soften the blow of a sudden departure.

Date

RESIGNATION LETTER FROM A CAR DEALERSHIP

Here is another resignation letter written by an individual who feels as though she is "leaving home," even though she is also thrilled about the new job. A great letter of resignation can do much to keep people speaking well of you for years.

TO: Ben Smith
     Howard Fine
     April Stevens

It is with much sadness as well as with great personal affection for all of you that I wish to inform you that I will be leaving Greenville Subaru Dealership. My final departure date is December 30, 1999.

A sales position has become available at *The Greenville Courier-Times* and I believe the hours of employment will be better suited to my needs as a single parent. I just became aware of this opportunity and there is an urgent need for the individual to begin employment on January 3. I am sorry I could not provide a longer notice.

Because I have been employed with Greenville Subaru Dealership for six years, I feel as though I am "leaving home," and in that nostalgic frame of mind, it is my desire to tell you how much I have appreciated your training me, helping me, and giving me opportunities to try new things and gain new skills. I am very truly grateful to you, and I hope you know that I always gave my best effort.

I can assure you that I will continue to be a highly productive source of referrals for you even when I am gone, because I believe wholeheartedly in the products and the product line we all have represented. If I can ever help any of you individually in any way, too, please let me know.

In the meantime, please accept my sincere thanks for all the kindnesses and professional courtesies you have shown me.

Yours sincerely,

Mary Tickner Mason

Date

Mr. Chris Brancaleone
Area Manager
Taco Bell
1226 S. Main Street
Smithfield, KS 78324

Dear Chris:

It is with great reluctance and some sadness that I am formally submitting my resignation, effective December 30, 1999. My association with Taco Bell has been a pleasant one, and I will miss the teamwork and friendships here that have become a valuable part of my life.

As you aware, my fiancee lives in Topeka and, although I had hoped to transfer to a job in Topeka with Taco Bell, a nonfood-industry company has recruited me for a position which involves a wider range of opportunities to be trained in numerous areas. The position I have accepted with that company will lead to a supervisory position, and after much consideration, I determined that I could not turn down the opportunity for training, rapid advancement, extensive benefits, and future potential which the company is offering.

I would like you to know that I am deeply indebted to you and to many others in the Taco Bell organization for helping me succeed in my job, and I can assure you that I will give "110%" in training my replacement in order to assure that individual's success.

Thank you in advance for your understanding of my decision to leave Taco Bell, and please be assured of my total loyalty to you and to the company during the remainder of my employment with you as well as afterwards, when I will certainly continue to speak highly of you and others in the fine organization which is Taco Bell.

Sincerely,

Janie Hitchcock

RESIGNATION FROM A RESTAURANT POSITION

The main point to take away from this section on resignation letters is that you should draft an elegant and thoughtful letter of resignation when you leave a company. You can see for yourself that it is a very nice way to finish off a relationship.

Writing to Publishers, Editors, and Literary Agents

If you have written a book or short story and wish to offer it for publication, you will find this section of the book useful. Here we will show you sample "query" letters that have worked to capture the attention of publishers, editors, literary agents, magazine editors, and others.

Most of the letters in this section were written by people who had a book they wanted to publish, and they used the letters in this section to introduce the book to likely publishers and literary agents. If you want to find out the names and addresses of publishers, magazines, and literary agents to whom you should address your letters, you can visit your library or bookstore. You will find dozens of books which will aid you in identifying the names and addresses of people and organizations. Many of the books are published annually, so you can be somewhat assured that the mailing address is as up-to-date as is possible. The books which you can consult will usually tell you what types of materials the publisher, literary agent, or magazine is interested in, and that will help you direct your query letter to the best source.

Date

Dear Sir or Madam:

The idea for this children's story, and for the series I am developing, occurred to me while I was living in the little town of Devon, England. The story tells of a body buried in a house on top of a high hill, and the house really does exist. I heard remnants of this tale and have embellished upon it a great deal.

As you will see from the story, which is for middle readers 4-6 grades, there is a hero which children will find appealing. While presenting children with a story that will inspire their imaginations and entertain them, the story is unusual because it presents a hero who is handicapped and who triumphs over many physical adversities in addition to the normal challenges faced by superhuman characters. The idea of a hero in a wheelchair may seem farfetched at first, but when you read the story, you will find it believeable—I assure you.

As the daughter of an international diplomat, I spent much of my childhood and teenage years in England, France, and Japan, and I learned to speak Japanese and French. Since my childhood was spent in those countries, I have chosen to set my hero's escapades in those cultures. I intend to write a series of books featuring the hero in a different mystery/escapade in each book, and I believe the series would be very educational for children and help them learn about other cultures while also—first and foremost—entertaining them and giving them a hero they can look up to.

As an adult, I have worked professionally as a teacher. I am very attuned to the attention span and tastes of children 4-6, and I feel I have a special talent for communicating with middle readers.

I hope you will give the enclosed story a read and let me know if you feel you could represent me.

Yours sincerely,

Penny Striker

LETTER FROM A PRE-PUBLISHED AUTHOR WHO WISHES TO WRITE A CHILDREN'S SERIES

This school teacher has been in the classroom with children in grades 4-6 for years, and she is writing a series of children's books which feature a hero who is handicapped or physically challenged. In books she has found at the library and bookstores, she has carefully read the guidelines provided by literary agents and publishers describing the types of materials which interest them, and she is sending this letter and the first story in the series to publishers and literary agents who seem to have an interest in fiction for children.

QUERY LETTER DESCRIBING A MANUSCRIPT

This letter is intended to accompany the synopsis which is on the facing page. The letter introduces the synopsis and the author's background, and it is designed to spark the agent's or publisher's interest in the book. Notice that the author does not send the entire manuscript to the publisher or agent. Consult reference books in bookstores and libraries which tell you what to send, but do not send unsolicited manuscripts (1) unless you know for sure that the agent or publisher accepts them and (2) you send a self-addressed stamped envelope (SASE) with sufficient postage for the return of your manuscript.

Date

Dear Sir or Madam:

With the enclosed synopsis of my novel, untitled as yet, I would like to introduce you to a story which explores themes related to genetics and hospital switching of babies at birth which are very much on the minds of Americans. Through the eyes and life of the protagonist, an attractive Asian woman named Kiser Jenkins, the novel treats readers to a fast-paced mystery which begins when Kiser's family dies in a mysterious fire in their family home. As the novel opens, the handsome detective Liam Fullingham is investigating the possible arson and murder.

As the story unfolds, the novel examines the nature of sibling relationships as it uncovers the complex relationships between two sets of twins. One set of twins is of mixed race, had different adoptive families from radically different socio-economic backgrounds, and never lived together; the other twins were orphaned early in childhood but grew up together. Throughout the novel, the reader is stimulated by insights into the age-old debate over which has more influence on a person's development—environment or genetics. As you will see when you read the story, the two sets of twins lived lives which shed light on that subject. The brothers were separated from birth, and then one lived in poverty while the other lived in luxury. The twin girls were orphaned from childhood through a tragic and accidental separation from their family, and they grew up together, although their environment bore no similarity to the environment of their father and mother.

The mystery of the fire is what draws the twins together in what becomes an elaborate tale of love lost, revenge sought, and love found. Readers are treated to an adventure of these two sets of twins as they unravel the secrets of their own origins while exploring clues to an apparent arson. In the rubble of the fire lie many secrets.

As a geneticist and practicing psychologist, I have come to understand the thirst most people have to understand the ultimate meaning of life and to figure out what their particular destiny might be. Considered a distinguished geneticist in the academic community and among my professional colleagues, I feel I have a gift for satisfying the public's appetite for genetics information through my ability to "translate" complex scientific concepts into understandable language.

Just as in real life, love and hate as well as greed and the desire for power are the primary passions driving the characters in this novel which I feel you would enjoy. While the novel is mainstream fiction, its themes could be of interest to any publisher developing a line geared to readers who are fascinated with genetics. Without revealing the plot, the protagonist becomes the subject for the sequel, which I am in the process of writing. Please let me know if you would like to see representative chapters.

Yours sincerely,

Kyle Drake

As the novel opens, Kiser Jenkins is on top of the world. She will soon be marrying her true love, Clayton Powers, a man of means from a southern family which traces its origins in America to the Mayflower. Just two weeks before the wedding, Kiser's family dies in a mysterious fire in their family home, and the reader (as well as Kiser's betrothed) is then introduced to the mysterious events surrounding Kiser's birth and subsequent upbringing. Right away the novel makes it clear to the reader that things are not always what they seem.

Kiser knows there is something "strange" about Liam Fullingham from the minute she meets him, but she cannot put her finger on what it is about him that bothers her. The reader senses that all is not as it seems with this detective as this astute and handsome young professional investigates the arson which caused the tragedy and probes into Kiser's background.

The reader meets two sets of twins in the novel. One set of twins was separated from birth, and then one lived in poverty while the other was settled in the lap of luxury. The other twins were abandoned at birth through a tragic and accidental hospital mishap, and the reader becomes fascinated with various theories of genetics as the lives of these twins are revealed.

A romance develops between two lovers whose love cannot be, as they eventually discover when they attempt to resolve the mystery of the fire through which the secrets of several families are revealed. Kiser's search for the clues to her birth and to her biological family takes her to a small town in Alabama, where she is drawn into a relationship with a man on death row whom she feels has been framed for a murder he didn't commit. As Kiser gets closer to the truth of "who done it" in the case of the death-row inmate, she gets dangerously close to the bitter secrets of an aristocratic southern family who despise her Asian roots and whose attitude of racial superiority will incense readers.

As Kiser gets closer to the truth, she becomes the target of influential folks whose wicked adoption business she threatens to expose. A fast-paced plot leads the reader through mishaps and misadventures in the West Indies, Tokyo, and Berlin.

At the end of the story, the two sets of twins have found the answers to numerous genetic and biological questions surrounding their origins, and they have also discovered some answers pertaining to their own destiny. At the end of the book, the reader feels satisfied that justice has been done and that key issues related to fate and biology have been resolved. As the book ends and the protagonist goes on to the sequel, the reader will be following her to the next book.

SYNOPSIS FOR A NOVEL

Many literary agents and publishers like to be approached with a short letter introducing the author and his or her background along with a synopsis. The synopsis gives sufficient details of the plot and scenery to interest the individual in requesting the entire manuscript or the first three chapters.

ABOUT THE EDITOR

Anne McKinney holds an M.B.A. from the Harvard Business School and a B.A. in English from the University of North Carolina at Chapel Hill. A noted public speaker, writer, and teacher, she is the senior editor for PREP's business and career imprint, which bears her name. Titles in the Anne McKinney Career Series published by PREP include: *Resumes and Cover Letters That Have Worked*, *Resumes and Cover Letters That Have Worked for Military Professionals*, *Resumes and Cover Letters for Managers*, *Cover Letters That Blow Doors Open*, *Letters for Special Situations*, and *Government Job Applications and Federal Resumes*. Her career titles and how-to resume-and-cover-letter books are based on the expertise she has acquired in 20 years of working with job hunters. Her valuable career insights have appeared in publications of the *Wall Street Journal* and other prominent newspapers and magazines.

Judeo-Christian Ethics Series

BACK IN TIME *Patty Sleem*
Also published in large print hardcover by Simon & Schuster's Thorndike Press as a Thorndike Christian Mystery in November 1998. (336 pages)
"An engrossing look at the discrimination faced by female ministers." – *Library Journal*
Trade paperback 1-885288-03-4—$16.00

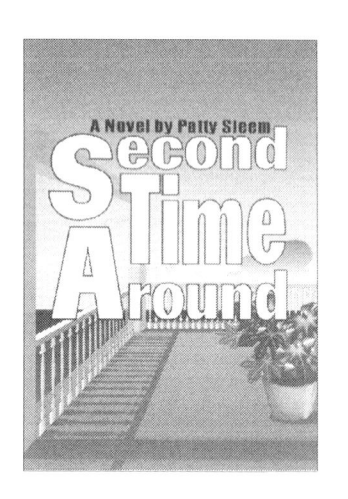

SECOND TIME AROUND *Patty Sleem*
"Sleem explores the ugliness of suicide and murder, obsession and abuse, as well as Christian faith and values. An emotional and suspenseful read reflecting modern issues and concerns." – *Southern Book Trade* (336 pages)
Foreign rights sold in Chinese.
Hardcover 1-885288-00-X—$25.00
Trade paperback 1-885288-05-0—$17.00

A GENTLE BREEZE FROM GOSSAMER WINGS *Gordon Beld*
Pol Pot was the Khmer Rouge leader whose reign of terror caused the deaths of up to 2 million Cambodians in the mid-1970s. He masterminded an extreme, Maoist-inspired revolution in which those Cambodians died in mass executions, and from starvation and disease. This book of historical fiction shows the life of one refugee from this reign of genocide. (320 pages)
"I'm pleased to recommend *A Gentle Breeze From Gossamer Wings*. Every Christian in America should read it. It's a story you won't want to miss – and it could change your life."
— Robert H. Schuller, Pastor, Crystal Cathedral
Trade paperback 1-885288-07-7—$18.00

BIBLE STORIES FROM THE OLD TESTAMENT *Katherine Whaley*
Familiar and not-so-familiar Bible stories told by an engaging storyteller in a style guaranteed to delight and inform. Includes stories about Abraham, Cain and Abel, Jacob and David, Moses and the Exodus, Judges, Saul, David, and Solomon. (272 pages)
"Whaley tells these tales in such a way that they will appeal to the young adult as well as the senior citizen." – *Independent Publisher*
Trade paperback 1-885288-12-3—$18.00

WHAT THE BIBLE SAYS ABOUT... Words that can lead to success and happiness *Patty Sleem*
A daily inspirational guide as well as a valuable reference when you want to see what the Bible says about Life and Living, Toil and Working, Problems and Suffering, Anger and Arguing, Self-Reliance and Peace of Mind, Justice and Wrong-Doing, Discipline and Self-Control, Wealth and Power, Knowledge and Wisdom, Pride and Honor, Gifts and Giving, Husbands and Wives, Friends and Neighbors, Children, Sinning and Repenting, Judgment and Mercy, Faith and Religion, and Love. (192 pages)
Hardcover 1-885288-02-6—$20.00

Business & Career Books

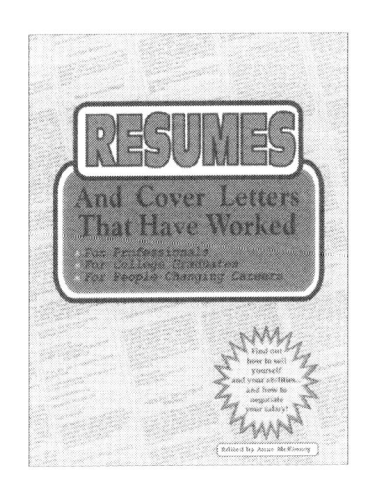

RESUMES AND COVER LETTERS THAT HAVE WORKED
Anne McKinney, Editor
More than 100 resumes and cover letters written by the world's oldest resume-writing company. Resumes shown helped real people not only change jobs but also transfer their skills and experience to other industries and fields. An indispensable tool in an era of downsizing when research shows that most of us have not one but three distinctly different careers in our working lifetime. (272 pages)
"Distinguished by its highly readable samples…essential for library collections." — *Library Journal*
Trade paperback 1-885288-04-2—$25.00

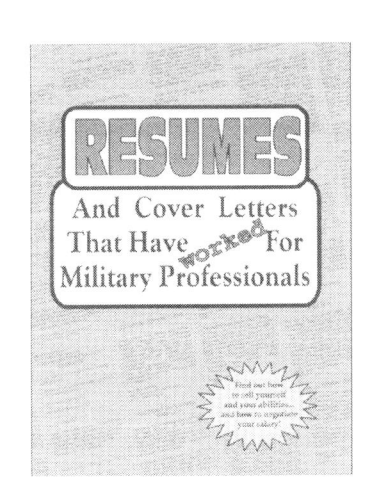

RESUMES AND COVER LETTERS THAT HAVE WORKED FOR MILITARY PROFESSIONALS
Anne McKinney, Editor
Military professionals from all branches of the service gain valuable experience while serving their country, but they need resumes and cover letters that translate their skills and background into "civilian language." This is a book showing more than 100 resumes and cover letters written by a resume-writing service in business for nearly 20 years which specializes in "military translation." (256 pages)
"A guide that significantly translates veterans' experience into viable repertoires of achievement." –*Booklist*
Trade paperback 1-885288-06-9—$25.00

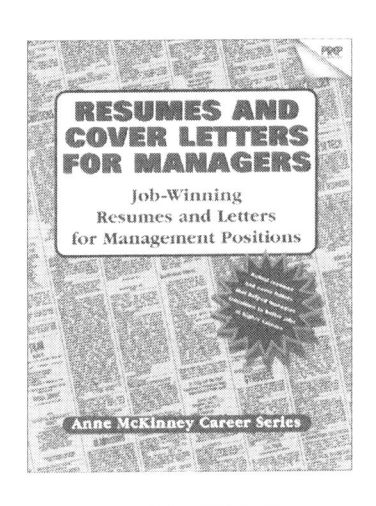

RESUMES AND COVER LETTERS FOR MANAGERS
Anne McKinney, Editor
Destined to become the bible for managers who want to make sure their resumes and cover letters open the maximum number of doors while helping them maximize in the salary negotiation process. From office manager to CEO, managers trying to relocate to or from these and other industries and fields will find helpful examples: Banking, Agriculture, School Systems, Human Resources, Restaurants, Manufacturing, Hospitality Industry, Automotive, Retail, Telecommunications, Police Force, Dentistry, Social Work, Academic Affairs, Non-Profit Organizations, Childcare, Sales, Sports, Municipalities, Rest Homes, Medicine and Healthcare, Business Operations, Landscaping, Customer Service, MIS, Quality Control, Teaching, the Arts, and more. (288 pages)
Trade paperback 1-885288-10-7—$25.00

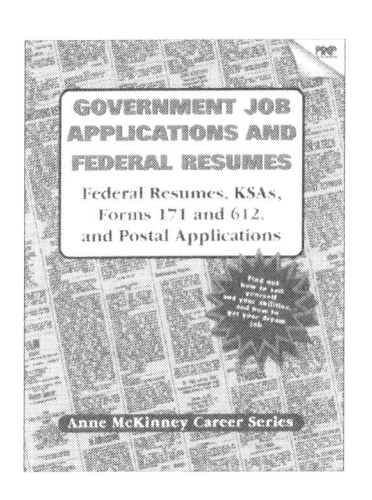

GOVERNMENT JOB APPLICATIONS AND FEDERAL RESUMES:
Federal Resumes, KSAs, Forms 171 and 612, and Postal Applications *Anne McKinney, Editor*
Getting a government job can lead to job security and peace of mind. The problem is that getting a government job requires extensive and complex paperwork. Now, for the first time, this book reveals the secrets and shortcuts of professional writers in preparing job-winning government applications such as these:
The Standard Form 171 (SF 171) – several complete samples
The Optional Form 612 (OF 612) – several complete samples
KSAs – samples of KSAs tailored to jobs ranging from the GS-5 to GS-12
Ranking Factors – how-to samples
Postal Applications
Wage Grade paperwork
Federal Resumes – see the different formats required by various government agencies. (272 pages)
Trade paperback 1-885288-11-5—$25.00

COVER LETTERS THAT BLOW DOORS OPEN *Anne McKinney, Editor*

Although a resume is important, the cover letter is the first impression. This book is a compilation of great cover letters that helped real people get in the door for job interviews against stiff competition. Included are letters that show how to approach employers when you're moving to a new area, how to write a cover letter when you're changing fields or industries, and how to arouse the employer's interest in dialing your number first from a stack of resumes. (272 pages) Trade paperback 1-885288-13-1—$25.00

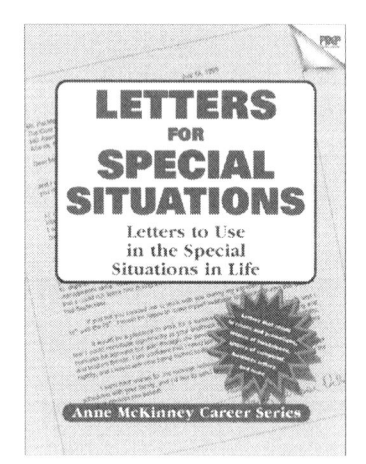

requesting reinstatement to an academic program, Follow-up letters after an interview, Letters requesting bill consolidation, Letters of reprimand to marginal employees, Letters requesting financial assistance or a grant, Letters to professionals disputing their charges, collections letters, thank-you letters, and letters to accompany resumes in job-hunting. (256 pages)
Trade paperback 1-885288-09-3—$25.00

LETTERS FOR SPECIAL SITUATIONS *Anne McKinney, Editor*

Sometimes it is necessary to write a special letter for a special situation in life. You will find great letters to use as models for business and personal reasons including: Letters asking for a raise, Letters of resignation, Letters of reference, Letters notifying a vendor of a breach of contract, Letter to a Congressman, Letters of complaint, Letters

PREP Publishing Order Form

You can order any of our titles from your favorite bookseller! Or just send a check or money order or your credit card number for the total amount*, plus $3.20 postage and handling, to PREP, Box 66, Fayetteville, NC 28302. If you have a question about any of our titles, feel free to e-mail us at preppub@aol.com and visit our website at http://www.prep-pub.com

Name: _____
Phone #: _____
Address: _____
_____
E-mail address: _____
Payment Type: ☐ Check/Money Order ☐ Visa ☐ MasterCard
Credit Card Number: _____ Expiration Date: _____

Check items you are ordering:

☐ $25.00—RESUMES AND COVER LETTERS THAT HAVE WORKED. Anne McKinney, Editor
☐ $25.00—RESUMES AND COVER LETTERS THAT HAVE WORKED FOR MILITARY PROFESSIONALS. Anne McKinney, Editor
☐ $25.00—RESUMES AND COVER LETTERS FOR MANAGERS. Anne McKinney, Editor
☐ $25.00—GOVERNMENT JOB APPLICATIONS AND FEDERAL RESUMES: Federal Resumes, KSAs, Forms 171 and 612, and Postal Applications. Anne McKinney, Editor
☐ $25.00—COVER LETTERS THAT BLOW DOORS OPEN. Anne McKinney, Editor
☐ $25.00—LETTERS FOR SPECIAL SITUATIONS. Anne McKinney, Editor
☐ $16.00—BACK IN TIME. Patty Sleem
☐ $17.00—(trade paperback) SECOND TIME AROUND. Patty Sleem
☐ $25.00—(hardcover) SECOND TIME AROUND. Patty Sleem
☐ $18.00—A GENTLE BREEZE FROM GOSSAMER WINGS. Gordon Beld
☐ $18.00—BIBLE STORIES FROM THE OLD TESTAMENT. Katherine Whaley
☐ $20.00—WHAT THE BIBLE SAYS ABOUT... Words that can lead to success and happiness. Patty Sleem

_____ TOTAL ORDERED (add $3.20 for postage and handling)

*PREP offers volume discounts on large orders. Call us at (910) 483-6611 for more information.

THE MISSION OF PREP PUBLISHING IS TO PUBLISH BOOKS AND OTHER PRODUCTS WHICH ENRICH PEOPLE'S LIVES AND HELP THEM OPTIMIZE THE HUMAN EXPERIENCE. OUR STRONGEST LINES ARE OUR JUDEO-CHRISTIAN ETHICS SERIES AND OUR BUSINESS & CAREER SERIES.

Would you like to explore the possibility of having PREP's writing team create a letter for you similar to the ones in this book?

For a brief free consultation, call 910-483-6611
or send $4.00 to receive our Job Change Packet to
PREP, Department SPE, Box 66, Fayetteville, NC 28302.

QUESTIONS OR COMMENTS? E-MAIL US AT PREPPUB@AOL.COM

Made in the USA
Lexington, KY
08 March 2014